Study Guide

LIFESPAN DEVELOPMENT

LIFESPAN DEVELOPMENT

Kelvin L. Seifert
Robert J. Hoffnung
Michele Hoffnung

Study Guide

Gregory Cutler
Bay de Noc Community College

Robert F. Rycek
University of Nebraska at Kearney

HOUGHTON MIFFLIN COMPANY   BOSTON   NEW YORK

Sponsoring Editor: David C. Lee
Senior Associate Editor: Jane Knetzger
Assistant Editor: Gwyneth V. Fairweather
Manufacturing Manager: Florence Cadran
Marketing Manager: Pamela J. Laskey

Printed in the U.S.A.

ISBN: 0-395-71143-6

123456789-VG-01 00 99 98 97

CONTENTS

TO THE STUDENT

This study guide was prepared to help you master the information provided in the text *Lifespan Development* and to facilitate your study and retention of the important theories, facts, and concepts related to developmental psychology.

In developing a study guide, we recognize that most students have devised their own ways of studying and learning new material. We encourage you to try those means you have found useful to make studying interesting and productive. At the same time, having access to a study guide developed especially for a text may help you study more efficiently and effectively, particularly as this may be introductory material for you.

Study guide content parallels textbook content and contains the following materials for each chapter:

1. A list of *learning objectives*, drawn specifically from the textbook's coverage. They describe what you are expected to be able to do to show that you have learned the material in the chapter.

2. A brief *overview* of chapter content.

3. A detailed *chapter outline* that summarizes the main points of the chapter and contains helpful hints for learning.

4. A series of *fill-in-the-blank statements* related to the key concepts of the chapter. The answers to these questions appear at the end of each chapter of this study guide.

5. A *Multiple-Choice Self-Test: Factual/Conceptual Questions* and *Multiple-Choice Self-Test: Application Questions*. These tests are designed to test your knowledge of chapter content and to give you practice in taking multiple-choice tests based on this content. The answers to the tests, along with a detailed explanation of why the correct choice is right and the other choices are not, appear at the end of each study guide chapter.

We hope that this study guide will help you to learn the material in your textbook more easily and thoroughly, and we wish you success in your study of developmental psychology.

Study Guide

LIFESPAN DEVELOPMENT

CHAPTER 1

Introduction: Studying Development

Learning Objectives

1. Define what is meant by development and describe the nature of developmental change.

2. Describe the three domains of developmental psychology and indicate how they interact.

3. Describe Bronfenbrenner's ecological framework for understanding development.

4. Discuss the reasons for studying development and what benefits developmental psychology provides to society.

5. Sketch the history of lifespan developmental psychology and describe how certain historical situations contributed to the emergence of this field.

6. Identify and discuss the basic issues in developmental psychology.

7. Describe the four features of the scientific method and explain how it is used in psychology.

8. Discuss the strengths and limitations of the cross-sectional approach.

9. Discuss the strengths and limitations of the longitudinal approach.

10. Differentiate between naturalistic and experimental studies.

11. Describe the experimental approach. Be able to differentiate between experimental and control groups, and between independent and dependent variables.

12. Describe what a correlation is and what it shows.

13. Identify and describe other methods for investigating developmental issues, including surveys, interviews, and case studies. Discuss the strengths, limitations, and usefulness of each technique.

14. Discuss the ethical constraints on conducting research.

15. Define what is meant by informed consent and describe the special concerns that exist when children are involved.

Chapter Overview

Development refers to changes in growth, feelings, and patterns of thinking. These changes can take place in the domains of physical, cognitive, and psychosocial development, and these domains interact in many ways, producing a whole, integrated person. Studying development is important for several reasons. First, it can help us have appropriate expectations about behavior and its changes. In addition, understanding development can help us respond appropriately to individuals' behavior and recognize when unusual behavior is a cause for concern. Self-understanding can also take place when studying development.

Historically, childhood and adolescence were not recognized periods of life. Urbanization and industrialization played important roles in making many people aware of childhood. The growing recognition of childhood led to new ways of studying children's behavior. Baby biographies and descriptive observation were early methods of inquiry.

Developmental psychology focuses on four major issues: nature and nurture, continuity and discontinuity, context and universality, and deficit and difference. Research about developmental psychology tries to follow the scientific method in terms of formulating a research question, stating a hypothesis, testing the hypothesis, and interpreting and publicizing the results. Of particular interest to developmental psychologists are the methods that vary the time frame of research: cross-sectional studies, longitudinal studies, and sequential studies. Cross-sectional studies compare people of different ages at a single point in time. Longitudinal studies observe the same subjects periodically over a relatively long period. Because cross-sectional and longitudinal studies have limitations, researchers use elements of each and conduct sequential studies. Naturalistic studies observe individuals in natural contexts, and experimental studies try to control extraneous conditions while varying only one or two specified variables. Correlation studies examine relationships between variables. Surveys, interviews, and case studies sample different numbers of people, and each has advantages and limitations. Research about human behavior must adhere to the ethical issues of confidentiality, full disclosure of purposes, and respect for the freedom to choose whether to participate in research. These ethical principles provide for informed consent, which is an understanding on the part of the people or group being studied of their rights as subjects and their right to decide whether they wish to participate. Studying people presents some unique challenges and opportunities to psychologists.

Chapter Outline

I. The nature of developmental change

   Development refers to changes in a person's long-term growth, feelings, and patterns of thinking.

   A. Three domains of development

   Domains refer to the type or form of change. There are three domains, and they interact in many ways with each other.

   1. **Physical development** includes bodily changes, the use of the body (e.g., motor skills, sexuality), and the effects of aging (e.g., eyesight, muscular strength).

   2. **Cognitive development** refers to changes in reasoning, thinking, language acquisition, and memory.

   3. **Psychosocial development** relates to changes in feelings or emotions, relationships with others, and development of a sense of self.

B. An example of development: Jodi

Bronfenbrenner's theory on ecological systems provides a framework of understanding the many contexts of development.

1. The microsystem consists of situations in which the individual experiences face-to-face contact with important individuals.

2. The mesosystem is the connections and relationships that exist between two or more microsystems.

3. Settings in which the person does not participate but that still have an influence are called the exosystem.

4. The macrosystem is the overall society, with its overarching institutions, practices, and patterns of belief.

II. Why study development?

A. Knowledge about development can lead to realistic expectations for children, adolescents, and adults.

B. Knowledge about development can aid appropriate responses to a person's actual behavior.

C. Developmental knowledge can increase recognition when departures from the normal are significant.

D. Developmental knowledge can enhance understanding of one's own development.

E. Knowledge about development can facilitate advocacy for the needs and rights of people of all ages.

III. The history of developmental study

A. Childhood and adolescence as concepts

1. Children were not always considered full-fledged members of society or even genuine humans. Children graduated to adulthood status early in life and took on major adultlike tasks.

2. Therefore, the period of adolescence was unknown, and teenagers assumed adult roles. Assuming major adultlike tasks was a factor in the early mortality of children.

• Perspectives: Wanted: A child and family policy

B. Early precursors to developmental study

Economic changes and the effects of industrialization made it known that children were working in factories and being abandoned.

C. The emergence of modern developmental study

1. Baby biographies were one of the earliest attempts to study development.

2.   Gesell developed **norms**, or standards of normal development, by observing children at precise ages doing specific tasks.

3.   Piaget observed behavior that illustrated cognitive skills.

IV. Basic issues in developmental study

A. Nature and nurture

Theorists have argued about the relative importance of genetics and inborn qualities (**nature**) and the skills and qualities acquired through learning and experience (**nurture**). Psychologists agree that most human traits and behaviors result from both nature and nurture, although it is still important to understand the relative contribution of both factors to development.

B. Continuity and discontinuity

Another issue around development involves whether human development is a gradual, continuous process (continuity) or progresses in relatively sudden leaps that lead to new and unprecedented behavior (discontinuity).

C. Universal and context-specific development

This issue explores the extent to which human development is universal or context-specific. Psychologists are recognizing that culture in which a person grows up determines when and how that person develops qualities and behaviors.

•   A multicultural view: Growing up in India

D. Deficit and difference

This issue involves questioning the value of certain developmental changes over other changes. Differences in development are sometimes perceived as desirable and sometimes as deficiencies.

V. Methods of studying developmental psychology

A. Scientific methods

The **scientific method** refers to systematic procedures for objective observations and interpretations of observations.

1.   Research begins with the formulation of research questions.

2.   Each question is stated as a **hypothesis**—a statement that precisely expresses the research question.

3.   After formulating hypotheses, researchers test them by conducting an actual study.

4.   Following the study, researchers analyze and report their results. Then they make reasonable interpretations and conclusions about these results.

B. Variations in time frame

Psychologists can study people of different ages at one point in time. In addition, the same people can be studied at several points in time.

1. A **cross-sectional study** compares people of different ages at a single point in time.

2. A **longitudinal study** observes the same subjects periodically over a relatively long period, often years.

3. Both types of studies have advantages and limitations. For instance, **cohorts** cannot be distinguished in cross-sectional studies. Subjects in longitudinal studies may drop out or move away.

4. **Sequential studies** combine elements of cross-sectional and longitudinal studies.

- Working with Marsha Bennington, speech-language pathologist: Communication difficulties across the lifespan

C. Variations in control: Naturalistic and experimental studies

Developmental studies vary in how much they attempt to control the circumstances in which individuals are observed.

1. **Naturalistic studies** observe behavior as it normally occurs in natural settings.

2. **Experimental studies** arrange circumstances so that only one or two factors or influences vary at a time.

    a. In experimental research, groups are arranged so that factors can be manipulated or held constant. A deliberately varied factor is called the **independent variable**. A factor that varies as a result of the independent variable is called the **dependent variable**.

    b. The population refers to the group being studied. When every member of the population has an equal chance of being chosen for the study, the individuals selected form a **random sample**. If no person has an equal chance of being selected, the sample is biased.

    c. Experimental studies use a number of precautions to ensure that their findings have **validity**, meaning they measure or observe what they are intended to measure or observe.

    d. One way to improve validity is to observe two sample groups, one an **experimental group,** or treatment group, and the other a **control group**. The experimental group receives the treatment or intervention related to the purposes of the experiment. The control group experiences conditions that are as similar as possible to the conditions of the experimental group but does not experience the crucial experimental treatment.

3. Most research studies look for correlations among variables.

    a. A **correlation** is a systematic relationship.

        b.   When the behaviors or characteristics change in the same direction, the relationship is a positive correlation; when they change in opposite directions, it is a negative correlation.

        c.   The correlation coefficient, which falls between +1.00 and –1.00, summarizes the degree of relationship between two characteristics.

D. Sampling strategies

Developmental studies vary in how many people are observed or interviewed.

    1.   **Surveys** are large-scale, specific, focused interviews of large numbers of people. Surveys have advantages and limitations.

    2.   **Interviews** are face-to-face directed conversations. Because interview studies take time, they usually focus on a smaller number of individuals than surveys do.

    3.   A **case study** examines one or a few individuals. In general, case studies try to pull together a wide variety of information about an individual case and then present the information as a unified whole. Case studies emphasize the relationships among specific behaviors, thoughts, and attitudes in the life of the subject.

VI. Ethical constraints on studying development

Sometimes ethical concerns limit the methods that can be used to study particular questions about development. Generally, researchers face four major ethical issues.

A. Confidentiality

If researchers collect information that might damage individuals' reputations or self-esteem, they should take care to protect the identities of the participants.

B. Full disclosure of purposes

Research subjects are entitled to know the true purpose of any research study in which they participate. Sometimes, however, telling subjects the truth about the study will make them distort their behavior. When this is the case, researchers need to balance dishonesty with making research more scientific. Purposeful deception may be permissible—but only when no other method is possible and when participants are fully informed of the deception and its reasons following the study.

C. Respect for individuals' freedom to participate

As much as possible, research studies should avoid pressuring individuals to participate.

D. Informed consent

With **informed consent**, each person shows that he or she understands the nature of the research, believes that his or her rights are protected, and feels free to either volunteer or refuse to participate.

VII. Strengths and limitations of developmental knowledge

Key Concepts

Directions: Identify each of the following key concepts discussed in this chapter.

1. _____ refers to the changes in a person's long-term growth, feelings, and patterns of thinking. Human development can take many forms, or _____.

2. Change in biological growth is called _____. Change in reasoning and thinking is called _____. The change experienced in feelings and emotions and how we relate to other people is referred to as _____.

3. The term _____ is used to refer to genetics and inborn qualities, while a person's experience and learning are known as _____. Most psychologists believe that the two _____ in determining behavior and traits.

4. Research studies of human development that begin by formulating specific research questions and hypotheses follow the _____.

5. A(n) _____ is a statement that expresses a research question precisely.

6. When a psychologist compares people of different ages at one point in time, a(n) _____ is being conducted. If a study compares a group of people at different times as they get older, it is called a(n) _____. A(n) _____ is a group of people born at the same time who have had similar developmental experiences.

7. A study that combines elements of cross-sectional and longitudinal studies is called a(n) _____ study.

8. Purposely observing behavior as it typically occurs in natural settings is termed _____ research. _____ research, on the other hand, involves arranging circumstances so that only a select few factors vary at one time.

9. In an experiment, the factor that is manipulated is called the _____ variable. The factor that varies as a result of the manipulation is called the _____ variable. It is important that the sample of individuals in an experiment be selected _____. In such a sample, each person has an equal chance of being selected for participation.

10. In an experiment, it is important that researchers measure or observe what they intend to measure. In order to ensure this type of _____, experiments include a(n) _____ group, to which a particular treatment is applied, and also a(n) _____ group, which receives no experimental treatment.

11. A(n) _____ is a systematic relationship between two behaviors, responses, or human characteristics.

12. Large-scale _____ are specific, focused interviews of a large number of people.

13. A sampling strategy that involves face-to-face directed conversations is called the _____.

14. When a study uses just one or a few individuals, a(n) _____ is being used.

15. A(n) _____ form notifies parents and children of the purposes of any research in which they might choose to participate, ensures the confidentiality of their results, and allows them the freedom to participate or not.

Multiple-Choice Self-Test

Factual / Conceptual Questions

1. The domain of development primarily concerned with changes in feelings, emotions, and how individuals relate together is the _____ domain.
   a. cognitive
   b. maturational
   c. physical
   d. psychosocial

2. The ecological systems approach is best associated with
   a. Bronfenbrenner.
   b. Freud.
   c. Gesell.
   d. Piaget.

3. Children in medieval times were
   a. pampered during childhood because not many survived.
   b. raised in large group homes or sold into slavery.
   c. treated quite harshly as compared with modern children.
   d. very much like modern children in their daily activities.

4. Which of the following is most consistent with the discontinuity view of development?
   a. Accumulation of the same skills
   b. Inborn skills
   c. Learning and experience
   d. Qualitative change

5. As compared to a research question, a hypothesis
   a. is more complex.
   b. is more general.
   c. is based on facts.
   d. makes a specific prediction.

6. Which of the following is true of a cross-sectional study?
   a. It always involves the manipulation of several independent variables.
   b. It compares age groups rather than individuals.
   c. It is expensive and time-consuming.
   d. It tests the same subjects repeatedly.

7. A study that tests the same subjects periodically across several years is best termed a(n)
   a. cross-sectional study.
   b. experimental study.
   c. longitudinal study.
   d. naturalistic study.

8. In a positive correlation, as one characteristic increases the other characteristic
    a. increases.
    b. decreases.
    c. stays the same.
    d. varies randomly.

9. Which of the following is a major limitation of the interview method?
    a. Too much data that can't be quantified may be collected.
    b. Subjects must be able to read and write.
    c. Responses may be affected by personal qualities of the interviewer or subject.
    d. Distinguishing between important and trivial behaviors is difficult.

10. All of the following are principles of informed consent *except*
    a. confidentiality.
    b. full disclosure of purposes.
    c. compensation for participation.
    d. respect for individuals' freedom to participate.

Application Questions

1. Which of the following best illustrates development within the psychosocial domain during the middle childhood period?
    a. Tanisha rides a bicycle for the first time.
    b. Roger prefers to associate with the boys in his class rather than the girls.
    c. Jorge learns to read out loud in front of a group.
    d. Tina gets her first job in a fast-food store.

2. The board of education at Jenny's school has decided that all students will now wear uniforms to school in order to decrease gang activities. Which level of Bronfenbrenner's ecological system is exerting its influence on Jenny?
    a. Exosystem
    b. Macrosystem
    c. Mesosystem
    d. Microsystem

3. If you were a student in Gesell's lab, your method of studying children would involve
    a. conducting experiments on children's visual perception.
    b. establishing norms of development.
    c. intensive interviewing of children.
    d. the use of psychotherapy.

4. A researcher studying motor development argues that crawling, walking, and running are qualitatively different and represent a stepwise progression in development. This researcher probably holds a _____ view of motor development.
    a. universal
    b. discontinuity
    c. genetic
    d. nurture

5. Professor Cohen wants to conduct systematic and objective studies of memory in five-year-olds. Her best approach would be to
   a. use quantitative methods whenever possible.
   b. develop a theory to explain her observations.
   c. do a cross-sectional study.
   d. follow the scientific method.

6. Andy is part of a study that looks at physical growth in over five hundred children. Every year for the past ten years, a scientist has measured various physical characteristics, tested his reflexes, and checked his performance in a number of physical tasks. Andy is participating in a(n)
   a. chronological study.
   b. cross-sectional study.
   c. experimental study.
   d. longitudinal study.

7. A psychologist looking at the effects of TV violence on aggression sets up a situation in which aggression is measured after a group of children watches either violent TV or nonviolent TV. In this study, the measure of aggression is the
   a. dependent variable.
   b. hypothesis.
   c. independent variable.
   d. natural variable.

8. In a study of the effects of playing video games on reaction time, one group actually plays video games for a half hour while the other group simply watches the games. Both groups are then tested using a standard reaction time measure. The group that simply watches a video game in this study would be considered the _____ group.
   a. control
   b. dependent
   c. experimental
   d. naturalistic

9. The relationship between children's age and number of words in their vocabulary would most likely be reflected by which of the following correlation coefficients?
   a. .00
   b. +.65
   c. −.55
   d. +1.75

10. Professor Singh is studying object identification in blind children by closely examining the activities of her own child, who is blind. She observes, records, and occasionally tests her four-year-old. She also talks to his special education preschool teacher, his sitters, and others who come in contact with her son. The method that best describes Professor Singh's approach is
    a. case study.
    b. experimental study.
    c. longitudinal study.
    d. naturalistic observation.

Answer Key

Key Concepts

1. Development, domains
2. physical development, cognitive development, psychosocial development
3. nature, nurture, interact
4. scientific method
5. hypothesis
6. cross-sectional study, longitudinal study, cohort
7. sequential study
8. naturalistic, Experimental
9. independent, dependent, randomly
10. validity, experimental, control
11. correlation
12. surveys
13. interview
14. case study
15. informed consent

Multiple-Choice Self-Test: Factual / Conceptual Questions

1. Choice (d) is correct. The psychosocial domain, by definition, covers all these issues while examining issues of family, peers, and personal relationships. Choice (a), cognitive, examines reasoning and thinking. Choice (b), maturational, is not considered a domain but rather a process. Choice (c), physical, is concerned with changes in the brain, sense organs, and muscles.

2. Choice (a) is correct. Bronfenbrenner developed the ecological systems approach. Choice (b), Freud, is the founder of the psychoanalytic approach; choice (c), Gesell, was an early developmental psychologist who established growth norms; and choice (d), Piaget, was a major cognitive developmental theorist.

3. Choice (c) is correct. In medieval times very young children were viewed as "talented pets" and were given adultlike responsibilities when they reached age seven or eight. It is true that many children did not survive, as indicated in choice (a), but those who did were not pampered. Instead, parents tried not to become too fond of them. Children were neither raised in group homes nor enslaved, choice (b). Nor were they viewed as children today are viewed, choice (d).

4. Choice (d) is correct. The discontinuity viewpoint holds that development consists of qualitative changes, as often represented by different stages of development. Choice (a), accumulation of the same skills, is most consistent with the continuity viewpoint in that quantitative, not qualitative, change is stressed. Choice (b), inborn skills, reflects the heredity, or nature, viewpoint (which can be either continuity or discontinuity), while choice (c), learning and experience, is consistent with the nurture viewpoint.

5. Choice (d) is correct. The main difference between a research question and a hypothesis is in the area of precision. A hypothesis is more precise and therefore makes specific predictions. Choices (a) and (b) are more descriptive of a research question, which tends to be more general and sometimes more complex than a hypothesis; choice (c) refers more to the outcome of testing a hypothesis in the hopes that it can be supported.

6. Choice (b) is correct. A cross-sectional study compares groups of individuals of different ages and does not directly compare one individual with another. Choices (c) and (d), expensive and

time-consuming and tests the same subjects repeatedly, respectively, are characteristics of a longitudinal study. Choice (a), involves the manipulation of several independent variables, could be included in a cross-sectional study to make it a more complex design. The variable of focus in a cross-sectional study, however, is always age.

7. Choice (c) is correct. By definition, a longitudinal study examines the same individuals repeatedly across time. Choice (a), cross-sectional study, looks at different people of different ages; choice (b), experimental study, involves the manipulation of certain variables to see their effect on other variables; and choice (d), naturalistic study, involves observation with minimal interference or manipulation.

8. Choice (a) is correct. In a positive correlation, as one variable increases, it is associated with an increase in the other variable. Choice (b), decreases, would be a negative correlation, and choices (c) and (d), stays the same and varies randomly, respectively, both describe a zero (or no) correlation since there is no systematic association.

9. Choice (c) is correct. The interviewer and subject may interact in positive or negative ways. Choice (a), too much data may be collected, is not necessarily a problem. You can never collect too much data. At times, quantification may be troublesome, but it is not viewed as an inherent problem with interviews. Choice (b), subjects must be able to read and write, is a limitation of surveys, and choice (d), distinguishing between important and trivial behaviors is difficult, is a limitation of the case study approach.

10. Choice (c) is correct. Choices (a), (b), and (d) are the three major aspects of informed consent. Choice (c), compensation, is not required of research even though participants are sometimes compensated.

Multiple-Choice Self-Test: Application Questions

1. Choice (b) is correct. One of the psychosocial developments during the middle childhood years involves gender segregation: boys prefer to be with boys, and girls prefer to be with girls. Choice (a) is within the physical domain; choice (c) would best be classified in the cognitive domain; and choice (d) is not a middle childhood issue, but rather an adolescent (or later) issue.

2. Choice (a) is correct. The exosystem involves a level in which significant decisions are made that affect the child even though he or she does not directly participate in the process. In Jenny's case, the school board exerts influence on what she will wear. Choice (d), microsystem, involves direct face-to-face influence, such as a family; choice (c), mesosystem, involves relationships between microsystems, such as the relationship between home and school, while choice (b), macrosystem, involves matters of society and social policy that are fairly removed but still exert influence.

3. Choice (b) is correct. Gesell was an early developmental psychologist who did extensive work in establishing norms for various motor abilities in children. He was not noted for conducting experiments, so choice (a) is incorrect; nor did he do much interviewing, making choice (c) also incorrect, or use psychotherapy, making choice (d) incorrect.

4. Choice (b) is correct. The discontinuity view holds that change occurs in qualitatively different steps or stages. Although choice (a), universal, could be correct because it is not inconsistent with the discontinuity view, universality of development implies that everyone develops in a similar fashion. This development, however, does not necessarily involve stages. Choices (c) and (d), genetic and nurture, respectively, refer to mechanisms of development based on heredity and environment.

5. Choice (d) is correct. The scientific method makes systematic and objective research possible by controlling certain variables while manipulating others. Choice (a), quantitative method, is also desirable in studying memory, but it does not guarantee either objectivity or systematic study; choice (b), develop a theory, is something Professor Cohen may want to do during or after her research, while choice (c), cross-sectional study, would be useful if she was concerned with looking at different ages.

6. Choice (d) is correct. A longitudinal study looks at the same individual repeatedly in order to determine changes over time. Choice (a), chronological study, is not a type of research study in developmental psychology; choice (b), cross-sectional study, looks at different individuals at different ages; and choice (c), experimental study, involves the manipulation of some variables and control of other variables. The study Andy is in seems only to be measuring different levels of performance.

7. Choice (a) is correct. A dependent variable depends on the subject's behavior; level of aggression is the measure. Choice (c), independent variable, is the variable manipulated by the experimenter; in this example, it is the type of TV watched. Choice (b), hypothesis, is the idea being tested; in this case, the hypothesis might be that children who watch violent TV will be more aggressive than those who watch nonviolent TV. Choice (d), natural variable, is not a meaningful term used in psychology.

8. Choice (a) is correct. Since the study is looking at the effects of video games on reaction time, an appropriate control group would consist of subjects who do not play. A control group experiences everything the experimental group does except for the critical variable that is being manipulated. Those who do play would be considered the experimental group, choice (c). Choices (b) and (d), dependent and naturalistic, respectively, are not terms used to define groups in experiments.

9. Choice (b) is correct. As age increases, so does vocabulary, which would indicate a positive correlation. That eliminates choice (a), which is a zero correlation, and choice (c), which is a negative correlation, indicating that as age increases, vocabulary decreases. Choice (d), although positive, is beyond the range of a correlation coefficient and probably means that a calculation error was made.

10. Choice (a) is correct. The case study approach usually involves the intensive examination of all aspects of a single subject. Choices (b) and (d), experimental and longitudinal studies, respectively, might be involved, but clearly Professor Singh's examination is not limited to simply those methods. Although the study is long-term, it is not considered a longitudinal study, choice (c), since that typically involves more than a single subject.

CHAPTER 2

Theories of Development

Learning Objectives

1. Define what is meant by a developmental theory and describe its characteristics.

2. Discuss how developmental theories differ on the issues of maturation versus experience, active versus passive, stages, and breadth of the theory.

3. Discuss the basic ideas in Freud's psychosexual theory of development, including the id, ego, and superego. Be able to describe each stage.

4. Discuss the basic ideas in Erikson's psychosocial theory of development and compare it to Freud's theory. Be able to describe each stage.

5. Describe alternative psychodynamic theories, including Mahler's infant stages and Stern's theory of the self, and contrast them with Freud's and Erikson's approaches.

6. Describe classical conditioning and be able to identify and define the key concepts, including conditioned stimulus, conditioned response, unconditioned stimulus, and unconditioned response.

7. Describe operant conditioning and be able to identify and define the key concepts, including reinforcement and punishment.

8. Describe Bandura's social cognitive theory. Be able to identify the roles of observational learning, modeling, and vicarious reinforcement in his theory.

9. Discuss the basic ideas in Piaget's theory of development, including the notion of schemes, the processes of assimilation and accommodation, and equilibrium.

10. Discuss the neo-Piagetian approaches and describe how they have influenced Piagetian thought.

11. Describe the basic features of the information-processing approach. Identify and describe the various components of memory.

12. Describe developmental changes according to information-processing theory, including changes in control processes, metacognition, and the knowledge base.

13. Describe the contextual approach to development, including Bronfenbrenner's ecological systems theory. Be able to describe each of the system levels within his theory.

14. Discuss Vygotsky's theory and other contextual theories, including transactional theory and ethological theory. Describe how these theories view development and contrast them with Bronfenbrenner's approach.

15. Describe the normative-crisis and timing of events models of development. Identify the major theories of adulthood that reflect these models.

16. Compare and contrast the major approaches and theories covered in the chapter. Be able to describe how each accounts for development.

Chapter Overview

Formal theories of development are helpful in organizing and understanding the process of development and in stimulating and guiding research, theory, and practice. A good theory has a number of characteristics: it possesses internal consistency, offers meaningful explanations, is open to scientific evaluation, and acts as a stimulus for new thinking, research, and practice. Theories are characterized and differentiated from each other by the degree to which they emphasize the role of maturation versus experience, the individual's active versus passive participation in his or her development, continuous versus stagelike development, and breadth of theoretical focus.

In the theories of Freud and Erikson, development is seen as a dynamic process that occurs in a series of stages, each involving psychological conflicts that the developing person must resolve. From the Freudian perspective, personality development is energized by the id, ego, and superego. Eight developmental stages characterize Erikson's psychosocial theory; each stage is defined by a psychological crisis that is never completely resolved.

Object relations approaches view development as the result of a child's mental representations of early social and emotional relationships with parents and important others. Learning is the focus of the behavioral views of development; it is seen as the source of developmental change. Pavlov's theory emphasizes learning through classical conditioning as the main process by which developmental changes occur. In operant conditioning, Skinner argues that reinforcement, punishment, extinction, and shaping determine developmental changes.

Bandura's social cognitive learning theory emphasizes the role of observation in developmental change. Cognitive development theories focus on how thinking and problem solving contribute to development. Piaget suggested that cognitive development occurs in stages, each of which incorporates and revises those that precede it. New ways of thinking and problem solving are achieved through assimilation and accommodation. A number of neo-Piagetian approaches emphasize the roles of mental space, skill acquisition, and information-processing capacity in cognitive development. The information-processing theory focuses on the steps involved in thought processes. Information is first stored in the sensory register, then in short-term memory, and last in long-term memory.

Contextual approaches view development as an interactive process between the child and his or her physical, social, and developmental contexts. Bronfenbrenner's ecological systems theory suggests that the microsystem, mesosystem, exosystem, and macrosystem form interactive and overlapping contexts for development. Vygotsky emphasizes the contributions of history and culture to development that takes place in the zone of proximal development. Ethology focuses on the developmental roles of behavioral dispositions and the traits that are thought to have evolutionary survival value for the human species. Normative-crisis theories of adult and lifespan development focus on fairly predictable changes that occur over the lifespan, particularly during the adult years. Vaillant's styles of coping and Levinson's seasons of life are examples of this approach. The timing of events theory emphasizes the role of both normative and nonnormative transitions in a person's life course and explains how social expectations may be internalized in a social clock against which we judge our own development. Although developmental theories differ in both focus and explanatory concepts, together they provide a fairly comprehensive view of developmental change and thus are very useful.

Chapter Outline

I. The nature of developmental theories

   A. What is a developmental theory?

   Theories help organize and make sense of information about development. A good theory has several characteristics.

   1. There is internal consistency, with the different parts fitting together in a logical way.

   2. It provides meaningful explanations of developmental change.

   3. The theory is open to scientific evaluation so that it can be revised or discarded.

   4. The theory stimulates new thinking and research.

   5. It provides guidance to parents and professionals in working with children, adolescents, and adults.

   B. How developmental theories differ: Four developmental themes

   1. Developmental theories differ in how much influence they attribute to maturation and how much to experience.

   2. They differ in their view of developmental change as being continuous or stagelike in nature.

   3. They differ in how broadly they define various factors and contexts in developmental change.

   4. They differ in their view of individuals as active or passive participants in their own development.

II. Psychodynamic developmental theories

   Psychodynamic theories propose that development is an active process influenced by inborn, biological drives and conscious and unconscious experiences.

   A. Freudian theory

   Freud, the creator of psychoanalysis, influenced psychodynamic theories of personality development and the causes and treatment of psychological problems.

   1. Freud described a three-part structure of personality.

a. The **id**, which is present at birth, is unconscious. It tries to satisfy a person's biological needs and desires by motivating behavior that instinctively seeks to maximize pleasure and avoid discomfort without regard for the realities involved.

b. The **ego** is the largely rational, conscious, reality-oriented, problem-solving part of the personality. It functions according to the reality principle.

c. The **superego** is the moral and ethical part of the personality. It includes the child's emerging sense of conscience.

2. Freud believed development occurs through id/ego/superego conflicts within a series of psychosexual stages.

a. Each stage focuses on a different area of the body.

b. Conflicts may result in these stages.

3. Defense mechanisms such as repression and projection protect the ego from conflicts.

4. Unresolved conflicts can lead to fixations. A fixation is a blockage in development

- Perspectives: Erik Erikson's identity crisis: An autobiographical perspective

B. Erikson's psychosocial theory

Erikson, who studied with Freud's daughter, Anna, believed personality development involves a lifelong process through which an individual attempts to achieve a sense of identity by mastering a series of conflicts created by three interrelated developmental forces: the person's biological and physical strengths and limitations; his or her unique life circumstances and developmental history; and the particular social, cultural, and historical forces at work during the individual's lifetime.

1. Each of Erikson's eight stages of development involves a particular psychosocial crisis that individuals must successfully master to achieve an adult identity.

a. **Trust versus mistrust** is the first stage (birth to one year). At this time, the child develops trusting relationships with others.

b. For successful resolution of the crisis of **autonomy versus shame and doubt** (one to three years), the child must learn control over bodily functions and activities.

c. During the **initiative versus guilt** stage (three to six years), the child tests the limits of self-assertion and purposefulness.

d. **Industry versus inferiority** (six to twelve years) is the stage where the child experiences the challenge of mastering many new social and intellectual tasks.

e. During the **identity versus role confusion** stage (twelve to nineteen years), individuals attempt to form an identity and coherent self-concept.

f. During the **intimacy versus isolation** stage (nineteen to twenty-five years), the young adult must develop close and committed relationships with others.

g. The crisis of **generativity versus stagnation** (twenty-five to fifty years) occurs in adulthood and midlife. Here the individual attempts to help future generations.

h. The older adult (fifty and older) confronts the crisis of **ego integrity versus despair**.

2. According to Erikson, people never fully resolve any of their psychosocial conflicts. Rather, they achieve more or less favorable ratios of positive to negative outcomes.

C. Other psychodynamic approaches

Other theories reflect Freud's belief in the significance of early childhood relationships and both conscious and unconscious inner experiences. An example is **object relations** theory.

1. Mahler proposed a four-phase model by which children learn to develop a psychological sense of self.

2. Kohut argued that a newborn's sense of self is initially fragmented and incomplete.

3. Stern described the infant's process of developing a sense of self in four overlapping, interdependent stages, each of which defines a different area of self-experience and social relatedness.

III. Behavioral learning and social cognitive learning developmental theories

Learning is generally defined as relatively permanent changes in observable behavior as a result of experience. Learning experiences that occur during the course of a person's life are the source of developmental change.

A. Pavlov developed the notion of **classical conditioning** while studying digestion in dogs.

B. Skinner pioneered the notion of **operant conditioning**.

1. Operant conditioning is based on the simple concept of **reinforcement**.

2. **Punishment** weakens a response by either adding an unpleasant stimulus or removing a pleasurable one.

3. Shaping occurs when small changes in behavior are reinforced to bring the behaviors closer to a desired behavior.

C. Bandura's social cognitive theory views developmental change as a process resulting from the **observational learning** and interactions between the child and the physical and social environment.

IV. Cognitive developmental theories

Cognitive theories examine the development of children's thinking and problem solving.

A. Piaget's cognitive theory

Piaget's theory of cognitive development describes cognition and intelligence.

1. Key principles of Piaget's theory

a. Piaget believed thinking develops in a series of increasingly complex stages, each incorporating and revising those that precede it.

b. People move from stage to stage through the processes of direct learning, social transmission, and physical maturation.

c. Direct learning occurs when the child experiences changes related to a **scheme,** which is a pattern of thought and action.

d. **Assimilation** is the process by which the child interprets experiences on the basis of concepts he or she already knows.

e. **Accommodation** occurs when the already existing schemes are modified to better fit new ideas or experiences.

f. **Adaptation** is the result of the interplay of assimilation and accommodation and refers to a deepening and modification of a scheme.

B. Neo-Piagetian approaches

These approaches to cognitive development are new or revised models of Piaget's basic approach.

1. Case proposed that cognitive development results from increases in the available capacity of the child's mental space.

2. Fischer's theory accepts Piaget's basic idea of stages, but instead of schemes uses the term *skills* to describe cognitive structures that apply to particular problem-solving tasks. These skills are more task specific than Piaget's schemes.

C. Information-processing theory

Precise, detailed steps involved in mental activities are the focus of **information-processing theory.**

1. There are several key principles in information-processing theory.

   a. The sensory register takes in information from the environment.

   b. Information that is attended to is transferred to short-term memory.

   c. Information is saved permanently in long-term memory.

2. Developmental changes in information processing

   a. As children grow older, they experience several cognitive changes that allow them to process information more efficiently and comprehensively.

   b. Changes take place in control processes, which direct attention toward particular input from the sensory register and guide the response to new information.

   c. As children grow older, they develop **metacognition,** or the awareness and understanding of how thinking and learning work. This understanding helps children assess task difficulty and plan strategies for approaching a task.

d.   As children grow older, they also increase their knowledge base.

V.   Contextual developmental theories

Contextual approaches view development as a process involving the pattern of reciprocal transactions between the child and the system of physical, social, and cultural developmental contexts in which those interactions occur.

A.   Bronfenbrenner's ecological systems theory

In Bronfenbrenner's ecological approach, the context in which the developing individual exists, the person's cognitive, socioemotional, and motivational capacities, and his or her active participation are central ingredients for developmental change. Bronfenbrenner describes four ecological settings in which development occurs.

B.   Vygotsky's sociohistorical theory

Vygotsky proposed that the development of cognitive ability is a function of individuals' social interactions with others more capable than themselves, and he asserts that learning occurs within the **zone of proximal development**, the range between what a person is capable of attaining alone and what she or he can achieve with the assistance of a more capable individual.

C.   Ethological theory, in the context of human development, focuses on an individual's innate behavioral and psychological characteristics that constrain physical and behavioral development.

•   A multicultural view: Cultural context and cognitive development

VI.   Adulthood and lifespan developmental theories

A.   **Normative-crisis model** of development

This model assumes that developmental changes occur in distinct stages and that all individuals follow the same sequence.

1.   Each stage is qualitatively unique, each becoming more complex and developed.

2.   Vaillant's styles of adult coping are based on longitudinal research; according to his model, development is a lifelong process influenced by relationships with others and coping styles.

3.   Levinson, using biographical data from men, identified three eras in male adult life: early adulthood, middle adulthood, and late adulthood. Each era is characterized by transitions.

B.   **Timing of events** model

1.   Life events are seen as markers of developmental change.

2.   Life events may be normative.

a.   Normative life events are transitions that follow an age-appropriate social timetable.

    b.   An internalized social clock tells the person if he or she is "on time."

  3.   Life events may be nonnormative.

    a.   Nonnormative life events occur at any point in time.

  4.   According to the timing of events model, changes during adulthood are less closely tied to the predictable physical and cognitive maturational changes that occur during childhood and adolescence. Adults play much more active and self-conscious roles in directing their own development through decisions and choices.

VII. Developmental theories compared: Implications for the student

  • Working with John Daviau, residential treatment program director: Understanding multi-problem adolescents

Key Concepts

Directions: Identify each of the following key concepts discussed in this chapter.

1. The purpose of any theory is to help us _____ and _____ of large amounts of sometimes conflicting information.

2. Four major themes by which we can both characterize and differentiate developmental theories are _____, _____, _____, and _____.

3. _____ theories believe development is an active, dynamic process that is influenced by biological drives and the conscious and unconscious.

4. Freud believed the personality consisted of three structures, _____, _____, and _____.

5. According to Freud, the _____ functions according to the pleasure principle, and the ego is regulated by the _____.

6. The ego uses _____ to protect itself from conflicts.

7. Whereas Freud's theory was considered a psychosexual theory, Erikson's was considered _____.

8. Unlike Freud, who looked only at developmental crises occurring during childhood, Erikson addressed the development of identity over _____ stages that occur over the course of the entire _____.

9. During Erikson's first stage, which coincides with Freud's oral stage, the child must develop the proper balance of _____ over _____ in order to handle later crises.

10. At the age when toilet training is typically an issue, the child must resolve the crisis of _____ versus _____.

11. The child takes _____ by gaining some measure of independence from the primary caregiver, but faces _____ when reprimanded for a new interest in the genitals as a source of pleasure.

12. Children who believe in their ability to master school tasks gain feelings of _____, while those who experience failure often feel _____ to peers.

13. Adolescents who explore their social, sexual, and intellectual roles as soon-to-be adults may begin to develop a sense of _____. On the other hand, premature choices of identity produce a sense of _____.

14. Young adults who develop the capacity to form close, committed relationships are able to experience _____, whereas those unable to form such associations experience _____.

15. Middle-age adults who derive personal satisfaction from work and family experience _____, while those who feel life has no purpose encounter _____.

16. During later adulthood and old age, individuals gain _____ when they are able to look back on their lives with dignity, optimism, and wisdom. Many of the elderly who are isolated socially or have economic or physical difficulties may feel _____ when facing the end of life.

17. Mahler's _____ approach proposes that infants progress through four phases in their development of _____. Stern suggests that infants develop a sense of _____ in four overlapping, interdependent stages.

18. _____ theories focus on observable behaviors and attribute learning to experience.

19. Pavlov's notion of _____ involves taking a stimulus that naturally elicits a response and pairing it with one that does not produce that same response.

20. In classical conditioning, the sight of the bottle and the mother's smile and voice are examples of _____.

21. Skinner's theory of _____ includes the effects of reinforcement, punishment, and extinction on behavior.

22. When parents praise a child for cleaning his or her room, with the intent of increasing the chances that the room-cleaning behavior will be repeated, they are using _____. However, when parents take away a favored activity from a child for misbehavior, they are administering _____.

23. _____ weakens a behavioral response.

24. When a child is no longer reinforced for a particular behavior, _____ often occurs, and the child's response disappears.

25. A technique to learn new responses by using reinforcement for successively better responses is called _____.

26. Bandura believed that developmental change occurs through _____.

27. According to Bandura's social cognitive learning theory, learning is _____.

28. Bandura stated that through _____, children are directly reinforced for repeating the actions of others.

29. Through _____, children are vicariously reinforced.

30. The development of thinking and problem-solving skills is the focus of _____ theories.

31. Piaget believed children have existing patterns of thought and action called _____.

32. According to Piaget, by _____ we incorporate new knowledge into preexisting ways of thinking about things; by _____ we modify our thinking to fit the new knowledge. The interplay of these two processes is termed _____.

33. When current schemes are used to interpret and respond to a new experience or situation, _____ takes place. A child changes an existing scheme when faced with a new experience or situation by _____.

34. A goal of intellectual activity, according to Piaget, is to establish _____.

35. Two theorists who expanded on Piaget's theories were _____ and _____; hence, these researchers are termed _____ theorists.

36. Case, in revising Piaget's theory, introduced the notion that cognitive development resulted from increased capacity within a child's _____. This term refers to the maximum number of schemes a child can apply at one time.

37. Fischer, also addressing weaknesses in Piaget's theory, proposed that within each developmental stage, a period of _____ occurs. At this time, the child gains new skills in specific contexts and integrates them with preexisting ones.

38. The _____ theory focuses on the precise, detailed features or steps involved in mental activities.

39. Information-processing theorists define _____ as the process of encoding, storing, and retrieving within the information-processing system.

40. The information-processing model describes a three-store memory system. In this system the _____ holds incoming stimuli from the environment for only seconds. The stimuli of which we are aware enter _____, where active thinking occurs. If the information is rehearsed, organized, or elaborated upon, it is stored in _____; otherwise it is lost.

41. Specific _____, such as attention or strategies used to remember new information, direct processing of information within and between the three memory stores.

42. _____ describes our capacity to know our own cognitive capabilities in light of specific cognitive tasks and to know what strategies are most effective in which situations.

43. Development is viewed as an interactive process of _____ transactions between children and their physical, social, and developmental contexts by _____ theorists.

44. Bronfenbrenner described four ecological settings in which developmental change occurs. The situations in which the young child interacts with immediate family members make up the _____. The _____ comprises the relationships between microsystems, such as home-school relationships. The _____ consists of situations in which decisions are made that affect the child, such as a parent's employment. The _____ involves social and cultural catalysts that have an impact on the other three systems.

45. Vygotsky proposed that learning occurs within the _____, that range of ability between what a child can accomplish alone and what he or she can do with the assistance of a more capable individual.

46. One area of interest to ethological theorists is the development of _____, the relationship between the infant and primary caregiver. Another of their interests is the way an individual responds to situations in the environment, or _____.

47. The adulthood and lifespan model that views developmental changes as occurring in distinct stages is called the _____. Two examples of this approach are the theories of _____ and _____.

48. _____ argued that developmental changes are indicated by life events. The life events that are less predictable are called _____ life events.

Multiple-Choice Self-Test

Factual / Conceptual Questions

1. Developmental theories that view an individual as progressing by resolving conflicts or by solving problems tend to view change as a(n)
   a. active process.
   b. conscious process.
   c. learning process.
   d. maturational process.

2. Whereas the id tries to maximize _____, the ego emphasizes _____.
   a. pleasure, the conscious
   b. pleasure, reality
   c. reality, logic
   d. the unconscious, the conscious

3. Which of Erikson's stages is most closely associated with Freud's oral stage?
   a. Autonomy versus shame and doubt
   b. Industry versus inferiority
   c. Initiative versus guilt
   d. Trust versus mistrust

4. A negative reinforcer
   a. follows the presentation of the conditioned stimulus.
   b. increases the likelihood of the response that preceded it.
   c. decreases the likelihood of the response that preceded it.
   d. always inflicts pain.

5. Social cognitive theory goes beyond learning theory by adding the concept of
   a. assimilation.
   b. libido.
   c. vicarious reinforcement.
   d. unconditioned response.

6. Piaget believed that infants understand the world through early reflexes called
   a. unconditioned responses.
   b. schemes.
   c. vicarious concepts.
   d. primary circular reactions.

7. According to Piaget, the process by which schemes are modified to incorporate new information is termed
   a. lateralization.
   b. assimilation.
   c. accommodation.
   d. conservation.

8. Short-term memory
   a. can hold about seven items.
   b. lasts approximately five minutes.
   c. replicates all information from the sensory register.
   d. contains strategies for learning information effectively.

9. Which of the following is *not* a characteristic of most contextual theories?
   a. They tend to be stage theories.
   b. They focus on experiences in multiple contexts.
   c. They view the child as highly active.
   d. They focus on interactions.

10. Which theorist hypothesizes the establishment of new life structures at each era of adulthood?
    a. Albert Bandura
    b. Erik Erikson
    c. Sigmund Freud
    d. Daniel Levinson

Application Questions

1. Professor Starsky believes that developmental change is caused by events in the environment that stimulate the person to respond. The professor's position can be described as a belief in
   a. conscious processes.
   b. discontinuity in development.
   c. maturational mechanisms of development.
   d. the passive role of the child.

2. Brett's mother remarked that her eighteen-month-old finally seems to be developing some patience when it comes to feeding. Brett is probably in Freud's _____ stage.
   a. anal
   b. latency
   c. oral
   d. phallic

3. Which phrase best captures Freud's notions of the conscience?
   a. "Thou shalt not . . . "
   b. "Anything goes!"
   c. "Do unto others . . . "
   d. "The sky's the limit."

4. Six-month-old Nathan's parents are fairly inconsistent in responding to his needs. He often spends a long time in wet and messy diapers, and his feeding schedule is somewhat unpredictable. According to Erikson, Nathan is likely to develop a
   a. strong sense of autonomy.
   b. strong sense of trust.
   c. weak sense of autonomy.
   d. weak sense of trust.

5. Armand, who is in Erikson's fifth stage, is trying to establish
   a. autonomy.
   b. identity.
   c. intimacy.
   d. trust.

6. Four-month-old Jamie has begun to form a mental image of her mother as an object that takes care of her needs. According to Mahler, Jamie is most likely in the _____ phase of development.
   a. autistic
   b. separation-individuation
   c. sensorimotor
   d. symbiotic

7. Immediately before breast-feeding her three-month-old, Raquel turns on the light next to the rocker she sits on. After a while, Raquel notices that her infant begins to suck as soon as the light is turned on even if the breast is not present. The infant's response to the light can be best described in terms of
   a. operant conditioning.
   b. classical conditioning.
   c. a reflex mechanism.
   d. unconscious conflict.

8. After repeatedly refusing to give her son candy so as not to spoil his dinner, Marge finally gives in and provides him with a piece of candy in order to stop his unrelenting whining. Her candy-giving behavior is thereby
   a. extinguished.
   b. negatively reinforced.
   c. positively reinforced.
   d. punished.

9. The first time Irene saw a platypus she called it a "duck." She is most likely
   a. accommodating.
   b. assimilating.
   c. imitating.
   d. misapprehending.

10. Which of the following best illustrates Vygotsky's notions concerning the zone of proximal development?
    a. Antonio is almost as tall as his brother, who is one year older.
    b. Amy cannot put on roller skates even though she can skate.
    c. Eddie cannot separate out different coins unless his father instructs him to first group the pennies, then the nickels, etc.
    d. Marika learned to jump before she could skip.

Answer Key

Key Concepts

1. organize, make sense
2. experience versus maturation, passive versus active role of a child, continuous versus stagelike development, breadth of focus
3. Psychodynamic
4. id, ego, superego
5. id, reality principle
6. defense mechanisms
7. psychosocial
8. eight, lifespan
9. trust, mistrust
10. autonomy, shame and doubt
11. initiative, guilt
12. industry, inferior
13. identity, role confusion
14. intimacy, isolation
15. generativity, stagnation
16. ego integrity, despair
17. object relations, psychological self, self
18. Behavioral learning theories
19. classical conditioning
20. conditioned stimuli
21. operant conditioning
22. reinforcement, punishment
23. Punishment
24. extinction
25. shaping
26. observational learning
27. reciprocally determined
28. imitation
29. modeling
30. cognitive developmental
31. schemes
32. assimilation, accommodation, adaptation
33. assimilation, accommodation
34. equilibrium
35. Case, Fischer, neo-Piagetian
36. mental space
37. skill acquisition
38. information-processing
39. cognition
40. sensory register, short-term memory, long-term memory
41. control processes
42. Metacognition
43. reciprocal, contextual
44. microsystem, mesosystem, ecosystem, macrosystem
45. zone of proximal development
46. attachment, temperament
47. normative-crisis model, Vaillant, Levinson (Erikson also acceptable)
48. Timing of events, nonnormative

Multiple-Choice Self-Test: Factual / Conceptual Questions

1. Choice (a) is correct. Active processes involve internal resolution or movements that bring about change in conflict situations and problem solving (as found in Freud's and Piaget's theories, respectively). Choice (b), conscious process, involves the question of whether a person is aware of the changes. Choices (c) and (d), learning and maturational processes, respectively, address the issue of whether change is environmentally or biologically motivated.

2. Choice (b) is correct. The id seeks immediate gratification through the pleasure principle. The ego places some restraints on the id based on the reality principle. Choice (a) is incorrect. The id does follow the pleasure principle, but there is no such thing as the "conscious principle," although the ego is represented at the conscious level. Choice (c) is also incorrect. The reality principle is associated with the ego, not with the id. In Freudian psychology, there is nothing called the logical principle. Choice (d), unconscious and conscious, names parts of the mind, not personality.

3. Choice (d) is correct. The oral stage is Freud's first stage, which deals with issues surrounding infancy and the development of dependence on others; Erikson's first stage deals with similar issues, including the establishment of trust. Choice (a), autonomy versus shame and doubt, corresponds to Freud's anal stage, choice (c), initiative versus guilt, is close to Freud's phallic stage, and choice (b), industry versus inferiority, is similar to Freud's latency stage.

4. Choice (b) is correct. A reinforcer (negative or positive) always increases the probability of the behavior that preceded it. Negative refers to the fact that a stimulus is turned off (positive involves the turning on of a stimulus). Choice (a) refers to a conditioned response; choice (c) defines what is meant by a punishment; and choice (d) is not true. In fact, a negative reinforcer often removes pain (an unpleasant stimulus or situation).

5. Choice (c) is correct. A major difference between learning theory and social cognitive theory involves the effects of indirect reinforcement based on the observation of others being reinforced (or punished). Choice (a), assimilation, is a concept from Piaget's theory; choice (b), libido, is a concept from Freud's theory; and choice (d), unconditioned response, is part of a learning theory.

6. Choice (b) is correct. Piaget believed that the early schemes (behaviors) were based on reflexes such as orienting, grasping, and sucking. Choice (a), unconditioned responses, is a term used in classical conditioning that is similar to innate reflexes. Choice (c), vicarious concepts, is not a real concept in psychology. Choice (d), primary circular reactions, is the term Piaget used for body-centered behaviors that actually come from the developing innate schemes.

7. Choice (c) is correct. Accommodation is the process by which a child changes his or her existing schemes when faced with new information. Choice (a), lateralization, is a process concerned with brain specialization. Choice (b), assimilation, is the process by which existing schemes are used to deal with new information. Choice (d), conservation, is a concept that holds that even though changes may occur in an object, certain aspects remain constant.

8. Choice (a) is correct; the short-term memory holds about seven bits of information. Choice (b) is incorrect because short-term memory lasts about twenty seconds, not five minutes. Only information that is attended to is passed from the sensory register to short-term memory; thus choice (c) is incorrect. The control processes, not the short-term memory, contain strategies for learning; thus choice (d) is also incorrect.

9. Choice (a) is correct. Most contextual theories hypothesize continuity in development, which is not characteristic of stages. Choices (b), (c), and (d) are all characteristics of the contextual

approach in that they consider multiple contexts and view individuals as highly active and interactive.

10. Choice (d) is correct. Levinson's theory describes what he terms the "seasons of life," in which each person needs to establish and reestablish his or her life structures at various points throughout adulthood. Bandura, choice (a), is associated with social learning theory; Erikson, choice (b), has a lifespan theory but hypothesizes certain crises at each of his psychosocial stages; and Freud, choice (c), does not focus on adulthood.

Multiple-Choice Self-Test: Application Questions

1. Choice (d) is correct. Professor Starsky's view seems to be close to a learning/conditioning approach in which the child is a reactor rather than an active initiator. Therefore, he seems to emphasize the passive role. Issues in choices (a), (b), and (c) are not addressed in the description; however, they all tend to be more consistent with an active rather than passive view of the child.

2. Choice (a) is correct, for two reasons. First, the oral stage generally begins at about one year of age and ends around three years; the eighteen-month-old falls within this span. Second, the development of patience during the feeding situation indicates an ability to delay gratification, which also develops during the anal stage, along with the ego. Choice (b), latency, does not begin until about five years of age; choice (c), oral, is Freud's first stage, in which the child wants immediate gratification of his or her needs. Choice (d), phallic, begins at about three years of age.

3. Choice (a) is correct. Freud divided the superego into two components: the conscience, which embodies all the rules that one must follow, and the ego ideal, which directs what one should do. Thus, "Thou shalt not . . . " would be the conscience, while choice (c), "Do unto others . . . ," would be the ego ideal. Choices (b) and (d), "Anything goes!" and "The sky's the limit," respectively, would be closer to something that the id would reflect.

4. Choice (d) is correct. A six-month-old would be in Erikson's first stage, which involves the crisis of trust versus mistrust. The inconsistent behaviors generally lead to a poor resolution, which in this case would be mistrust. Choices (a) and (c) focus on Erikson's second stage. Choice (b) is indicative of a successful resolution of the trust-versus-mistrust conflict as evidenced by fairly consistent and appropriate parental responses.

5. Choice (b) is correct. Erikson's fifth stage occurs during adolescence and centers around the establishment of an identity. Choice (a), autonomy, corresponds to stage two; choice (c), intimacy, to stage six, and choice (d), trust, to Erikson's first stage.

6. Choice (d) is correct. Mahler's second phase, which covers ages two to six months, involves a "dim awareness of the need-satisfying object," which is typically the primary caretaker. Choice (a), autistic, refers to Mahler's first phase, which is a transition phase between the womb and the outside world with little recognition; choice (b), separation-individuation, is Mahler's third phase, which involves quite definite recognition of the primary caretaker and others; and choice (c), sensorimotor, is Piaget's first stage of development, not a term used by Mahler.

7. Choice (b) is correct. The situation involves an initially neutral stimulus (the light) that elicits an already established stimulus-response pair (breast and sucking). Choice (a), operant conditioning, involves a response followed by a reinforcer, which is not the case here; and choice (c), reflex mechanism, is descriptive of the stimulus-response pair (breast and sucking), not the light. There is no conflict, so choice (d), unconscious conflict, is not appropriate.

8. Choice (b) is correct. Negative reinforcement occurs when the ending of an obnoxious stimulus increases the probability of the event that immediately preceded it. In this case, the giving of the candy ended the whining and thus if Marge is in this whining situation in the future, she will be more likely to give her son candy. Choice (c), positively reinforced, is what is happening from the son's perspective: he is being positively reinforced and will be likely to whine for candy in the future. Choice (d), punishment, always involves the decreased probability of a behavior, while just the opposite has happened to the candy-giving behavior. Similarly the candy-giving behavior is not being extinguished, choice (a); in fact, it is being strengthened.

9. Choice (b) is correct. Assimilation involves the application of already established behaviors or schemes to new information. Presumably Irene is familiar with ducks and simply fits the platypus into that scheme because it has some similarity. Choice (a), accommodating, is not occurring since Irene is just fitting the platypus into what she knows without changing anything. If, however, she had called it a "beaver-duck" or a "four-legged duck," this would be modifying a scheme to fit new information. Choice (c), imitating, does not apply, since there is nothing to imitate, and although Irene is making a mistake, she is not misapprehending, choice (d), because she has never seen a platypus before.

10. Choice (c) is correct. The zone of proximal development involves the notion that a person is unsuccessful at a task unless an older, more experienced person helps him or her. This help then leads to successful performance. Eddie cannot sort coins by himself, but when given minor directions, he can do it. Choices (a) and (d) are not relevant; choice (b) does not give us information on whether or not Amy can get her skates on with minor assistance and therefore is not correct.

CHAPTER 3
Genetics, Prenatal Development, and Birth

Learning Objectives

1. Identify and describe the mechanisms and means through which genetic information is transferred. Describe the roles of DNA, genes, chromosomes, and cell division.

2. Distinguish between genotype and phenotype.

3. Describe dominant and recessive genes and how these mechanisms influence the expression of various traits. Identify what is meant by polygenic transmission of traits.

4. Describe how and when gender is determined. Discuss sex-linked recessive disorders and how they are transmitted.

5. Describe the characteristics of the major genetic disorders, including chromosomal abnormalities and gene-based abnormalities.

6. Describe the methods used for detecting genetic disorders during the prenatal period and identify the circumstances in which genetic counseling is recommended.

7. Describe the role of behavioral genetics, including the concepts of canalization and range of reaction.

8. Describe various methods for studying the heredity-environment issue, including adoption and twin studies.

9. Describe the process of conception and the factors that affect it.

10. Identify and describe the three stages of prenatal development, including the major events that occur at each stage.

11. Discuss the various issues concerning pregnancy, including infertility and the physical and psychological adjustments associated with pregnancy.

12. Identify and describe the major biological risk factors associated with each trimester during the prenatal period.

13. Discuss the physical and biological risk factors associated with the mother during pregnancy.

14. Identify and describe the effect that various teratogens have on prenatal development, including alcohol, smoking, and drugs. Discuss the role of diet and nutrition, violence, teenage pregnancy, stress, and other environmental hazards on prenatal development.

15. Describe the birth process and identify the characteristics of the three stages of labor. Identify and describe alternative birthing techniques. Explain how drugs are used in childbirth, and describe the consequences.

16. Describe the problems that can occur during birth that are associated with faulty power, faulty passageway, and faulty passenger, and discuss their solutions.

Chapter Overview

Genes, DNA, and chromosomes play important roles in the transmission of human traits. Genetic information is contained in deoxyribonucleic acid (DNA). Reproductive cells divide by meiosis, resulting in one-half their normal number of chromosomes until conception, when the number of chromosomes returns to normal; all other cells divide by mitosis. A person's genotype is the specific pattern of genetic information inherited in his or her chromosomes and genes at conception. Phenotype refers to the physical and behavioral traits the person actually shows during his or her life. Phenotype is the product of the interaction of genotype and environmental variables. Some genes are dominant, which means they may influence the phenotype if only one member of the pair occurs. Other genes may be recessive; their influence occurs only when both members of the pair are present in a particular form. Many traits are inherited by the combined actions of several genes and are called polygenic. Sex is determined by one particular pair of chromosomes called the X and Y chromosomes.

There are a number of genetic abnormalities; these can be caused by abnormal numbers of chromosomes (e.g., Down syndrome), dominant gene disorders (e.g., Huntington disease), recessive gene disorders (e.g., sickle-cell disease), or multifactorial (genetic plus environmental) causes. Genetic counseling is an option for couples who may carry genetic disorders; the counseling may include testing for genetic problems before the baby is born, including ultrasound, fetoscopy, amniocentesis, chorionic villus sampling, and various blood tests.

According to behavior geneticists, every characteristic of an individual is the result of the unique interaction between genetic inheritance and the sequence of environments through which he or she passes during development. The concept of range of reaction describes the strength of genetic influence under different environmental conditions. Studies of identical twins and of adopted children suggest that heredity and environment operate jointly to influence developmental change. Linkage and association studies use repeated DNA segments as genetic markers to locate abnormal genes. Neither biogenetic nor environmental determinism is likely to give us an adequate understanding of human development, which is the product of both genes and environment.

The first step in prenatal development is conception, whereby a sperm cell fertilizes an ovum. Prenatal development takes place in three stages: germinal, embryonic, and fetal. From the germinal to fetal stage, important developmental landmarks take place. At the end of nine months, the average fetus weighs 7.5 pounds and is 20 inches long. Some couples experience infertility, which is the inability to conceive or carry a pregnancy to term after one year of unprotected intercourse.

Pregnancy brings many new experiences for both mother and father. There are critical periods in prenatal development when development is highly vulnerable to disruption from teratogens. Teratogens are substances or other environmental influences that can permanently disrupt and damage an embryo's growth. Their effects depend on the timing, intensity, and duration of exposure, the presence of other risks, and the biological vulnerability of the baby and the mother. Environmental hazards also pose risks for pregnant women. The mother's age and health may also influence the development of the fetus. Other factors that may negatively affect development include environmental hazards, domestic violence, pregnancy in teenagers, diet and nutrition, prenatal health care, and stress.

The birth process occurs in three stages, beginning with contractions that open the cervix and ending with the expulsion of the placenta and umbilical cord. Women have a number of options with regard to childbirth settings and methods, including birthing rooms, freestanding birth centers, and home births. Many women participate in prepared childbirth such as the Lamaze method. Most mothers feel pain during labor contractions, and some may request pain relief. Problems such as weak contractions, placenta previa, abruptio placenta, and baby size or position may pose problems in childbirth. In these cases, a cesarean section may be performed. Fetal monitoring can record uterine contractions and the fetal heart rate to identify if the fetus is in distress. Having a baby can create new challenges for the family and can be especially difficult for adolescent parents and parents who are educationally and economically disadvantaged.

Chapter Outline

I. Genetics

Inheritance affects a large number of human qualities.

II. Mechanisms of genetic transmission

Genetic information is combined and transmitted through gametes (i.e., **ovum** and **sperm**), which contain genetic information in molecular structures called **genes**, which form threads called **chromosomes**.

A. The role of DNA

1. The genes are made of deoxyribonucleic acid (DNA) molecules, which have a double helix (spiral) chemical structure that allows their division and duplication.

2. DNA transmits genetic information at conception, when the sperm and ovum unite creating a **zygote**.

B. Meiosis and mitosis

1. Gametes divide through meiosis, resulting in twenty-three chromosomes.

2. All other cells divide by mitosis, resulting in forty-six chromosomes.

III. Individual genetic expression

A. Genotype and phenotype

1. The **genotype** of an individual is the set of genes he or she inherits that may influence a particular trait.

2. The **phenotype** is the physical and behavioral characteristics a person actually exhibits at a particular point in development. The phenotype results from all of the interactions of the genotype with environmental influences.

B. Dominant and recessive genes

1. A **dominant gene** will influence a phenotype even when paired with a recessive gene.

2. A **recessive gene** must be paired with another recessive gene to be able to influence the phenotype.

3. Traits that exhibit the phenotype of recessive genes, such as blue eye color, result from the pairing of two recessive genes.

C. Transmission of multiple variations

1. The genes responsible for eye color, or any other specific trait, often take on a variety of forms called **alleles**.

2. When a person inherits identical alleles from each parent for a specific trait, he or she is said to be homozygous for that trait.

3. When a person inherits different alleles for a trait, he or she is said to be heterozygous for that trait.

4. Codominance is a situation where the characteristics of both alleles are independently expressed in a new phenotype.

D. Polygenic transmission

1. Some traits seem to result from the combined influence of many genes, each of which contributes a small part to the trait.

2. Since the influence of these genes is small, the environment can influence phenotypes.

E. The determination of sex

1. One chromosomal pair determines development as a male or a female.

2. Females have a matched pair of longer chromosomes, called XX; males have one longer and one shorter chromosome, or an XY pair.

3. A large number of genetic abnormalities are linked to genes on the X chromosome and are called **sex-linked recessive traits**. One of these traits is hemophilia, for which males are at greater risk because there is no location on the shorter Y chromosome for a dominant gene to block the influence of the abnormal hemophilia gene.

IV. Genetic abnormalities

A. Disorders due to abnormal chromosomes

1. Many individuals with **Down syndrome** have abnormalities of the heart and intestinal tract and facial deformities. They are also at risk for developing other serious diseases.

2. They may reach normal developmental milestones, but do so more slowly than normal children.

3. Down syndrome is much more frequent in babies of mothers over age thirty-five and among older fathers.

B. Abnormal genes

Even though transmitted through a normal pattern of forty-six chromosomes, abnormal genes may create serious medical problems for the child after birth.

1. Dominant gene disorders

   These disorders require only one abnormal gene to affect a child (e.g., Huntington disease)

2. Recessive gene disorders

   These disorders require a pair of recessive genes. **Sickle-cell disease** is a recessive gene disorder and causes the oxygen-carrying protein in the red blood cells to take on an abnormal shape. These cells get caught in the blood vessels, cutting off circulation, reducing oxygen supply, and causing pain.

3. Multifactorial disorders

   Disorders that result from a combination of genetic and environmental factors are called multifactorial.

V. Genetic counseling and prenatal diagnosis

Some genetic problems can be reduced or avoided through counseling for couples who may carry genetic disorders. The parents' medical and genetic histories and tests are used to estimate the chances of having a healthy baby.

- A multicultural view: Cultural differences and genetic counseling

VI. Relative influence of heredity and environment

Research supports the important role heredity, as well as environmental factors, plays in individual developmental differences. Behavior genetics is the study of how genotype and environmental experience jointly influence phenotype.

A. Key concepts of behavior genetics

Range of reaction refers to the range of possible phenotypes a particular genotype might exhibit in response to environmental influences.

B. Adoption and twin studies

1. **Adoption studies** measure the effects of genetics and environment on development.

2. **Twin studies** compare pairs of identical twins raised in the same family with pairs of fraternal twins raised in the same family.

3. **Twin adoption studies** compare pairs of identical twins who are raised apart since birth in different environments.

4. Linkage and association studies allow research to identify polymorphisms, which are certain segments of DNA that are inherited together, and those polymorphisms that are coinherited with a particular trait in families unusually prone to that trait.

C. Cautions and conclusions about the influence of heredity and environment

There is substantial evidence that genetic inheritance plays at least a moderate role in differences in physical, intellectual, and personality traits. It is likely that such differences are due to both heredity and environmental experience.

VII. Prenatal development and birth

VIII. Stages of prenatal development

Prenatal development takes place in the **germinal, embryonic,** and **fetal** stages.

A. Conception

Conception occurs when a sperm cell penetrates and fertilizes an egg cell.

B. The germinal stage (first two weeks)

1. The blastocyst is differentiated into three layers: the ectoderm, the endoderm, and the mesoderm.

2. The blastocyst moves down the fallopian tube into the uterus for implantation.

3. The embryonic stage begins with implantation, and the fully implanted blastocyst is referred to as the embryo.

C. The embryonic stage (third through eighth weeks)

1. Growth in the embryonic and fetal stages follows a cephalocaudal (head-to-tail) and a proximodistal (near-to-far) pattern.

2. The head, blood vessels, heart, and most vital organs begin to develop before the arms, legs, hands, and feet.

3. The **placenta** forms, through which oxygen and nutrients reach the fetus.

4. The **umbilical cord** connects the embryo to the placenta; it provides nutrients and carries away waste products.

5. The **amniotic sac** surrounds the embryo and protects it.

D. The fetal stage (ninth week to birth)

1. The fetal stage is marked by the development of the first bone cells. The embryo is now called the fetus.

2. By the third month, the fetus is able to move its head, legs, and feet. By the fourth month, the mother may feel quickening, or fetal movement.

3. The beginning of the seventh month is considered the age of viability.

4. At the end of nine months, the fetus is on average 7.5 pounds and almost 20 inches long.

E. Infertility

   1. About 15 percent of couples are unable to conceive or carry a pregnancy to term after one year of unprotected intercourse.

   2. In about 80 to 90 percent of couples receiving medical treatment, it is possible to discover a clear medical reason for infertility.

   3. New technologies are now available to help couples deal with infertility.

- Perspectives: Technological alternatives to normal conception

   F. The experience of pregnancy

   1. Physical complaints such as nausea are common.

   2. Normal weight gain is about 30 pounds and is dispersed in organs, baby, and bodily fluid.

   3. Pregnancy is a powerful experience for both mother and father. It raises the question "Am I ready to be emotionally and economically responsible for this baby?"

- Working with Katie Glover, ob-gyn, nurse practitioner: Preparing for childbirth

IX. Prenatal influences on the child

   A. Key concepts

   1. **Canalization** is seen in prenatal development.

   2. Risk factors can interfere with canalized processes that lead to the development of specific organs.

   3. The **critical period** refers to a limited period of time during which certain developmental changes are particularly sensitive to disruption.

   4. Any substance or other environmental influence that can interfere with or permanently damage an embryo's growth is called a **teratogen.**

   5. A teratogen's effect is dependent on several factors, such as timing of exposure, intensity and duration of exposure, the number of other harmful influences, and biogenetic vulnerability.

   B. Maternal age and physical characteristics

   The mother's age and health can lead to complications at birth.

   C. Maternal diseases

   1. Syphilis may cause fetal death, and gonorrhea may cause blindness.

   2. About three-fourths of AIDS cases in children involve perinatal transmission from an infected mother to her baby.

a. IV drug use by the mother causes most cases of perinatal AIDS.

b. Most children infected perinatally show symptoms before age one, but some remain free of symptoms for several years.

c. The drug AZT administered to an AIDS-infected woman during late pregnancy and labor and given to her child immediately after birth may help reduce the chance of having an HIV-infected baby.

D. Medicinal drugs

Drugs that may cure illness and relieve pain may negatively affect fetal development.

1. Thalidomide

a. Thalidomide was widely prescribed for reducing morning sickness in the late 1950s and early 1960s.

b. Babies of mothers who took thalidomide had deformed arms, legs, and faces and suffered deafness and brain damage.

2. Diethylstilbestrol (DES)

a. DES was taken by pregnant women to prevent miscarriages.

b. Babies of mothers who took DES seemed normal but developed serious problems later in life such as structural abnormalities in the vagina and uterus in girls and an increased risk for testicular cancer in boys.

E. Nonmedicinal drugs

1. Babies born to mothers who consume too much alcohol may have fetal alcohol syndrome (FAS) and fetal alcohol effects (FAEs).

2. Symptoms of FAS include central nervous system damage, physical abnormalities of the heart, head, face, and joints, and mental retardation.

3. Even moderate drinking during pregnancy can be dangerous.

F. Environmental hazards

There are physical and biological hazards to the developing fetus present in the workplace.

G. Domestic violence

Seven to eight percent of pregnant women are beaten by their partners. One percent of all pregnant women with no history of being battered will be abused during pregnancy.

H. Teenage pregnancy

1. The United States has the highest rate of teenage pregnancy in the industrialized world.

2. Pregnant teenagers often have nutritional deficiencies and may not get adequate prenatal care.

3. Babies born to teenage mothers are more likely to be premature and have low birth weight.

I. Diet and nutrition

1. Poor nutrition leads to increased risk of prematurity and infant mortality.

2. Babies of mothers with poor diets have lower birth weights and have an increased risk for congenital malformations.

J. Prenatal health care

1. Adequate early prenatal health care is critical to infant and maternal health.

2. Race and socioeconomic status play a major role in determining whether adequate early prenatal health care is obtained.

3. Programs can help high-risk mothers. These programs involve regular home visits and education.

K. Stress

1. Prolonged anxiety just before or during pregnancy is likely to increase medical complications.

2. Emotional stress is related to spontaneous abortion as well as to labor and birth problems.

X. Birth

After about thirty-eight weeks in the womb, the baby is considered "full term," or ready for birth. **Fetal presentation** refers to the body part closest to the mother's cervix. There are three types of presentation: cephalic, breech, and transverse.

A. Stages of labor

1. During the last weeks of pregnancy, it is common for the mother to experience false labor, or Braxton-Hicks contractions.

2. The first stage of labor usually begins with relatively mild contractions, leading to stronger contractions and the dilation of the cervix to accommodate the baby's head.

3. Toward the end of the first stage, which may take from eight to twenty-four hours, a period of transition begins, and the baby's head begins to move through the birth canal.

4. The second stage of labor is from complete dilation of the cervix to birth, lasting from one to two hours.

5. During the third stage of labor, which lasts between five and twenty minutes, the afterbirth (consisting of the placenta and umbilical cord) is expelled.

B. Childbirth settings and methods

Traditionally, childbirth was attended by a midwife and was seen as a natural process. With the advent of modern technology, more births took place in medical settings. This resulted in decreased mortality rates, but birth was now seen as a medical event controlled by physicians.

1. Hospital births

Birthing rooms are becoming more popular in hospitals.

2. Nonhospital settings

   a. Freestanding birth centers are nonhospital facilities that provide family-centered maternity care.

   b. Home births are another birthing alternative, with a nurse-midwife or physician monitoring labor if the pregnancy has been predetermined to be low risk.

3. Prepared childbirth

Methods of **prepared childbirth** help parents rehearse the sensations of labor.

   a. Programs emphasize educational, physical, and emotional preparation for the birth process and use of a coach.

   b. Women who participate in the Lamaze method report more favorable effects.

   c. Fathers' involvement in preparing for and participating in delivery has positive effects.

4. Medicinal methods

Despite good psychological preparation, the mother may experience considerable pain, which can be made bearable through pain-reducing drugs such as narcotics or other sedatives.

   a. The most common anesthetics are epidural and spinal, which allow the mother to remain awake and alert during birth.

   b. A general or local anesthetic delays the recovery of the mother as well as the bonding between mother and child.

C. Problems during labor and delivery

1. Faulty power is the failure of the uterus to contract strongly enough to make labor progress to actual delivery. Induced labor can be stimulated by the hormone oxytocin.

2. A faulty passageway condition occurs when the placenta develops so close to the cervix that it blocks the baby's passage down the birth canal during labor. This condition is called placenta previa.

3. A faulty passageway occurs when the placenta partly separates from the wall of the womb.

4. A faulty passenger condition is when problems exist with the baby's position or size. Usually babies enter the birth canal headfirst, but occasionally one turns in the wrong direction during contractions. Forceps are sometimes used to remedy the situation.

5. In a cesarean section, the mother receives a general anesthetic and the baby is removed surgically. Techniques for this surgery have improved; however, a common criticism is that too many cesareans are performed.

6. In most hospitals, electronic fetal monitoring is used to record uterine contractions and the fetal heart rate.

D. Birth and the family

1. The majority of births occur without significant problems.

2. A newborn can create stress in the family.

XI. From biological to psychological development

Key Concepts

Directions: Identify each of the following key concepts discussed in this chapter.

1. The reproductive cells are called _____. The gamete the father contributes is the _____ cell, while the mother's contribution is a(n) _____. These cells are formed through a process called _____.

2. Genetic information is contained in molecular structures known as _____. which form threads called _____. Genetic codes are transmitted through an acid called _____.

3. The _____ is the result of conception, a single cell from which all other body cells derive. It contains forty-six _____, twenty-three from each parent. Through the process of _____, the zygote creates body cells.

4. All humans are characterized by _____, or our genetic endowment, and _____, or our observable traits that result from the interaction of our genetic make-up and environmental influences.

5. When paired, some genes dominate others and influence individual characteristics. In this situation, _____ genes control or block the effects of _____ genes.

6. Genes responsible for a trait that takes on two or more alternative forms are called _____. If someone is _____ for a particular trait such as eye color, he or she has inherited two identical alleles for that trait. When different alleles are inherited for a trait, an individual is said to be _____ for that characteristic. Human traits that display themselves in varying degrees, such as height, are considered _____ because individuals do not inherit such characteristics in an all-or-none fashion.

7. Males have a(n) _____ sex chromosome, and females have a(n) _____ sex chromosome.

8. Abnormalities that are transmitted on the single complete X chromosome are called _____. An inability of the blood to clot is called _____.

9. A disorder in which increased maternal age is a factor and that involves degrees of mental retardation is called _____.

10. When red blood cells take on an abnormal shape instead of the normal round shape, _____ is present.

11. The scientific study of how genotype and the environment influence phenotype is called _____.

12. _____ is all the possible phenotypes an individual with a particular genotype might exhibit.

13. Genetics studies that use twins are called _____ and _____.

14. The two types of twin pairs studied are _____ and _____ twins.

15. Three discrete stages typify prenatal development. The _____ stage occurs during the first two weeks, followed by the _____ stage, from weeks three to eight. The period from week eight to birth is called the _____ stage.

16. To create a fertilized egg cell, or _____, at least one of a large number of _____ must fertilize one _____, or an egg cell in the female. At this point, _____ occurs.

17. During the first two weeks of pregnancy, the dividing zygote forms a tiny sphere called a(n) _____. The cells of this tiny sphere differentiate into three layers, the _____, the _____, and the _____, which correspond to various organs and systems in the developing fetus. About one week following conception, _____ occurs, when the blastocyst adheres to the uterine wall and is now considered a(n) _____.

18. Two patterns of growth mark both the embryonic and fetal stages, a head-to-tail, or _____ pattern, and a center-outward, or _____ pattern. These patterns explain why organ development precedes development of the fingers and toes.

19. The mother supplies oxygen and nutrients to the developing child through the _____. The embryo and placenta are connected by the _____, which contains three large vessels that carry nutrients to the embryo and waste from the embryo to the mother. A tough, spongy, fluid-filled bag called the _____ develops by the end of the eighth week. This structure stabilizes the fetus's temperature and protects it from sudden jolts.

20. When the embryonic cells no longer differentiate into major structures, about eight weeks following conception, the embryo becomes a(n) _____ and begins to develop humanlike features.

21. Around the fourth month, most pregnant women feel the movement of the fetus inside the womb. This is called _____.

22. About _____ percent of American couples are infertile.

23. The concept of _____ refers to the tendency of genes to direct or restrict development of a particular characteristic to a single phenotype and to resist environmental factors that push development in other directions.

24. _____ refers to a time-limited period during which certain developmental changes are particularly sensitive to disruption.

25. Of the three _____, or three-month divisions of pregnancy, the baby is most susceptible during the first three months. Substances such as alcohol, cigarette smoke, and medications, which can permanently damage the embryo at this early stage, are called _____.

26. _____ are at greater risk of having low-birth-weight infants, stillbirths, or problems during delivery.

27. About _____ of AIDS cases in children involve perinatal transmission from an infected mother to her child.

28. A drug called _____ was used for morning sickness but was found to cause severely malformed limbs. _____ was taken to prevent miscarriages but caused abnormal development in the vaginal cells of female babies.

29. Babies born to mothers who have consumed too much alcohol during pregnancy develop _____, which displays itself in symptoms such as sluggishness, physical abnormalities, heart defects, mental retardation, and slowed motor development.

30. The safe amount of alcohol for a pregnant woman is _____.

31. The body part of the fetus that is closest to the mother's cervix is called _____.

32. Prior to birth, the mother experiences three _____, beginning with mild, irregular uterine contractions. Toward the end of the first stage, _____ begins, at which time the _____ dilates and the baby's head moves into the birth canal. Complete cervical dilation and birth mark the second stage of labor. During the third stage, the _____ and the _____ are expelled from the mother's body.

33. The option of _____ allows mother and baby to stay together until both are ready to leave the hospital.

34. _____ are nonhospital facilities organized to provide family-centered maternity care for low-risk pregnancies.

35. To alleviate the mother's discomfort and stress during delivery, methods of _____ have been devised so that parents may rehearse before the actual delivery date. The _____ method uses no drugs during labor and trains both parents in relaxation and breathing techniques for each stage of labor.

36. Two forms of anesthesia are available during the final stages of delivery: _____ and _____.

37. The surgical removal of a baby, called _____, is recommended when either the fetus or the mother is at risk.

Multiple-Choice Self-Test

Factual / Conceptual Questions

1. Phenotype refers to
   a. a map or photo of all twenty-three chromosomal pairs.
   b. the genetic make-up of an individual.
   c. traits actually displayed by an individual.
   d. traits that a person can potentially pass on to offspring.

2. In order for a recessive gene to influence phenotype it must be
   a. a sex-linked trait.
   b. paired with another recessive gene.
   c. paired with a dominant gene.
   d. polygenic.

3. Traits such as height, which are determined by the action of a number of genes, are said to be
   a. heterozygous.
   b. magnagenis.
   c. polygenic.
   d. homozygous.

4. Which of the following is a sex-linked recessive trait?
   a. Blue eyes
   b. Hemophilia
   c. Down syndrome
   d. Klinefelter syndrome

5. Which of the following disorders is carried by a dominant gene?
   a. Down syndrome
   b. Sickle-cell anemia
   c. Huntington's chorea
   d. Tay-Sachs disease

6. Identical twins may show similarities in a number of characteristics because of their common
   a. genotype only.
   b. phenotype only.
   c. maturation only.
   d. genotype and phenotype.

7. Which of the following events occurs during the germinal stage?
   a. The heart begins to beat.
   b. Bone cells appear.
   c. The blastocyst is formed.
   d. The amniotic sac is formed.

8. During pregnancy, quickening refers to
   a. the rapid cell division experienced shortly after conception.
   b. the movement of the fetus inside the womb.
   c. the process by which substances readily pass across the placental barrier.
   d. early contractions prior to the first stage of labor.

9. Of the following teratogens, which one tends to show a delayed reaction?
   a. Cocaine
   b. DES
   c. Rubella
   d. Thalidomide

10. The second stage of labor is characterized by
    a. Braxton-Hicks contractions.
    b. birth.
    c. mild and irregular contractions.
    d. expulsion of the placenta.

Application Questions

1. David and Seth have identical phenotypes for eye color. Which of the following statements is most accurate?
   a. They may have the same genotype.
   b. They must have the same genotype.
   c. They cannot have the same genotype.
   d. It is impossible to conclude anything about their genotype.

2. Carson's blood type is A, and his mother's blood type is also A. His father's blood type must
   a. only be A.
   b. only be AB.
   c. only be O.
   d. be either A, AB, or O.

3. John's genotype is XXY, so he
   a. is really a girl.
   b. has Down syndrome.
   c. has Klinefelter syndrome.
   d. has Turner syndrome.

4. All of the following are likely candidates for prenatal counseling *except*
   a. Ashley, who is married to her first cousin.
   b. Gina, who has a family history of breast cancer.
   c. Naomi, who has a daughter with spina bifida.
   d. Sarah, an Ashkenazi Jew.

5. Julie knows the sex of her unborn child based on a television image of her entire baby she saw in her physician's office. What procedure was most likely done?
   a. Amniocentesis
   b. Fetoscopy
   c. Ultrasound
   d. Videoprobe

6. A person's skin originates from the _____ layer of cells in the blastocyst.
   a. ectoderm
   b. endoderm
   c. extoderm
   d. mesoderm

7. While in her physician's office, Tammy heard the heartbeat of her unborn child. What is the earliest gestational age that this event could occur?
   a. One week
   b. Three weeks
   c. Six weeks
   d. Nine weeks

8. Albert has fetal alcohol syndrome (FAS); he will probably show all of the following *except*
   a. central nervous system damage.
   b. hyperactivity.
   c. missing or severely misshapen arms or legs.
   d. poor impulse control.

9. Rena, who is pregnant with her first child, asks her physician what amount of weight change is best. Her physician will most likely say that normally she should
   a. lose five to ten pounds.
   b. gain five to ten pounds.
   c. gain twenty-five to thirty pounds.
   d. gain forty-five to fifty pounds.

10. _____ is the hormone used to artificially induce labor if progression of normal labor is insufficient.
    a. Epidural
    b. Oxytocin
    c. Dystocia
    d. Thalidomide

Answer Key

Key Concepts

1. gametes, sperm, ovum, meiosis
2. genes, chromosomes, DNA
3. zygote, chromosomes, mitosis
4. genotype, phenotype
5. dominant, recessive
6. alleles, homozygous, heterozygous, polygenic traits
7. XY, XX
8. sex-linked recessive traits, hemophilia
9. Down syndrome
10. sickle-cell disease
11. behavior genetics
12. Reaction range
13. adoption studies, twin studies
14. identical, fraternal
15. germinal, embryonic, fetal
16. zygote, sperm cells, ovum, conception
17. blastocyst, ectoderm, endoderm, mesoderm, implantation, embryo
18. cephalocaudal, proximodistal
19. placenta, umbilical cord, amniotic sac
20. fetus
21. quickening
22. 15
23. canalization
24. Critical period
25. trimesters, teratogens
26. Very young mothers
27. three-fourths
28. thalidomide, DES
29. FAS
30. none
31. fetal presentation
32. stages of labor, transition, cervix, placenta, umbilical cord
33. rooming in
34. Freestanding birth centers

35. prepared childbirth, Lamaze
36. epidural, spinal
37. cesarean section

Multiple-Choice Self-Test: Factual / Conceptual Questions

1. Choice (c) is correct. Phenotype refers to our outward appearance, in other words what characteristics are actually expressed. Choice (a) is a karyotype; choice (b) is genotype, and choice (d) refers to dominant and recessive genes.

2. Choice (b) is correct. The only way a recessive gene can be expressed is if it is paired with another recessive gene of the same type. It does not need to be sex-linked, so choice (a) is incorrect; however, there is a special case where sex-linked recessive traits are expressed when there are no other genes blocking them. If a dominant gene is present, choice (c), it will block the expression of a recessive gene. Choice (d), polygenic, refers to traits that are determined by multiple genes, in which case the action of dominant and recessive genes acts in multiple combinations.

3. By definition, when a number of gene pairs determine a specific trait, the trait is termed *polygenic*, choice (c). Choice (a), heterozygous, refers to the situation where one gene is dominant and the other recessive, in which case the dominant gene is the expressed characteristic. Choice (d), homozygous, refers to the situation where the two genes are identical and thus express the same characteristic. Choice (b), magnagenis, is not a term used in genetics.

4. Choice (b) is correct. Hemophilia, the inability of the blood to clot, is a sex-linked recessive trait. Choice (a), blue eyes, is a recessive trait but not sex-linked; choice (c), Down syndrome, is caused by an extra twenty-first chromosome, while choice (d), Klinefelter syndrome, is caused by an extra X chromosome (XXY).

5. Choice (c) is correct. Huntington's chorea, the gradual deterioration of the central nervous system, is determined by a dominant gene and persists because it does not manifest itself until later in life (often after the childbearing years). Choice (a), Down syndrome, is determined by an extra chromosome; choices (b) and (d), sickle-cell anemia and Tay-Sachs disease, respectively, are both determined by recessive genes.

6. Choice (d) is correct. Identical twins have the same genotype and very similar phenotype, especially if they are raised in similar environments. Therefore, choices (a) and (b) are incorrect. Identical twins should also show similar maturation, choice (c), but this is primarily because of genotype and phenotype.

7. Choice (c) is correct. The blastocyst is formed shortly after cell division begins. Choices (a), (b), and (d) all occur toward the end of the embryo stage.

8. Choice (b) is correct. By the fourth month, the mother may begin to feel movement of the fetus within the womb, which is referred to as quickening. Choice (a) is simply rapid cell division; choice (c) involves the process of osmosis; and choice (d) refers to Braxton-Hicks contractions (sometimes called false labor).

9. Choice (b) is correct. DES-exposed mothers have children who show normal development up until puberty, at which time they have problems with the maturing of their reproductive organs. Choice (a), cocaine, often results in addiction problems at birth, while choices (c) and

(d), rubella and thalidomide, respectively, typically result in physical abnormalities during the prenatal period.

10. Choice (b) is correct. Birth occurs at the end of the second stage of labor once the cervix is fully dilated. Choice (a), Braxton-Hicks contractions, also known as false labor, often occurs prior to true labor. Choice (c), mild and irregular contractions, occurs during the first stage, which begins with mild and irregular contractions and continues until the cervix is completely dilated. Choice (d), expulsion of the placenta, occurs during the third, and last, stage of labor.

Multiple-Choice Self-Test: Application Questions

1. Choice (a) is correct. David and Seth have the same eye color, but this could have happened for a number of reasons depending on what color eyes they actually have. Therefore, it is possible that they have the same genotype for eye color, but it is also possible that they don't. Thus, choices (b), (c), and (d) are not correct.

2. Choice (d) is correct. Since A and B are both dominant and O is recessive, Carson's father cannot be B, otherwise Carson would be AB; but his father could contribute a dominant A by being either A or AB, or he could be recessive O and let his wife's A determine their child's blood type.

3. Choice (c) is correct. Klinefelter involves the presence of an extra X sex chromosome. Genetically, a person with Klinefelter syndrome is considered a male, so choice (a) is wrong. Down syndrome, choice (b), also involves an extra chromosome but not an extra sex chromosome, and Turner syndrome, choice (d), involves the absence of a chromosome.

4. Choice (b) is correct. Gina is at a lower risk for a genetic disorder than the others listed. Although some forms of cancer do have genetic links, the links and consequences are not strong enough to merit prenatal counseling. On the other hand, choice (a), Ashley, is a strong candidate for prenatal counseling because marriage between cousins can produce offspring with genetic abnormalities, while choice (c), Naomi, is also at risk because she already has a child with a prenatal disorder that has genetic links; and Sarah, choice (d), is a member of an at-risk ethnic group for Tay-Sachs.

5. Choice (c) is correct. Ultrasound produces a visual image of the infant using sound waves and is commonly done in a physician's office. Choice (a), amniocentesis, involves sampling the amniotic fluid; choice (b), fetoscopy, involves the use of a probe, and although it does produce images, they are usually not of the entire baby. Choice (d), videoprobe, is not a medical procedure.

6. Choice (a) is correct. The outermost layer of the blastocyst cells, the ectoderm, differentiates to form skin, hair, and nails. Choice (b), endoderm, is the innermost layer, which becomes the organs, and choice (d), mesoderm, is the middle layer which becomes connecting parts like muscles, circulatory system, bones, etc. Choice (c), extoderm, is not one of the layers.

7. Choice (b) is correct. A primitive heartbeat occurs as early as three weeks' gestational age, although it is difficult to detect. Choice (a), one week, is too early because the heart is not formed at this time. By choices (c) and (d), six and nine weeks, respectively, the heartbeat is already well established.

8. Choice (c) is correct. Although some minor physical abnormalities are associated with FAS (especially in facial features), great distortions such as those found with thalidomide are not evident. A number of behavioral problems, such as hyperactivity, choice (b), and poor impulse control, choice (d), are associated with FAS, as is central nervous system damage, choice (a).

9. Choice (c) is correct. Current recommendations for weight gain during pregnancy are that a woman should gain twenty-five to thirty pounds and increase her calorie intake by two hundred to one thousand calories per day. Choices (a) and (b) are too low and could harm the infant by supplying too few carbohydrates and protein. Choice (d) is too high and could lead to other problems.

10. Choice (b) is correct. Oxytocin is a hormone that can either induce or strengthen contractions. An epidural, choice (a), is an injection used to eliminate pain during labor. Dystocia, choice (c), is the term used for failure to progress in labor. Thalidomide, choice (d), is a mild sedative that was found to cause severe birth defects.

CHAPTER 4

The First Two Years: Physical and Cognitive Development

Learning Objectives

1. Describe the physical characteristics of an infant at birth. Discuss the procedures used to assess newborn functioning.

2. Describe infant sleep patterns in terms of type and duration.

3. Discuss the infant's sensory and reflex abilities at birth and throughout the first two years.

4. Describe the development of motor skills during the first year. Discuss the roles of learning and maturation in motor development.

5. Discuss the nutritional requirements during infancy. Outline the pros and cons of breast versus bottle feeding.

6. Describe current trends in infant mortality in the United States and elsewhere. Identify the differences found with respect to socioeconomic status.

7. Define perception and cognition and describe ways of studying these processes.

8. Describe habituation and indicate how it is used to study perceptual development.

9. Characterize early infant perceptual abilities, including size and shape constancy and depth perception. Describe the infant's ability to localize sounds.

10. List the major characteristics and achievements of each of Piaget's six stages of sensorimotor development.

11. Describe infant learning, including operant conditioning and imitation.

12. Trace phonological development in the infancy period. Indicate the kinds of sounds infants can understand and produce.

13. Trace semantic development in the infancy period. Describe the characteristics of the first words infants can understand and produce.

14. Describe the individual differences in language development and explain how parents influence early language.

Chapter Overview

Right after birth, the newborn's skin is often covered with a waxy substance and its skull is somewhat compressed on top. The Apgar scale is a test used to quickly determine the health of the newborn by assessing five characteristics. The average newborn at full term weighs about 7.5 pounds, and its body proportions make the infant look appealing to adults. Infants sleep almost twice as much as adults do, but the amount of sleep gradually decreases as they get older. They experience six states of arousal and move through each state each day. At birth, infants already can see and hear, but with less accuracy or acuity than adults do. There are two dozen inborn reflexes in the newborn, but most disappear during the first few months. Motor skills appear during the first year of infancy and include reaching, grasping, and walking; motor skills develop differently depending on cultural background and sex.

One of the most important impairments to early growth is low birth weight. Low-birth-weight infants often have difficulties with breathing, digestion, and sleep, and their reflexes may be poorly developed.

Compared to formula and bottle feeding, breast-feeding has a number of advantages. After weaning, infants need a diet rich in protein and calories. Most North American families can provide these requirements, but many cannot. A common problem in North American diets is overnutrition, which can make infants seriously overweight, or obese. For a variety of reasons, some infants fail to thrive normally. Although mortality in infants has decreased in recent years, it is still higher in the United States than it should be.

Infants' arousal and attention can be studied by noting changes in their heart rates. Using habituation, scientists are able to study infants' responses. Studies of visual perception and object perception show that infants under six months of age perceive or at least respond to a variety of patterns and show size constancy. Researchers have concluded that infants do perceive depth, but show little fear of it. Infants also have the ability to localize sounds to some extent, but do not accurately do so until about six months. Cultural background probably plays a small role in infant perception, at least during the first year of life.

Piaget's theory of cognitive development in infants emphasizes six stages, during which the child's schemes become less egocentric and increasingly symbolic and organized. Research on these six stages generally confirms Piaget's observations, but also raises some questions about the effects of motor skills, memory, and motivation on infants' cognitive performance. Like older children and adults, infants can learn through behavioral conditioning and imitation. Behavioral learning tends to be ambiguous in infants less than three months old because it is difficult to distinguish true learning from general, automatic excitement.

Infants acquire language and its component parts such as phonology. They start to babble around four to eight months of age and appear to be intrinsically motivated to do so. Deaf infants babble, too, but not in the same way that hearing babies do. Infants show individual differences in their first words, but generally they use words for objects in their environment that are distinctive in some way. Adults influence language acquisition mainly through modeling simplified utterances, recasting their infant's own utterances, and directing considerable language at the child.

Chapter Outline

I. Physical development

II. Appearance of the young infant

    A. The first few hours

        1. The **neonate** may be covered with vernix and lanugo.

2. The head may be elongated from the compression of the skull bones at the fontanelles.

B. Is the baby all right?

The **Apgar scale** helps determine the health status of the newborn by measuring heart rate, efforts to breathe, muscle tone, skin color, and reflex irritability at one and five minutes.

C. Size and bodily proportions

1. At birth, a typical baby weighs about 7.5 pounds and is about 20 inches long.

2. Babies' physical appearance may have consequences for attachment.

III. Development of the nervous system

The **central nervous system** consists of the brain and spinal cord. The brain grows rapidly from before birth through the second year. Weight gain in the brain results from the development of fibers to form connections among **neurons** and the formation of myelin—a fatty sheath encasing neurons and nerve fibers—by certain brain cells called glia.

A. States of sleep and wakefulness

1. Infants sleep an average of sixteen hours per day.

2. Newborns divide their sleeping time about equally between active sleep, or **REM sleep**, and quieter sleep, or **non-REM sleep**, and they waken frequently but unpredictably.

3. An attempt should be made for a regular routine.

4. Infants show various states of arousal; however, the largest share of time goes to deep sleep. As they get older, their patterns of arousal begin to resemble those of older children.

• Perspectives: Sudden infant death syndrome

IV. Visual and auditory acuity

A. Infants can see at birth, but without the clarity of focus or acuity characteristic of adults with good vision. Infant vision is nearsighted but improves rapidly.

B. Auditory acuity refers to sensitivity to sounds.

1. Infants can hear at birth, but not as well as adults can.

2. Sudden noises produce a dramatic startle reaction called the Moro reflex.

V. Motor development

A. Early reflexes

There are more than two dozen inborn **reflexes**, most of which disappear in the first few months.

B. The first motor skills

  1. **Motor skills** are voluntary bodily movements and can be divided into gross motor skills and fine motor skills.

  2. Skills generally develop according to the **cephalocaudal principle** (head to tail) and **proximodistal principle** (near to far).

  3. Gross motor development in the first year is increasingly marked by purposefulness.

  4. Early, crude reaching disappears fairly soon after birth, only to reappear at about four or five months as two separate skills, reaching and grasping.

  5. By the age of twelve or thirteen months, babies typically take their first independent steps.

  6. Differences exist in motor development among cultures.

  7. During the first two years, the genders do not differ in competence.

    a. Boys and girls pass major developmental milestones at about the same time.

    b. Boys show more activity than girls and girls spend more time using their emerging fine motor skills, perhaps due to differences in parental encouragement and genetics.

VI. Impairments in infant growth

  A. Newborns are considered **low-birth-weight** infants if they weigh less than twenty-five hundred grams, or 5.5 pounds. There are two major reasons for low birth weight.

  B. Causes of low birth weight include maternal factors such as malnourishment during pregnancy, smoking, drinking alcohol, or consuming drugs. Teenage mothers or poor mothers who lack prenatal care also tend to have low-birth-weight babies. Multiple births also tend to result in small-for-date babies.

  C. Consequences of low birth weight include neurological development that contributes to weak organization of reflexes such as grasping and startling, immaturity of muscle development, and difficulty regulating sleep.

  D. Neurological limitations may persist for the first two or three years of life.

VII. Nutrition during the first two years

Compared with older children, infants eat less in absolute amounts, but in proportion to body weight they need to consume much more than children or adults do.

  A. Breast milk versus formula

1. Health experts generally recommend human milk as the sole source of nutrition for the first six months of life, because it seems to give infants greater protection from diseases and other ailments.

2. There are several reasons why pediatricians recommend breast-feeding.

B. Nutrition in later infancy

1. Infants can be gradually introduced to solid foods (e.g., cereals and fruits) after about six months. This shift is gradually completed over many months.

2. Malnutrition in North America is related to dietary deficiencies in vitamin A, vitamin C, and iron. Vitamin A and C deficiencies seem to create deficits in motor ability. Iron deficiency appears to create deficits in cognitive performance.

3. In calorie-loving societies, overeating can lead to becoming **obese**.

4. Contrary to what some parents fear, weight in infancy correlates very little with weight in childhood and even less with weight in adulthood.

5. **Failure to thrive** occurs when an infant or preschooler fails to grow at normal rates for no apparent reason. Causes of failure to thrive are complex.

C. Infant mortality

1. In the past several decades, health-care systems have improved their ability to keep infants alive.

2. The **infant mortality rate** in the United States and Canada is two or three times lower than in many Third World countries. However, mortality in the United States is higher than in nineteen other developed nations.

VIII. Cognitive development

Perception is a psychological process that involves the brain's immediate organization and interpretation of sensation. **Cognition** refers to all the processes involved in thinking and other mental activities.

IX. Studying cognition and memory in infants

A. Arousal and infants' heart rates

1. One way to understand an infant's cognition is to measure heart rate (HR) with a small electronic stethoscope.

2. The changes in HR are taken to signify variations in arousal, alertness, and general contentment.

3. When HR slows down, it suggests heightened attention or interest.

B. Recognition, memory, and infant habituation

1. Babies' responses to the familiar and the unfamiliar provide infant psychologists with a second means of understanding infant perception and cognition.

2. Psychologists study infants' tendency to get used to and therefore ignore stimuli as they experience them repeatedly; this tendency is called **habituation**.

3. Typically the researcher presents the baby with a study stimulus to which the infant habituates. Then the study stimulus is presented along with other stimuli. If the baby recognizes the original stimulus, she or he will look at the new stimuli longer and HR will slow down.

X. Infant perception

The automatic quality of perception has made many psychologists suspect that it is either genetically programmed or learned in early infancy.

A. Visual perception

Early studies suggested that two-day-old infants recognize human faces; more recent studies have shown that infants are drawn more to the interesting contours, complexity, and curvature of the face than to its humanness.

1. Object constancy refers to the perception that an object remains the same in some way despite constant changes in the sensations it sends to the eye.

2. Size constancy is the perception that an object stays the same size even when viewed at different distances.

3. Depth perception refers to a sense of how far away objects are or appear to be. The **visual cliff** experiment demonstrates that infants acquire this skill at about two or three months.

4. Babies old enough to crawl show significant fear of the visual cliff.

B. Auditory perception

1. Infants just two months old have a limited ability to locate sounds, as shown by the way they orient their heads toward the noise of a rattle. But several seconds are needed before orienting toward the sound.

2. Infants are better able to locate relatively high-pitched sounds than low-pitched sounds. Infants prefer sounds in the middle range of pitches.

3. Babies appear to be able to coordinate what they see with what they hear.

4. Whether culture influences the visual and auditory perception still remains unclear.

XI. Infant cognition

At first, infant cognition, or thought, has little to do with the symbolic forms that develop in most children and adults. Instead, it emphasizes active experimentation with and manipulation of materials. Truly symbolic thought does not emerge until the end of infancy.

A. Piaget's theory of sensorimotor intelligence

1. Piaget's theory of cognitive development outlines infant intelligence, describing infant thought in terms of sensory perceptions and motor actions, or **sensorimotor intelligence.**

2. Two major trends are demonstrated across Piaget's six stages of infancy.

   a. Infants show a trend toward symbolic thinking.

   b. Infants form cognitive structures called **schemes,** organized patterns of actions or concepts that help them make sense out of and adapt to their environment. These initial schemes lead to later cognitive structures that Piaget called operations.

3. Piaget argued that sensorimotor intelligence develops by means of two complementary processes: **assimilation,** which consists of interpreting new experiences in terms of existing schemes, and **accommodation,** which involves modifying existing schemes to fit new experiences.

   a. Stage 1: early reflexes (birth to one month). Inborn reflexes are quickly modified in response to the newborn's experiences.

   b. Stage 2: primary circular reactions (one to four months). The baby begins building and differentiating action schemes quite rapidly. Within a month or so, these schemes become very repetitive—hence, the term **circular reactions.** Also at this time, babies begin to vary in their preferences for schemes.

   c. Stage 3: secondary circular reactions (four to eight months). The infant expands attention beyond his or her own body to include objects and events in the surrounding environment. New, repetitive actions motivated by external objects and events, called secondary circular reactions, show that the infant is beginning to acquire **object permanence**—the belief that objects have an existence separate from the baby's own actions and continue to exist even when she or he cannot see them.

   d. Stage 4: combined secondary circular reactions (eight to twelve months). Here the infant intentionally chooses a scheme as a means toward an end and uses this means-end connection purposefully. The relatively fixed quality of schemes at this stage may derive from a heavy reliance on motor actions.

   e. Stage 5: tertiary circular reactions (twelve to eighteen months). At this stage, the infant deliberately varies schemes to produce interesting results. The baby can now use trial and error in learning about properties of new objects by running through his or her repertoire of schemes. These variations involving systematic scheme applications are termed tertiary circular reactions.

   f. Stage 6: the first symbols (eighteen to twenty-four months). At this time, the motor schemes previously explored and practiced begin to occur symbolically; that is, the child can begin to imagine actions and their results without actually trying them beforehand. Mental representational skill allows for true object permanence and deferred imitation. Mental representation allows the child to form and maintain thoughts and memories of relevant experiences that later become available for expression again.

- Working with Gillian Luppiwiski, infant care provider: Fostering infants' thinking

B. Assessment of Piaget's theory of infant cognition

Piaget's theory has stimulated research on infant cognition, much of which confirms the main features of his theory. Some research, however, has pointed out additional aspects of infancy that complicate Piaget's original presentation.

1. One question is whether infants begin life with fundamentally separate sensorimotor schemes, as Piaget argued, or whether there are connections among early schemes and a high degree of integration of schemes.

2. Another question concerns Piaget's emphasis on motor limitations versus cognitive limitations. Some infant psychologists question Piaget's six stages because they believe that the stages confuse the child's motor abilities with his or her cognitive abilities. Object permanence, for example, implicitly depends on a child's capacity to conduct a search. Perhaps younger infants lack classic object permanence because they lack motor skills or use them clumsily.

3. Piaget may have failed to account properly for the effects of memory. He explained most infant thinking in terms of motor schemes: repeated, familiar actions that allow infants to know their environment.

4. By emphasizing the nature of competence, Piaget's theory tends to neglect the immediate causes of performance. Even an infant who shows high competence in one situation may fail to do so in a situation that differs from the first one only slightly.

XII. Behavioral learning in infancy

One framework for studying the specific performance of infants is based on **behaviorism**, or learning theory, which focuses on changes in specific behaviors and covers three types of learning: classical conditioning, operant conditioning, and imitation. All three types may be exhibited in infancy.

A. Operant conditioning

1. Studies have found that infants are capable of learning through operant conditioning. For instance, newborns will learn to suck on a pacifier more rapidly if doing so yields a tiny amount of sugar water.

2. Infants are predisposed to learn these particular behaviors. All examples of operant conditioning in infants rely on those few behaviors that young babies can already do, which are mainly reflexive. Since reflexes occur easily, one may question whether infant responses constitute learning or general excitement.

B. Imitation

1. Research generally shows that babies engage in different kinds of imitation at different points during infancy.

2. Infants imitate actions they can see themselves perform sooner than they imitate actions they can observe only in a model.

3. Infants sometimes imitate actions that are relatively invisible to themselves.

XIII. Language acquisition

Infants must acquire all three major aspects of language to become verbally competent and to listen with comprehension: language sounds (phonology), meaning (semantics), and organization (syntax). Parents and other adults also influence language acquisition.

A. Phonology

1. Sounds that speakers of a language consider distinctive and use to make the words of that language are called **phonemes**. English has about forty-one phonemes.

2. Perceiving phonemes is important because it helps infants ignore meaningless variations. Language specialists suspect that humans are genetically and physiologically predisposed to notice phonemic differences.

3. Sometime between four and eight months, infants begin babbling with increasing complexity and with the purpose of hearing themselves vocalize.

4. Babbling seems to be intrinsically motivated. Studies involving babbling in deaf infants revealed that babies babble with their hands in ways analogous to the oral babbling of hearing infants.

5. Parents and others appear to have an influence on babbling. Deaf babies babble months later than hearing babies and only when they hear sound that is amplified.

B. **Semantics** and first words

1. First words learned by children are nominals, particularly those that are used frequently or that stand out.

2. Children's language differs in style, which is encouraged by differing family environments.

C. Influencing language acquisition

1. Asking questions and pausing, even when a child is too young to answer, can facilitate the child's learning turn-taking in language.

2. By simplifying their language with the infant and keeping just ahead of the infant's own linguistic skill (**infant-directed speech**), parents can stimulate further development of language.

3. The Harvard Preschool Project has shown that the most intellectually and socially competent infants have parents who direct large amounts of language at them.

4. Professional caregivers can also influence language acquisition even though differences of intensity and frequency exist. The forms of influence resemble those of parents.

• A multicultural view: Cognitive effects of talking to infants: A cross-cultural perspective

XIV. The end of infancy

Key Concepts

Directions: Identify each of the following key concepts discussed in this chapter.

1. The newborn baby, or *neonate*, is born covered with a white, waxy substance called *vernix* and *lanugo*, or fine, downy hair. Gaps in bones of the skull are _____, or "soft spots." *fontanelles*

2. To identify neonates that may need immediate medical attention, the *Apgar* is used to determine heart rate, breathing, muscle tone, color, and reflex irritability at one- and five-minute intervals following delivery.

3. The way a baby looks may have psychological consequences by fostering *attachments*.

4. The brain and nerve cells of the spinal cord, or *neurons*, make up the *central nervous system* of the infant. The neurons are gradually covered with a(n) *myelin* sheath, a fatty covering manufactured by the *glial* cells of the brain. This sheath allows faster and more reliable transmission of neural impulses.

5. Periods of infant sleep are divided almost equally by active (or *REM*) sleep, in which the infant appears restless, and *non REM* sleep, in which functions such as breathing become more regular.

6. At birth, infants can see, but they lack *Acuity*.

7. The infant's earliest innate movements are called *reflexes*. Voluntary movements of the body or parts of the body are called *motor skills*.

8. The baby's *Gross* motor skills, involving large muscle groups, develop prior to *fine* motor skills, or those involving the smaller muscles of the body. As the infant's motor skills develop, the *cephalocaudal* principle allows upper-body skills, such as head turning, before lower-body skills, such as walking. Because of the *proximidistal* principle, central body parts become skilled before outlying parts.

9. Baby boys show *more activity* than baby girls. Throughout childhood, girls excel at *fine motor skills* and boys excel at *gross motor skills*.

10. A low-birth-weight baby weighs *5.5 lbs* or less.

11. Health experts recommend *breast milk* as the sole source of nutrition for at least the first six months.

12. One reason for preferring breast over bottle feeding of infants is that breast-feeding seems to foster more secure *attachment* between the mother and infant.

13. Many diets lack enough *Vit A*, *Vit C*, and *Iron*.

14. *Failure to thrive* occurs when an infant or preschooler fails to grow at normal rates for no apparent reason.

15. The proportion of babies who die during the first year of life is called *infant mortality rate*.

16. *Perception* is a psychological process that refers to the brain's immediate organization and interpretation of sensation. *Cognition*, on the other hand, is a more general term that refers to processes by which we acquire knowledge.

17. The tendency of infants to get used to and ignore stimuli that they come in contact with frequently is termed _habituation_. A common measurement used to assess an infant's cognition is _heart rate_.

18. Infants enjoy looking at the human face's _contours_, _complexity_, and _curvature_. _Object constancy_ is the perception that an object remains the same in some way in spite of constant changes in the sensations that it sends to the eye.

19. The sense of how far away objects appear to be is _depth perception_. The _Visual Cliff_ experiment demonstrates two- to three-month-old infants' ability in this sense.

20. When localizing sounds, young infants _take longer_ than older infants.

21. Infants are better at locating _high pitched sounds_.

22. Piaget described infant thought in terms of sensory perceptions and motor actions, or _sensorimotor intelligence_. The organized patterns of actions that help an infant make sense of and adapt to the environment are called _schemes_. Interpreting new experiences in terms of existing schemes is called _assimilation_. Modifying existing schemes to fit new experiences is known as _accommodation_.

23. Behavior that is repeated endlessly for no apparent reason is called _circular reaction_. When the infant experiences pleasure at these behaviors, they become _primary circular reaction_.

24. New repetitive actions motivated by external objects are termed _secondary circular reactions_ and show that the infant is beginning to acquire _object permanence_, a belief that objects have an existence of their own, separate from that of the infant.

25. A criticism of Piaget's theory is that the stages confuse the child's motor abilities with _cognitive abilities_.

26. Ways of studying infant performance have come from _behaviorism_, or _learning theory_, which focuses on changes in specific behaviors and covers three types of learning: classical conditioning, operant conditioning, and imitation.

27. _operant conditioning_ can explain why a behavior such as looking at an interesting toy occurs again.

28. Children can copy what they see others do through _imitation_.

29. The sounds of the language are called _phonology_.

30. A child's first words are generally _nominals_.

31. _Infant directed speech_ is speech that is simplified to the level just ahead of the infant's speech and can stimulate further development of language.

32. A parent can facilitate language acquisition by using routine language embedded in a highly familiar situation. This is called _textual dialogue_.

Multiple-Choice Self-Test

Factual / Conceptual Questions

1. At birth, the infant is often covered with a white, waxy substance called
    a. myelin.
    b. vernix.
    c. fontanelles.
    d. lanugo.

2. The average newborn infant spends about _____ percent of his or her time sleeping.
    a. 25
    b. 50
    c. 66
    d. 80

3. A sudden loss of support (for example, if a person trips while carrying the infant) is likely to elicit the _____ reflex in a newborn.
    a. Moro
    b. rooting
    c. stepping
    d. sucking

4. With respect to reaching and grasping, newborn infants
    a. show no abilities in this area.
    b. can reach and grasp, but unsuccessfully.
    c. show limited abilities that gradually improve.
    d. are remarkably good at both abilities.

5. Weight in infancy is _____ correlated with weight in adulthood.
    a. slightly
    b. moderately
    c. strongly
    d. negatively

6. Newborns tend to prefer looking at objects that
    a. are high in contour.
    b. have simple shapes.
    c. they have seen before.
    d. are innately preprogrammed.

7. Object constancy refers to
    a. the fact that infants show consistent preferences for certain kinds of objects.
    b. the notion that objects exist even when they are out of sight.
    c. the perception that an object stays the same despite changes in sensation.
    d. none of the above.

8. Which of Piaget's sensorimotor stages is characterized by the development of secondary circular reactions?
    a. First
    b. Second
    c. Third
    d. Sixth

9. Recent studies of object permanence using habituation suggest that
   a. Piaget's original research was quite accurate.
   b. Piaget overestimated the level of object permanence in infants.
   (c.) Piaget underestimated the level of object permanence in infants.
   d. object permanence is a false concept and should be viewed instead as object relationships.

10. When are the semantics of a language fully mastered?
    a. By about two years of age
    b. By about five years of age
    c. By about twelve years of age
    (d.) Never

Application Questions

1. Beth and Rick have just been told that their newborn's Apgar score is 4; this means that their baby
   a. is probably in good health.
   b. will probably have above-average intelligence.
   (c.) is in immediate need of special medical attention.
   d. is not likely to survive.

2. Megan is one month old; by the time she is six months old she should have lost the _____ reflex.
   a. Babinski
   b. eyeblink
   c. sucking
   (d.) tonic neck

3. Liam has just learned to walk holding on to furniture. He should be able to do all of the following *except*
   a. pull himself up to sit.
   b. sit up without assistance.
   (c.) stand alone well.
   d. stand holding furniture.

4. When a two-month preterm infant is four months of age, the infant's behavior is probably close to that of a normal
   a. newborn.
   b. one-month-old.
   (c.) two-month-old.
   d. four-month-old.

5. Six-month-old Brianne has an iron deficiency; if this is not remedied soon she could
   a. lose muscle strength.
   b. lose some of her eyesight.
   (c.) suffer cognitive deficits.
   d. suffer motor and coordination problems.

6. When a mobile was first placed in her crib, Katie spent much of her time watching it. As time passed, she spent less and less time watching it. Her behavior best illustrates
   a. operant conditioning.
   b. object constancy.
   (c.) habituation.
   d. stimulus overload.

7. Which of the following best illustrates a primary circular reaction?
   a. Carlos fans his toes outward after someone strokes the bottom of his foot.
   b. Carrie kicks her feet repeatedly in her crib.
   c. Carl taps his spoon repeatedly on his plate.
   d. Chrissie picks up a small cracker and eats it.

8. While playing with his favorite ball, Danny, who is in sensorimotor stage four, watches as it rolls off his chair, disappears under the couch, and reappears just before it bounces down the steps out of sight into the basement. Danny will most likely
   a. not search for his ball.
   b. search for his ball under the couch.
   c. search for his ball between the couch and the basement stairs.
   d. search for his ball in the basement.

9. Rob repeatedly sticks his tongue out at his newborn brother, Ned. Ned is likely to
   a. cry.
   b. babble.
   c. stick his tongue out at Rob.
   d. call his mother.

10. If a child had a referential style, which of the following words would she be more likely to utter before the others?
    a. Diaper
    b. Dog
    c. Goody
    d. Hello

Answer Key

Key Concepts

1. neonate, vernix, lanugo, fontanelles
2. Apgar scale
3. attachments
4. neurons, central nervous system, myelin, glial
5. REM, non-REM
6. acuity
7. reflexes, motor skills
8. gross, fine, cephalocaudal, proximodistal
9. more activity, fine motor skills, gross motor skills
10. 5.5 pounds
11. breast milk
12. attachment
13. vitamin A, vitamin C, iron
14. Failure to thrive
15. infant mortality rate
16. Perception, Cognition
17. habituation, heart rate
18. contours, complexity, curvature, Object constancy
19. depth perception, visual cliff
20. take longer
21. high-pitched sounds

22. sensorimotor intelligence, schemes, assimilation, accommodation
23. circular reaction, primary circular reaction
24. secondary circular reactions, object permanence
25. cognitive abilities
26. behaviorism, learning theory
27. Operant conditioning
28. imitation
29. phonology
30. nominals
31. Infant-directed speech
32. textual dialogue

Multiple-Choice Self-Test: Factual / Conceptual Questions

1. Choice (b) is correct. Vernix is a white, waxy substance that covers the skin at birth, especially if the infant is born a bit early. Myelin, choice (a), is a fatty sheath that develops on neurons. Fontanelles, choice (c), refers to the "soft spot" on the baby's head. Lanugo, choice (d), refers to the fine, downy hair present at birth.

2. Choice (c) is correct. Newborns spend about sixteen hours (about 66 percent) per day sleeping, with a range of as little as eleven hours and as much as twenty-one hours. Therefore, choices (a) and (b), 25 and 50, respectively, are below average and choice (d), 80, is above average, although (b) and (d) fall near the extremes of the range.

3. The Moro reflex, choice (a), a startle response characterized by spreading the arms, shaking, and making a horrible face, is produced in response to a loss of support. The rooting reflex, choice (b), is initiated by stimulation to the cheek. The stepping reflex, choice (c), occurs when an infant is held upright—the infant lifts his or her legs as if to step. The sucking reflex, choice (d), occurs when something is placed in the infant's mouth.

4. Choice (b) is correct. Newborns will reach and grasp for an object; however, although they may touch it, they often fail to close their hands on the object. This ability disappears soon after birth and then reappears at about four or five months of age as two separate abilities. Choice (a), no abilities, is incorrect since they have some abilities (although they are probably reflexive); choice (c), limited abilities that gradually improve, is incorrect because the abilities do not continue to develop gradually but rather disappear and then reappear later; and choice (d), remarkably good at both abilities, is incorrect because most early reaching and grasping are unsuccessful.

5. Choice (a) is correct. Contrary to popular belief, weight in infancy is only slightly related to weight in adulthood. In other words, weight in infancy does not predict adult weight.

6. Choice (a) is correct. Studies have found that newborn infants tend to look at and prefer stimuli with a high degree of contour, such as the human face. Infants tend to prefer the most complex stimulus they are capable of perceiving, so choice (b) is incorrect. Items they have seen before seem to be preferred later, so choice (c) is also incorrect. There does not seem to be strong evidence for innately preprogrammed stimuli, choice (d).

7. Choice (c) is correct. Object constancy, which includes size and shape constancies, is the notion that although something may look different from different distances or angles, we perceive it as the same object. Choice (a) refers to object preferences, and choice (b) to object permanence.

8. Choice (c) is correct. Piaget's third stage is the stage of secondary circular reaction, in which the infant focuses on repeated actions of objects. Piaget's first stage is the stage of early reflexes, choice (a). The second stage is the stage of primary circular reactions, choice (b). The sixth stage involves the first symbols, choice (d).

9. Choice (c) is correct. Studies by Baillargeon (1991) have found evidence of sophisticated object permanence in infants as young as three and one-half months of age. Choices (a), (b), and (d) are all inconsistent with these findings.

10. Choice (d) is correct. The purposes and meaning (semantics) of a language are so complex that one never really masters it, although one does get better at understanding the language as one gets older.

Multiple-Choice Self-Test: Application Questions

1. Choice (c) is correct. A score of 4 indicates that something is wrong and the newborn is in need of immediate medical attention. Infants with scores of 8 and above are probably in good health, choice (a). Infants with scores of 3 and below need immediate intensive care and may not survive, choice (d). The Apgar sheds no light on later intelligence, choice (b).

2. Choice (d) is correct. The tonic neck reflex typically drops out at about two or three months of age. Choice (c), sucking, disappears at about eight to twelve months of age, and choices (a) and (b), Babinski and eyeblink, respectively, are both permanent reflexes that do not fully disappear.

3. Choice (c) is correct. Walking while holding furniture typically appears between seven and ten months of age, while standing alone well first appears at about ten months of age. Choices (a) and (b), which involve sitting, appear between six and nine months, and choice (d), stand holding furniture, appears between five and nine months.

4. Choice (c) is correct. A preterm infant shows delays in infancy equal to that of its gestational age. Had the infant been born on time, he or she would have been two months old. Choices (a) and (b), newborn and one-month-old, respectively, are incorrect since there is development, although slower, in the preterm infant about equal to the infant's gestational age. Choice (d), four-month-old, is incorrect since some delays are found.

5. Choice (c) is correct. Iron deficiencies have been associated with problems in cognitive performance while choices (a) and (b), loss of muscle strength and loss of eyesight, respectively, have not. Choice (d), motor and coordination problems, is a symptom of vitamin A and C deficiencies.

6. Choice (c) is correct. With repeated presentation, an infant tends to look less and less at a stimulus, or habituate to it. Choice (a), operant conditioning, would need to involve some sort of reinforcement or punishment; choice (b), object constancy, is the notion that an object stays the same even though the view of that object may change; and, actually, the opposite of choice (d), stimulus overload, is occurring.

7. Choice (b) is correct. A primary circular reaction is one that is body-centered (and does not involve other objects) and endlessly repeated; Carrie's description fits that definition best. Choice (a), fanning of toes, is a reflex; choice (c), tapping a spoon, would be a secondary circular reaction; and choice (d), eating a cracker, involves objects.

8. Choice (b) is correct. Children in stage four sensorimotor development make the AnotB error in that they look for an object in the first place it disappeared, not the last place. Therefore, Danny will search under the couch. Choice (d), search for the ball in the basement, is something a stage five child would do; a stage three child would not search, choice (a); and we rarely see children searching between the hiding places, choice (c).

9. Choice (c) is correct. Newborns are capable of imitating tongue protrusions if they observe them repeatedly. It is doubtful that Ned will cry, choice (a), and a newborn is not likely to babble, choice (b); since he can't talk, he certainly won't call his mother, choice (d).

10. Choice (b) is correct. A referential style refers to objects and events. Choices (b) and (a) are both common objects within an infant's world, but it seems that words like *dog* occur more often than words like *diaper* even though babies have more exposure to diapers. Choices (c) and (d), goody and hello, respectively, are found in children who have an expressive style.

CHAPTER 5

The First Two Years: Psychosocial Development

Learning Objectives

1. Describe the early emotions of the infant, including the range of expression and developmental patterns.

2. Define what is meant by temperament and describe the three types found in infants.

3. Discuss the short- and long-term effects of temperament. In particular, describe how it interacts with parent characteristics.

4. Describe the special relationship parents and infants develop. In particular, discuss the synchrony in behavior.

5. Describe the special relationship fathers and infants develop. Discuss how this role is similar to and how it differs from the mother-infant relationship.

6. Discuss the roles that siblings, peers, and other caregivers play in social interactions, and contrast these roles with mother-infant and father-infant relationships.

7. Identify and describe the four phases of attachment. Cite the major characteristics of each phase and be able to generate examples.

8. Describe the "Strange Situation" and indicate how it is used to assess attachment level.

9. Describe the three common outcomes of attachment, how they are assessed, and what the long-term consequences of each are.

10. Discuss the similarities and differences in mothers' and fathers' roles in attachment.

11. Describe the effects of maternal employment and day care on attachment.

12. Define what is meant by the development of autonomy and indicate how parents might influence it.

13. Differentiate among the four major theoretical positions (identification, operant conditioning, observational learning, and social referencing) concerning the development of autonomy.

14. Describe the development of self-knowledge and self-awareness during the first two years.

15. Describe the development of competence in the infant and explain how it contributes to self-esteem.

Chapter Overview

Infants appear to be capable of a complex range of emotional responses and are quite sensitive to the feelings of the caregivers. Research has revealed that even at birth, infants exhibit differences in temperament, patterns of physical and emotional responsiveness, and activity levels. These differences both influence and are influenced by the feelings and responses of their caregivers. Caregiver-infant synchrony is the closely orchestrated social and emotional interactions between an infant and his or her caregiver; it provides an important basis for the development of attachment relationships. Newborn infants have a natural tendency to actively participate in their social world. Parents undergo a transition to parenthood that is marked by a shift from self-centeredness, changing social relationships, declining marital satisfaction, and changing husband-wife relations. The child's interaction with the father is more similar to than different from his or her interaction with his or her mother. The effects of nonmaternal care and maternal employment on infant and toddler development depend on the specific circumstances, but in general do not appear to be negative. High-quality care for infants is associated with caregiver motivation, competence, and training. Infants can engage in active social interactions with their older siblings and peers and often prefer them to the parents as playmates and become more social with experience. Nonparent caregivers and family day-care homes are becoming more utilized and therefore more critical.

Attachment is the tendency of young infants and their caregivers to seek and maintain physical and emotional closeness with each other; it develops in a series of phases. The development of attachment can be assessed by the Strange Situation method. Three patterns of attachment have been identified: secure attachment, anxious-resistant attachment, and anxious-avoidant attachment. The mother's relationship with her infant is a major determinant of attachment. Secure attachment is most likely to develop when the caregiver responds sensitively and appropriately to the infant, and the infant can use the caregiver as a safe base for exploration. Insecurely attached infants tend to be less able than securely attached infants to get help from parents when they need it or to accept it when it is offered. Infants can be equally attached to both mother and father, and to other caregivers as well, even though in the majority of families the mother is the primary caregiver. Most infants of mothers who are employed either full- or part-time are securely attached, but the effects of maternal employment depend on a number of variables. Infants are capable of developing multiple attachments and tend to be independent of attachments with parents.

Sources of the growing autonomy that characterizes the second year of infancy include identification, operant conditioning, observational learning, and social referencing. Researchers have used a number of innovative methods to examine self-knowledge and self-awareness and have concluded that children go through different levels of self-awareness. Competence is achieved as a child's natural curiosity and desire to explore the world inspires him or her. A competent child can do a number of things, such as compete with peers and show pride in personal achievement. Parents play an important role in the development of competence by supporting curiosity and the desire to explore. Self-esteem is an outcome of growing up in this type of supportive environment.

Chapter Outline

I. Emotions and temperament in infancy

Infants are capable of expressing emotions and needs through four different kinds of cries. Caregivers respond with basic routines to an infant's different cries.

A. Emotions in infancy

1. Babies' expectations and understandings influence the degree of specificity of emotional expression.

2. There is general agreement that emotions can reliably be expressed at different ages from a few weeks through toddlerhood.

3. Expressions of emotion are thought to play an important role in development by providing vital information to infants and their caregivers about ongoing experiences and interactions.

4. Infants become increasingly able to regulate their emotional states to a comfortable level to maintain interaction with their surroundings.

B. Temperament

Temperament refers to an individual's pattern or style of reacting to a broad range of environmental events and situations. These patterns are present at birth; whether temperament is due solely to genetics is unclear.

1. In the now classic study of temperament, infants were rated on nine dimensions. Three patterns of temperament were found: easy babies, difficult babies, and slow-to-warm-up babies. A fourth group, mixed-pattern babies, did not fall neatly into the first three groups.

2. Temperament can be useful for predicting problems, but only for a minority of children with difficult or slow-to-warm-up temperaments.

3. Predictions of later temperament based on differences observed toward the end of the first year are somewhat more accurate than those made early.

4. Environmental influences (e.g., infant-family fit, culture) play a major role in supporting or modifying temperament throughout development.

5. Temperament differences may be as much a product of the mother's behavior as the infant's.

II. Early social relationships

Infants seem to have a natural tendency to be social participants and are capable of many social responses shortly after birth.

A. Transition to parenthood

Having a child represents a major life transition.

1. There are changes in relationships with other adults, family roles, and interactions between father and mother.

2. Becoming a parent can be associated with a decline in marital satisfaction for both spouses.

3. Participation by the husband in child care and housework can increase his empathy and appreciation of his wife's experience.

B. Caregiver-infant synchrony

1. Social interactions between parent (or other caregiver) and infant involve an intricate pattern of close coordination and teamwork called **caregiver-infant synchrony**.

2. Mothers and babies have "conversations" that resemble adult dialogues.

3. Coordinating these "conversations" is the caregiver's responsibility until the baby is a few months old and capable of initiating social exchange.

4. Problems with this synchrony may reflect childrearing difficulties and can place the infant at risk for developmental problems.

C. Social interactions with fathers and siblings

Children live in a network of social relationships where other people make contributions to their social lives.

1. Fathers spend about two or three hours per day in the care of infants and young children and play more actively with their children.

2. Most children grow up with siblings. They spend more time with siblings than with mothers or fathers. Conflict among siblings is most likely when parents are seen as giving preferential treatment.

D. Interactions with nonparental caregivers

Infants also interact with nonparental caregivers, including day-care teachers, other relatives, and family friends. Several factors that affect the quality of infant and toddler care have been found.

1. High-quality care for infants is best ensured by employing caregivers who are well-trained and supervised and responsive to the physical, cognitive, social, and emotional needs of infants and their families.

2. Grandparents are often secondary sources of advice and child care.

E. Interaction with peers

1. Even young babies show considerable interest in other babies and in much the same way they show interest in their parents.

2. Infants become more social with experience.

3. Repeated contact with a peer in a familiar setting with a familiar caregiver and minimal adult interference appears to facilitate the development of peer friendship.

III. Attachment formation

Attachment refers to the strong and enduring emotional bond that develops between infant and caregiver during the infant's first year of life and is characterized by reciprocal affection and a shared desire to maintain physical closeness. Most developmental psychologists believe that attachment relationships develop over time as a result of repeated infant-caregiver interactions.

A. Phases of attachment formation

Attachments are thought to develop in a series of phases, which are partly determined by cognitive changes and partly by interactions that appear to develop quite naturally between infants and their caregivers.

1. Phase I: Indiscriminate sociability (birth through two months). In this phase, an infant uses her limited attachment behaviors less selectively than she will as she grows older.

2. Phase II: Attachments in the making (two through seven months). In this phase, most babies still generally accept certain forms of attention and care from comparative strangers and will tolerate temporary separation from parents.

3. Phase III: Specific, clear-cut attachments (seven through twenty-four months). In this phase, the baby's preference for specific people becomes stronger; therefore, separation anxiety and stranger anxiety appear near the beginning of this phase.

4. Phase IV: Goal-corrected partnerships (twenty-four months and onward). By age two, the baby is capable of mental representation and is better able to understand the feelings and points of view of parents and to adjust his own accordingly.

B. Assessing attachment: The "Strange Situation"

1. The most widely used method for assessing attachment is the **Strange Situation**, in which infants are confronted with a cumulative series of stressful experiences such as being in an unfamiliar place, meeting a stranger, or being separated from a parent.

2. Based on infant patterns of behavior in this situation, about 70 percent of infants showed **secure attachment** to the parent, about 10 percent displayed an **anxious-resistant attachment** pattern, and about 20 percent showed an **anxious-avoidant attachment** pattern.

C. Consequences of different attachment patterns

1. Secure attachment early in infancy leads to babies who tend to cooperate best with parents, comply with rules, and seek help from parents.

2. Anxious-resistant infants may not learn as well from their parents, responding with anger and resistance to parental efforts to teach or help them.

3. Anxious-avoidant infants often avoid interaction with their parents and miss out on parent efforts to teach or help them.

4. Such differences persist into the preschool years.

- A multicultural view: Cross-cultural variations in attachment

    D. Influences on attachment formation

        1. The quality of the infant-mother relationship is a strong determinant in the attachment process. A mother's capacity to respond sensitively and appropriately to her baby is more important than the amount of contact.

        2. Differences in infant temperament are likely to affect the mother-infant relationships and the quality of attachment.

        3. Being securely attached herself makes the mother more likely to have a child who is securely attached.

        4. Children can form equally strong attachments with their fathers. Studies have found no differences in most babies' preferred attachment during their first two years.

        5. The quality of fathers' interaction with their infants, their attitudes, and time spent are important variables.

        6. The effects of maternal employment on the child are almost always influenced by a number of factors such as economic and cultural differences, the mother's "morale," the father's satisfaction with his wife's employment, husband-wife relationships, and other factors. Working mothers who experience high levels of separation anxiety are more likely to have infants who develop anxious-avoidant attachments.

        7. There are many variables that determine the effects of day care and other forms of nonmaternal care on attachment. The majority of infants receiving full-time center care appear to be quite securely attached to one or both parents. The two sets of attachment, one for parent and the other for caregiver, tend to be independent of each other. Multiple attachments in other contexts are not only possible but may contribute to the child's well-being.

- Perspectives: Family-leave policies in the United States

- Working with Rachelle Turner, infant day-care coordinator: Understanding infant social development

    E. Limitations of attachment theory

        1. One concern about the Strange Situation is that it is a single occurrence of a limited number of specific interactions and may not reflect the overall relationship.

        2. Studying caregiver-infant interactions longitudinally over the entire first year has been suggested as an alternative assessment method.

IV. Toddlerhood and the emergence of autonomy

By the second year of life, the relatively secure base of attachment that most infants have achieved with their parents allows them to shift attention outward to the physical and social world. **Autonomy** is the ability to be independent and self-directed and to balance one's own demands for self-control with demands for control from others. Parents must support their child's efforts to be autonomous without overestimating or underestimating the child's capabilities, external dangers, and internal fears.

A. Sources of autonomy

   1. Identification is the process by which children wish to become like their parents and other important attachment figures in their lives.

   2. Operant conditioning stresses the importance of reinforcement for desirable behaviors, including behaviors that reflect self-control.

   3. Observational learning espouses the view that the key to autonomy lies in the child's inherent tendency to observe and imitate parents and other nurturant individuals.

   4. **Social referencing**, a common denominator in all three explanations of autonomy, refers to children's sensitivity to how their parents are feeling and their ability to use those cues as a basis for guiding emotional response.

B. Development of self-knowledge and self-awareness

   The sense of self that develops late in infancy shows up in everyday situations as well as in situations involving self-control. Researchers have used mirrors and television images of infants to assess infants' self-recognition capability.

   1. Self-recognition never occurs in infants younger than fifteen months and increases to 100 percent at twenty-four months.

   2. Infants initially use contingent cues and then noncontingent cues.

   3. By the end of their second year, most children show an increasing appreciation of the standards and expectations of others about how they should behave toward people and things. For children, satisfaction is gained by initiating challenging activities or behaviors, and they often smile at the results. A two-year-old may also direct adults' behavior by inviting them to play, requesting help, or other such behaviors. Children frequently use language to express needs and wants, implying awareness of themselves as individuals.

C. Development of competence and self-esteem

   Competence (skill and capability) develops out of a child's natural curiosity and desire to explore the world and the pleasure experienced in successful mastery and control of that world.

   1. A number of capabilities are observed in a socially competent toddler.

   2. Social competence is influenced by the parent-toddler relationship. Mothers support and encourage their toddler's curiosity and desire to explore.

   3. A natural outcome of such parenting is a strong sense of **self-esteem**—the child's feeling that he or she is an important, competent, powerful, and worthwhile person whose efforts toward autonomy and initiative are respected and valued by those around him or her.

V. Looking back/looking forward

Key Concepts

Directions: Identify each of the following key concepts discussed in this chapter.

1. The earliest emotional expression observed in infants is _____. An infant's typical way of reacting to events and situations is termed _____. According to a classic study, children are classified _____ if they are adaptable and readily develop secure relationships, _____ if they are inactive and rarely show their moods, or _____ if they are irregular in activity patterns and react intensely to new situations.

2. _____ can influence the degree to which temperament remains stable.

3. Marital satisfaction _____ following the birth of a child.

4. Social interactions between parents and infant involve a complex pattern of close coordination and teamwork, called _____.

5. When fathers play with their infants, they tend to be _____.

6. In talking to their younger siblings, children use _____.

7. Grandparents can be a good resource for advice and child care, especially when they are in _____.

8. _____ refers to the strong and enduring emotional bond between infant and caregiver. Although this bond cannot be directly observed, it can be inferred from commonly observed behaviors such as _____ (crying, cooing, babbling) and _____ (smiling, clinging).

9. Harlow's studies of rhesus monkeys produced findings suggesting that _____ may be a primary need in infancy that is relatively independent of what was traditionally thought to be the basis of emotional development.

10. When the infant makes specific, clear-cut attachments, his or her preference for specific people becomes stronger; therefore, the infant often expresses _____ at leaving the primary caregiver and _____ at meeting a new person.

11. The four stages of attachment formation are _____, _____, _____, and _____.

12. The most widely used method for assessing attachment is the _____, in which infants are confronted with a cumulative series of stressful experiences.

13. Three patterns of infant behavior are typically seen in the Strange Situation: _____ attachment, _____ attachment, and _____ attachment.

14. The mother's _____ is important in determining individual differences in attachment.

15. Differences in infant _____ can affect the mother-infant relationships and the quality of attachment.

16. Most infants of mothers who are employed either full- or part-time are _____. Most infants who receive full-time center care seem to be _____ to one or both of their parents.

17. The attachments that an infant develops with caregivers and parents are _____.

18. A problem with the Strange Situation is that researchers tend to _____ on it as the standard for measuring mother-child relationships.

19. Parents may help their infant develop _____, or the ability to regulate one's own thoughts, feelings, and actions while overcoming shame and doubt, by continually devising situations in which the child can play independently and safely.

20. The process of children wishing to become like their parents is called _____. The child's sensitivity to the feelings of parents and others and use of this ability to guide his or her own responses is called _____.

21. _____, or skill and capability, develops as a result of a child's natural curiosity about the world and his or her pleasure in mastering or controlling it.

22. A natural outcome of quality parenting is a strong sense of _____, a child's feeling that he or she is competent, powerful, and worthwhile.

Multiple-Choice Self-Test

Factual / Conceptual Questions

1. Psychosocial development during early infancy is characterized by the development of
   a. autonomy.
   b. basic trust.
   c. emotions.
   d. self-esteem.

2. Early infant coping skills that involve such things as self-comforting and self-stimulation are termed
   a. conditioned responses.
   b. self-directed regulatory behaviors.
   c. attachment behaviors.
   d. temperament.

3. Observation of young infant behavior indicates that
   a. there is synchrony between parent and infant responses.
   b. there is an inborn tendency to trust the parent.
   c. infants have very little social awareness.
   d. infants are capable of expressing emotions like fear, guilt, envy, and pride.

4. As compared with the amount of time mothers spend interacting with their families, fathers tend to spend
   a. more time.
   b. about the same amount of time.
   c. less time.
   d. less total time but more quality time.

5. Studies of monkeys indicate that a key attachment behavior seems to be
   a. feeding.
   b. physical closeness.
   c. grooming.
   d. rocking.

6. During which phase of attachment does the infant begin to actively seek proximity to his or her caregiver and develop clear-cut attachment?
   a. Phase 1
   b. Phase 2
   c. Phase 3
   d. Phase 4

7. The Strange Situation is used to assess
   a. creativity.
   b. level of attachment.
   c. perception of novelty.
   d. tolerance level of stimulation.

8. Which approach describes the development of autonomy as a function of parental reinforcement of a child's grown-up behavior or independent exploration and self-restraint?
   a. Classical conditioning
   b. Identification
   c. Observational learning
   d. Operant conditioning

9. A common feature in all the major theories of the development of autonomy is
   a. the use of reinforcement.
   b. social referencing.
   c. innate predispositions.
   d. conflict as a source of motivation.

10. The "rouge test" is used to assess
    a. level of attachment.
    b. self-esteem.
    c. self-recognition.
    d. depth perception.

Application Questions

1. Which emotional expression is newborn Inga likely to exhibit the earliest?
   a. Fear
   b. Pleasure smile
   c. Social smile
   d. Surprise

2. When two-month-old Kiley took her first bath in the bathtub, she responded by crying through most of it. The following day, she still showed some apprehension but did not cry. By the third day, she started to enjoy her bath. Kiley's temperament would most likely be classified as
   a. difficult.
   b. easy.
   c. impulsive.
   d. slow to warm up.

3. Since Steve and his wife had their new baby, he has helped more around the house by washing the dishes and clothes and helping in the care of the baby. Chances are that
   a. Steve is competing with his baby for his wife's attention.
   b. Steve is frustrated with the added responsibility.
   c. Steve has more and better quality time with his wife.
   d. Steve's wife is happy, but Steve is somewhat depressed.

4. When Ramona smiles at her infant, he tends to smile back; when she verbalizes to him, he coos back. This behavior illustrates
   a. caretaker-infant synchrony.
   b. habituation.
   c. motherese.
   d. operant conditioning.

5. Two-year-old Emily is in the most common form of day care for a child her age. She is
   a. at her home with a sitter.
   b. at a sitter's home.
   c. in a child-care facility.
   d. at home with older sibling.

6. When his mother gets ready to leave the house to go shopping, Leon gets apprehensive. Once she leaves, Leon cries and doesn't play very much. Leon is most likely in the _____ phase of attachment.
   a. specific, clear-cut attachment
   b. attachment-in-the-making
   c. goal-coordinated partnership
   d. indiscriminant sociability

7. Which of the following best describes the behavior of an anxious-resistant attached toddler?
   a. Jack runs to a stranger when he enters the room but not when his mother enters.
   b. Danielle gets upset when her mother prepares to leave the room and clings to her when she returns.
   c. Patrice ignores both a stranger and her mother when they enter a room.
   d. Huong stops playing with his toys when a stranger enters the room.

8. Zack gets easily frustrated when he can't succeed at things, especially when his mother tries to help him. His attachment is probably
   a. aggressive.
   b. anxious-avoidant.
   c. anxious-resistant.
   d. secure.

9. At about what age will Jason recognize himself in the mirror?
   a. Three months of age
   b. Six months of age
   c. Twelve months of age
   d. Eighteen months of age

10. Eighteen-month-old Javier seems to be developing into a competent person with a good sense of self. Chances are his parents use _____ techniques in childrearing.
    a. authoritative
    b. permissive
    c. power-assertive
    d. protective

Answer Key

Key Concepts

1. social smile, temperament, easy, slow to warm up, difficult
2. Infant-family fit
3. declines
4. parent-infant synchrony
5. more physical
6. baby talk
7. good health (a cultural group that values their participation)
8. Attachment, signaling behaviors, approach behaviors
9. contact comfort
10. separation anxiety, stranger anxiety
11. indiscriminate sociability, attachments in the making, specific attachments, goal-coordinated partnerships
12. Strange Situation
13. secure, anxious-avoidant, anxious-resistant
14. sensitivity
15. temperament
16. securely attached, securely attached
17. independent of each other
18. over rely
19. autonomy
20. identification, social referencing
21. Competence
22. self-esteem

Multiple-Choice Self-Test: Factual / Conceptual Questions

1. Choice (b) is correct. Erikson, who is the primary psychosocial theorist, characterizes infancy as a time to deal with the conflict of trust versus mistrust. Choice (a), autonomy, involves development during late infancy/early childhood; and although both emotions, choice (c), and self-esteem, choice (d), are also developing, they are viewed as occurring in childhood rather than infancy.

2. Choice (b) is correct. Self-directed regulatory behaviors are often used by infants to control negative feelings during the first year of life. Choice (a), conditioned responses, is a concept from classical conditioning denoting a learned behavior; attachment behaviors, choice (c), are behaviors (such as greeting and proximity maintaining) used to promote bonding; and temperament, choice (d), refers to primitive personality or disposition found in infants.

3. Choice (a) is correct. Social interactions between parent and infant involve close coordination in which each waits for the other to finish before beginning to respond. There is no evidence to suggest innate trust, choice (b). Rather, trust seems to develop over the first year. Even young infants show a remarkable ability in the area of social competency and awareness, so choice (c) is incorrect. Infants do seem to be able to express fear, choice (d), but more sophisticated emotions, such as pride, guilt, and envy, are not found in young infants.

4. Choice (c) is correct. Studies have shown that fathers spend about two or three hours per day interacting with the infant and mothers spend about nine hours. Choices (a) and (b) are not true. Although fathers' interactions are somewhat different from mothers', both tend to be of good quality, so choice (d) is also incorrect.

5. Choice (b) is correct. Harlow found that contact comfort (physical closeness) was the primary need independent of food, choice (a), or any other behaviors, such as grooming and rocking, choices (c) and (d), respectively.

6. Choice (c) is correct. Phase 3, which occurs from seven to twenty-four months, is characterized by greater mobility, separation anxiety, and stranger anxiety. Choice (a), phase 1, is the phase of indiscriminate sociability; choice (b), phase 2, is attachment in the making; and choice (d), phase 4, is goal-coordinated partnership.

7. Choice (b) is correct. The Strange Situation is a series of eight brief social episodes involving an infant, his or her mother, and a stranger; it is used to assess attachment. The Strange Situation has nothing to do with creativity, choice (a); perception of novelty, choice (c); or tolerance level of stimulation, choice (d).

8. Choice (d) is correct. The use of reinforcement by parents to shape desirable behavior is characteristic of an operant conditioning approach. Choice (a), classical conditioning, would involve pairing a stimulus with an already established reflexlike response. Choice (b), identification, involves autonomy based on the adoption of the behaviors and values of the same-sex parent. Choice (c), observational learning, involves imitation of parental and other adult autonomous behavior.

9. Choice (b) is correct. The psychoanalytic, operant conditioning, and observational learning theories all acknowledge the child's sensitive awareness of how his or her parents and others are feeling, and use of those cues to guide his or her own behavior. Choice (a), use of reinforcement, is emphasized by operant conditioning and observational learning theories (to some degree) but not psychoanalytic theory; choices (c) and (d), innate predispositions and conflict as a source of motivation, respectively, would be characteristic of the psychoanalytic approach.

10. Choice (c) is correct. The "rouge test" involves placing red rouge on an infant's nose and observing the infant's response when he or she looks in a mirror. If the infant touches his or her nose, it is an indication of self-recognition. Choice (a), level of attachment, is typically assessed using the Strange Situation; choice (b), self-esteem, is assessed in various ways but typically using older children; and choice (d), depth perception, often involves the use of the visual cliff.

Multiple-Choice Self-Test: Application Questions

1. Choice (c) is correct. The social smile is found as early as two weeks of age. Choice (b), pleasure smile, is found at three months; choice (d), surprise, begins at four months, and choice (a), fear, begins at about five months.

2. Choice (d) is correct. Kiley showed some initial reluctance about her bath; however, as time passed, her response became more positive. This is the behavior of a slow-to-warm-up infant. The difficult infant, choice (a), is likely to show continued negative reactions (crying) for some time; three days would not be enough time to adjust. The easy infant, choice (b), may show initial apprehension but would adapt quickly during the first bath. Impulsive, choice (c), is not a temperament style; impulsiveness would be characteristic of an infant who would act without much caution.

3. Choice (c) is correct. Studies have found that fathers who are involved in coparenting and helping around the house when the new child arrives actually have more time to spend in

quality interactions with their wives and are generally happier. Choices (a), (b), and (d) all imply negative consequences.

4. Choice (a) is correct. A rhythm of responding seems to develop between the infant and primary caretakers so that their behaviors become synchronized. Choice (b), habituation, would indicate lack of responding and getting bored with one another; some of choice (d), operant conditioning, might be occurring, each mutually reinforcing the other, but the pattern of responding indicates synchrony, not mere conditioning. Choice (c), motherese, is seen especially with older infants, where a mother adjusts her speech when talking to an infant.

5. Choice (b) is correct. Over 41 percent of children in child care are at the sitter's home. About 32 percent are at their own home, choice (a); and about 18 percent are in a child-care facility, choice (c). Only a few are cared for by older siblings, choice (d).

6. Choice (a) is correct. Leon is exhibiting separation anxiety, which is common once attachment is established in the third phase. In choices (b) and (d), attachment-in-the-making and indiscriminate sociability, respectively, separation anxiety is typically not found. Choice (c), goal-coordinated partnership, could also be correct, but Leon would need to take a more assertive role in his interactions with his mother for this to be true. This does not seem to be the case given the information provided.

7. Choice (b) is correct. The anxious-resistant attached toddler shows signs of anxiety even before separation, is intensely upset during separation, actively seeks close contact upon reuniting, but resists attempts to be comforted. Choices (a) and (c) are similar to patterns found in anxious-avoidant attachment. Choice (d) is similar to what might be found in a securely attached child.

8. Choice (c) is correct. The anxious-resistant infant is insecure and at times ambivalent about his or her relationship with primary caretakers. This is particularly true when parents try to assist their child in a task that is difficult and potentially frustrating. Secure infants, choice (d), do not show this frustration. Anxious-avoidant infants, choice (b), are also insecure, but generally do not show the same level of frustration in these situations. Choice (a), aggressive, is not an attachment style.

9. Choice (d) is correct. Studies like the "rouge test" indicate that self-recognition does not appear until about eighteen months of age. All the other choices (a), (b), and (c), are too early.

10. Choice (a) is correct. The authoritative parent exerts control but seeks information from the child and is very nurturant. This approach has been found to produce children who are generally well-adjusted, independent, competent, and have high self-esteem. Choice (b), permissive parents, has produced children who are sometimes directionless and incompetent; similarly, choice (c), power-assertive, is a method often used by authoritarian parents and does not tend to produce a high degree of self-esteem and competence. Choice (d), protective parents, produces children who are not assertive or self-confident and who show lower competence.

CHAPTER 6

Early Childhood: Physical and Cognitive Development

Learning Objectives

1. Describe normal physical development in the preschool years, including the various characteristics and patterns of growth.

2. Discuss the nutritional, health, and social factors that influence growth during the preschool years.

3. Describe the development of bladder control during the preschool period.

4. Identify and describe the changes that occur in motor skills, indicate how they come about, and discuss the effects of training.

5. Describe how drawing changes over the preschool period. Differentiate between prerepresentational and representational drawing.

6. Discuss the gender differences in physical development during the preschool years, including information on real and perceived changes.

7. Describe how parents change in response to physical changes and growth, including changes in surveillance and patience.

8. Describe Piaget's stages of preoperational thinking and identify the three major developments during this stage.

9. Discuss the development of thought in early childhood, including symbolic and egocentric thought.

10. Describe the work on classification skills and conservation. Indicate how extensions of these studies differ from Piaget's original work.

11. Describe how a child's concept of number develops over the preschool period and distinguish between cardinality and ordinality.

12. Identify and discuss the changes in Piaget's original ideas proposed by neostructuralists.

13. Describe the basic features of language acquisition during early childhood, with particular focus on the development of syntax.

14. Discuss the errors related to the understanding of syntax, including undergeneralization and overgeneralization.

15. Discuss the two major theories of language development and review the basic assumptions and concepts of each. Evaluate the two theories.

16. Describe the role that parents, gender, and socioeconomic status play in the acquisition of language.

17. Discuss the development of language in deaf children. Explain how their language development compares to that of hearing children.

18. Describe the characteristics of a good early education program.

Chapter Overview

Between the ages of two and five, physical growth slows down and children take on more adultlike bodily proportions. Physical growth is usually smooth and predictable and is influenced to some extent by genetic, social, and nutritional differences. The nutritional needs of a preschooler may be different from those of an infant. Parents should encourage variety in the child's diet and avoid using coercion or sweet foods as rewards. Failure to thrive is a condition where the child does not grow normally. Although family stress seems to be a factor, it is difficult to pinpoint the condition's causes. Although high-socioeconomic-status preschoolers tend to be very healthy, substantial percentages of preschoolers live in poverty and consequently lack adequate health care. Education appears to help parents ensure adequate diet and health care for children.

Preschoolers develop bladder and bowel control, with daytime control appearing before nighttime control. Fundamental motor skills, such as walking, running, jumping, throwing, and catching, become more smooth and adultlike. Fine motor skills emerge during the preschool years. Drawing appears to follow two overlapping phases of development, moving from prerepresentational drawing to representational drawing. Boys and girls in preschool are more similar than different when it comes to physical development and motor skills. On average, there are only slight gender differences in physical development and motor skills, with boys tending to be bigger, stronger, and faster. It is important to note that these differences are slight and refer to averages. Preschoolers' facial features and changing size and motor skills influence parents' responses and methods of childrearing to some extent.

The preoperational stage of thinking, defined by Piaget, is characterized by increased symbolic thinking and understanding identities and functional relationships. Because the child can engage in symbolic thought, he or she can recall experiences, solve problems more effectively, and communicate with others about his or her experiences. Preschoolers can also classify objects accurately as long as the system or criteria for classifying is relatively simple. At age three, preschoolers have some knowledge of how the number system works, but they do not achieve full understanding until about age four or five. Preschoolers often cannot solve problems that require reversible thinking, such as tasks of conservation. Vygotsky's zone of proximal development has been suggested as an explanation for how development occurs. The neostructuralist perspective uses Piaget's belief in stages but focuses on relatively specific cognitive skills of the child.

Another significant area of development is preschoolers' major strides in acquiring the syntax, or grammar, of their native language. Young children's first word combinations are related by semantics and omit syntactic relationships. Initially, children speak in duos and then telegraphic speech. One important syntactic error preschool children make is overgeneralization. Research indicates that children infer grammatical relationships and do not just copy what they hear from others. Children also seem to learn some syntactic rules and language by rote. Explanations presented for the mechanisms of language acquisition include the role of reinforcing utterances, imitation and practice, and the child's language acquisition device. The LAD is the innate tendency to acquire language. Infant-directed speech appears to help children acquire language sooner and better. Techniques such as recasting provide scaffolding within which children can build their own language structures. Language varies between girls and boys in ways that support gender stereotypes and according to socioeconomic class in ways that prepare middle-socioeconomic-status children better than low-socioeconomic-status children for school settings. Other language differences are less clear. Children who are deaf or hearing impaired often learn American Sign Language, which has all of the properties of an oral language.

Effectiveness of early childhood education is related to a number of characteristics, such as staff competence, seeing education as an integrated whole, and involving parents. Developmentally appropriate practices consist of ways of assisting children's learning that are consistent with the developmental needs and abilities of children. These practices should consider cultural differences and values.

Chapter Outline

I. Physical development

II. Influences on normal physical development

Physical development in the preschool years is relatively easy to measure. For any preschool child who is reasonably healthy and happy, physical growth is remarkably smooth. Physical growth lacks discrete stages, plateaus, or qualitative changes.

A. Genetic background

1. Most dimensions of growth are influenced substantially by heredity.

2. Both parents contribute equally to growth tendencies.

3. Races and ethnic groups differ in growth patterns such as height and body shape.

B. Disease

1. Children with serious illnesses often have other conditions that retard growth.

2. Some conditions, like small for date, may lead to illness, which may contribute to hindered growth.

C. Nutritional needs during the preschool years

1. The amount of food consumed by preschoolers may be less than that of toddlers.

2. Eating a variety of foods is important to ensure nutrition.

D. Social influences on growth

1. **Failure to thrive** may be related to stress in the family, although the causes are poorly understood.

2. The effects of failure to thrive may be reversed if the condition has not persisted for too long.

III. The connections between health and poverty

Children from middle- and high-socioeconomic-status settings are generally very healthy.

A. About 30 percent of families in the United States have poor access to medical care because of poverty.

B. Illness and malnourishment put children at risk for additional illnesses.

C. Strategies can focus on individuals and their communities and on systematic reorganization of the health-care system.

D. Education in health and nutrition can build on the knowledge of low-income parents.

• Perspectives: Reforming children's health care

IV. Bladder and bowel control

Sometime during the preschool years, most children acquire control of their bladder and bowels. Daytime control usually precedes nighttime control, sometime before the third birthday. Bladder and bowel control reflects the large advances children make in controlling their bodies.

V. Motor skill development

A. Fundamental motor skills

Young children experiment with simple voluntary actions. Older children use action usually as means to other ends.

1. After a year or so of practice, most children can walk without looking at their feet. Their steps are more regular and their feet get closer together. They move to running shortly after walking has smoothed out.

2. Early jumping may look like a fast stretch and may improve to the lifting of one foot off the ground. Around age three, efficient arm movement enables the preschooler to gain upward momentum.

3. For infants and toddlers, first throws may happen by accident and be followed by more intentional and stereotyped throws. Children proceed through stages in throwing that also appear in catching.

B. Fine motor coordination: The case of drawing skills

Not all motor activities of young children involve strength, agility, and balance of the whole body. Many require **fine motor coordination**. The fine motor skill of drawing serves a number of purposes. There appears to be two overlapping phases of development in drawing.

1. Prerepresentational drawing emerges at the end of infancy, when children begin to scribble. The focus of this activity is initially on the activity itself. Later a child's interest in the results will appear in the patterns she or he imposes on scribbling.

2. Representational drawing emerges as children develop an interest in representing people, objects, and events in their drawings. This interest precedes their ability to do so. Only as children reach school age do their drawings of persons become relatively realistic.

C. Gender differences in physical development

Aside from wide individual differences, preschool boys and girls develop at almost exactly the same average rate. By the time children begin kindergarten at around age five, slight gender differences in physical development and motor skills exist but are noticeable only as averages based on large numbers of children. Gender differences in physical development may be related to social roles.

VI. Effects of children's growth on adults

A. Changes in facial features

1. Having a young-looking face depends on having large features and a large forehead.

2. Younger-looking children are rated as more attractive than older-looking children by both adults and their peers.

3. Adults tend to expect more mature behavior from older-looking children; these children may not be developmentally ready to fulfill these expectations.

B. Changes in size and motor skills

1. Small children can be handled and carried from place to place. By age five, children have outgrown these physical interactions and must assume more responsibility for themselves. By age five, the child has not only gained in physical growth but has also improved various motor skills and gained increasing physical competence.

2. By the end of the preschool years, minute-by-minute surveillance of children recedes in importance; however, the concern for safety remains and is reflected in rules set by caregivers.

3. During the preschool years, many parents discover a special need for patience in dealing with their children.

VII. Cognitive development

VIII. Thinking in preschoolers

Preschoolers extend their ability to represent objects and experiences into many new areas of activity and thinking, or cognition.

A. Piaget's preoperational stage

1. According to Piaget, at about age two children enter a new stage of cognitive development.

2. Preoperational children become increasingly proficient at using symbols, recognizing identities, and sensing functional relationships or variations in their environment.

    3. Piaget focused on the limitations as well as the achievements of preoperational children.

B. Symbolic thought

    1. Probably the most significant achievement of the preoperational stage is the emergence of **symbolic thought.**

    2. Symbolic thinking helps children organize and process what they know by providing them with convenient ways of remembering objects and experiences.

    3. Symbols help children communicate what they know to others; communication helps them learn from the experiences of others.

C. Egocentrism in preschool children

    1. **Egocentrism** is the tendency of a person to confuse his or her own point of view with that of another person.

    2. Piaget used the three mountains test to assess egocentrism.

    3. Using more familiar test materials and settings, preschool children can adopt others' spatial perspectives.

    4. Preschoolers show distinct but incomplete egocentrism in oral communications.

D. Other aspects of children's conceptual development

Preschool children develop specific cognitive skills as a result of their growing symbolic ability.

    1. **Classification** skills refer to the placement of objects in groups or categories according to some specific standards or criteria. Young preschoolers can reliably classify objects that differ in just one dimension.

    2. **Reversibility** is the ability to undo a problem mentally and go back to its beginning.

    3. **Conservation** is the ability to perceive that certain properties of an object remain the same despite changes in the object's appearance; this skill appears around age six.

       a. Often preschoolers either cannot or do not use reversible thinking, even when the situation calls for it.

       b. Tasks of conservation are affected by how they are described to the child.

    4. Children do not fully grasp how the conventional number system works. For the preschooler it is a rote activity. Piaget probably underestimated preschoolers' knowledge of numbers. Young children acquire the notion of numerosity whether or not they can count yet.

E. How cognitive development occurs

    1. Children learn within their social contexts and experiences and acquire cognitive skills in conjunction with adults or more experienced peers.

2. The gap in difficulty between independent thinking and socially supported thinking is the **zone of proximal development,** the area in which problems are too difficult to solve alone but are solvable with support from more competent individuals. The concept originated with Soviet psychologist Lev Vygotsky. It suggests how stages and skills may emerge and evolve.

F. Neostructuralist theories of cognitive development

1. Much of the research on children's conceptual development does not really contradict Piaget's general approach. Other research suggests that Piaget underestimated children's abilities.

2. There is a commitment to keep Piaget's notion of development occurring in stagelike progression but revise the content or details of those stages.

3. This newer view of cognitive stages is sometimes called **neostructuralist** or neo-Piagetian.

4. This view has also paid more attention to how, or by what processes, children acquire new cognitive skills.

IX. Language acquisition in the preschool years

For most children, language expands rapidly after infancy. Dramatic development occurs in syntax, or the way the child organizes utterances. Significant changes also occur in semantics (meaning) and communicative competence.

A. The nature of syntax

1. The **syntax** of language is a group of rules for ordering and relating its elements, or morphemes. Morphemes are the smallest meaningful unit of language.

2. Syntactic rules can change the meaning of sentences.

3. Some syntactic rules have only a small range of application, and others are completely irregular. In acquiring syntax, a child confronts a mixed system of rules.

B. Beyond first words: Semantic and syntactic relations

Before age two, words seem connected by their semantic relations—their intended meanings—rather than by syntactic relations—the relations among grammatical classes of words, such as nouns, verbs, and adjectives.

1. Before age two, the child begins forming duos, or linking two words together, when she or he speaks. Leaving out syntactic indicators makes the speech sound stilted and ambiguous; it is therefore also called **telegraphic speech**.

2. After highly individual beginnings, certain aspects of syntax develop in universal and predictable patterns. Sometimes early syntax becomes too regular, and children make **overgeneralizations**.

3. Young children seem to infer grammatical relationships rather than simply copy others' speech. A classic study of early syntax showed the importance of the child's own inferences about grammatical rules.

4. Much syntax must be learned by rote, because rules do not cover many specific cases of language usage. Although children eventually rely on rule-governed syntax, they probably still learn a lot of language by rote, especially idiomatic expressions that bear no logical relation to normal meanings or syntax.

C. Mechanisms of language acquisition

1. One view, the behavioral perspective, is that children learn to speak through reinforcement by caregivers of vocal sounds that approximate genuine words or utterances. Analysis of conversations between parents and children shows that parents are more likely to elaborate on the child's topic if the utterance is a grammatical one.

2. Children must imitate their native language to acquire it. Most children copy only certain selected utterances rather than everything they hear. Imitation may also help children acquire language by initiating playful practice with new expressions.

D. Innate predisposition to acquire language: LAD

1. Some experts conclude that children have an innate predisposition to learn language called the language acquisition device, or LAD.

2. The idea of the LAD is supported by the poverty of content in the speech to which most infants and preschoolers are exposed. Language learned later in life is limited in amount and complexity.

3. Preschoolers do not simply copy their parents' language directly. Certain other experiences with language may be crucial in language development.

4. Experiences affect the version of language that children acquire, even if they grow up in the same general language community.

5. The fairest conclusion about language acquisition is that children are both predisposed to acquire language and also rely on experiences with it.

E. Parent-child interactions

Certain kinds of verbal interactions apparently help children acquire language sooner and better than other kinds do.

1. **Infant-directed speech,** or "motherese," is a simplified version of language.

2. Recasting a child's utterances is repeating or reflecting on what the child has said. Recasting is a form of scaffolding, or providing a temporary structure within which young children can build their own language structures.

X. Language variations

A. Gender differences in language

1. Within any community, girls learn nearly the same syntax as boys but acquire very different ways of using language, which may reflect societal stereotypes.

2. The sexes reinforce their differences in language with certain nonverbal gestures and mannerisms.

3. Gender differences in discourse may contribute to gender segregation.

B. Socioeconomic differences in language

   1. Most research has found that low-income children are less verbal than middle- or high-income children.

   2. Most tests of language skills favor middle-class versions of English in both vocabulary and style of discourse, or conversational patterns.

   3. Low-income children more often lack prior experience with test question exchanges.

C. Language of deaf and hearing-impaired children

   1. Children with hearing impairments often do not develop oral language skills as fully as other children do.

   2. **American Sign Language (ASL)** is a true language.

   3. Children growing up learning ASL experience the same steps in language development that speaking children do.

   4. Children learning ASL and English become bilingual.

- Working with Carolyn Eaton, preschool teacher: Introducing sign language to young children

XI. Early childhood education

A. Early education and cognitive theories of development

   High-quality early education programs are usually based on some sort of developmental perspective.

B. Effective childhood education

   1. Staff of program are competent observers of children's educational needs and can make important decisions.

   2. Curriculum is an integrated whole rather than independent subject areas.

   3. Programs involve parents directly or indirectly.

C. Cultural diversity and best practice in early education

   1. **Developmentally appropriate practices** are ways of assisting children's learning that are consistent with developmental needs and abilities.

   2. Some developmentally appropriate practices are culture-bound rather than universally beneficial to children.

3. Best practices need to take into account cultural differences and values regarding children's development.

- A multicultural view: Parents' beliefs about intelligence: A cross-cultural perspective

XII. From preschooler to child

Key Concepts

Directions: Identify each of the following key concepts discussed in this chapter.

1. The physical growth of a preschooler is _____ and _____. Physical growth does not progress by _____.

2. A condition thought to be related to a poor match between parental expectations and a child's inherent styles of responding is known as _____.

3. Daytime control of the bladder and bowels occurs _____.

4. _____ control often takes much longer to achieve than _____ control.

5. Motor activities that require the coordination of small movements but not strength are called _____.

6. Scribbling at the end of infancy is _____ drawing. The preschooler tends to draw in a(n) _____ manner.

7. The differences in motor skills between boys and girls might be more accurately called _____.

8. A young-looking face has _____ features and a(n) _____ forehead.

9. The handling of a preschooler consists mostly of _____ rather than physically moving her.

10. During the preschool period, _____ is a special need for parents when dealing with children.

11. Children in the preoperational stage also extend their belief in object permanence to include _____. Variations in the environment that normally occur together are called _____.

12. One of the most significant achievements of the preoperational stage is the emergence of the child's _____, or the ability to think by making one object or action stand for another.

13. A preschooler may not be able to take the perspective of another person. This is called _____.

14. Preschool children have trouble with _____, which is typically learned in early grades and consists of the ability to undo a problem mentally and go back to its beginning. This ability is necessary to a major cognitive achievement of middle childhood, _____, the ability to perceive that certain properties of objects remain the same regardless of appearance.

15. A child who can place objects in groups or categories according to some specific standards or criteria can do _____.

16. _____ developed the idea called _____, which is the area in which problems are too difficult to solve alone, but not too hard to solve with support from adults or more competent peers.

17. _____ theories represent newer views of cognitive stages but are rooted in the ideas of Piaget.

18. _____ is a group of rules for ordering and relating its elements. The _____ is the smallest meaningful unit of language.

19. Two-word utterances are called _____. Stilted and ambiguous speech where syntactic indicators are left out is called _____.

20. When early syntax becomes too regular, children make _____.

21. We use _____ when we praise a child for vocalizations.

22. The innate tendency to acquire language is called the _____. The language to which children are exposed is marked by incompleteness and grammatical errors, or what linguists call _____, making it unsatisfactory as a guide to learning grammatical structure.

23. Motherese is sometimes called _____. When a child's utterance is repeated or reflected back, _____ is being used. Techniques to help children acquire language that invite them to try new, unfamiliar language are called _____.

24. With regard to language, boys and girls differ in _____, which may contribute to _____.

25. Deaf children acquire the language of gestures known as _____.

26. High-quality early childhood education is usually based on _____. Parental involvement was important in the success of the federal program _____.

27. Ways of assisting children's learning that are consistent with children's developmental needs and abilities are called _____.

Multiple-Choice Self-Test

Factual / Conceptual Questions

1. Physical growth during the preschool years tends to be
   a. rapid and erratic.
   b. rather smooth and predictable.
   c. slower than at any other time in childhood.
   d. slow at the beginning and fast at the end.

2. Failure to thrive has been associated most often with
   a. family stress and parental conflict.
   b. genetic predispositions.
   c. hormonal imbalances.
   d. poor nutrition.

3. Changes in a preschooler's gross motor skills indicate
   a. considerable vacillation.
   b. deterioration and regression in development.
   c. general improvement.
   d. little or no improvement.

4. True running develops at about age
   a. three.
   b. five.
   c. seven.
   d. nine.

5. Piaget's second stage of development, which extends across the preschool years, is called the
   a. concrete operational stage.
   b. prelogic stage.
   c. preoperational stage.
   d. primary circular reaction stage.

6. Which of the following develops during the preoperational stage?
   a. Identities
   b. Object permanence
   c. Reversibility
   d. Sensory integration

7. The term *functional relationships* refers to
   a. the ability to undo a problem mentally.
   b. cause-and-effect behaviors.
   c. constancies within objects.
   d. variations in an environment that normally occur together.

8. The lack of reversibility in thinking is one of the reasons preschoolers
   a. can't solve mathematical problems.
   b. lack object permanence.
   c. lack conservation skills.
   d. can't play games with rules.

9. The statement "Piaget's grand stages should probably be replaced by stages of more focused content" would most likely be made by a(n)
   a. information-processing theorist.
   b. behaviorist.
   c. neostructuralist.
   d. Freudian.

10. Syntax refers to
    a. contextual adjustments in language production.
    b. the purposes and meaning of language.
    c. the organizational rules and grammar of language.
    d. the smallest meaningful unit of sound.

Application Questions

1. Three-year-old Stacie wets the bed at night. Her parents should
   a. seek medical attention.
   b. consider using conditioning techniques to control the problem.
   c. make her change the sheets at night to make her aware of the problem.
   d. not worry; most children at this age wet the bed sometimes.

2. André is three years old. He is most likely able to
   a. balance on one foot.
   b. catch a large ball.
   c. make simple representational drawings.
   d. jump in the air with both feet.

3. Of the following skills, which would be most difficult for a five-year-old?
   a. Catching a baseball
   b. Jumping from a standing point
   c. Running
   d. Throwing a baseball

4. Scribbling by preschoolers is a characteristic of
   a. abstract drawing.
   b. prerepresentational drawing.
   c. associative drawing.
   d. primitive drawing.

5. Asad realizes that since he has dark hair and dark skin now, he will have dark hair and dark skin when he grows up. He is exhibiting
   a. conservation.
   b. functional relationships.
   c. identity permanence.
   d. object permanence.

6. Will crosses two sticks and begins to move them overhead while saying, "Clear for landing" and making noises like a jet. He is displaying
   a. assimilation.
   b. false-belief syndrome.
   c. functional relationships.
   d. symbolic thought.

7. Both Miranda and Tanya have 200-gallon round swimming pools in their yards. Tanya's pool is taller but not as wide as Miranda's. Tanya claims that her pool has more water than Miranda's even though both pools actually hold the same amount. Tanya's thinking represents
   a. an inability to use classifications.
   b. lack of conservation.
   c. lack of identity permanence.
   d. lack of symbolic thinking.

8. Rachel counts each car she sees in front of her house and then says, "There are four cars." Her concept of number illustrates
   a. ordinality.
   b. cardinality.
   c. reversibility.
   d. one-to-one correspondence.

9. When nine-year-old Billy speaks to his three-year-old sister, Sylvia, in a slow, deliberate manner using simple words, he is demonstrating his use of
   a. pragmatic speech.
   b. semantic anticipation.
   c. speech recognition.
   d. sibling speech.

10. Miriam, who has been deaf since birth, uses American Sign Language (ASL). Her language development
    a. should be severely impaired.
    b. should parallel the development of hearing children.
    c. will be very primitive since ASL is not a true language.
    d. will be much slower than that of hearing children.

Answer Key

Key Concepts

1. smooth, predictable, stages
2. failure to thrive
3. at very nearly the same time
4. Nighttime, daytime
5. fine motor coordination
6. prerepresentational, representational
7. gender differences
8. large, large
9. negotiating and discussing
10. patience
11. identities, functional relationships
12. symbolic thought
13. egocentrism
14. reversibility, conservation
15. classification
16. Vygotsky, zone of proximal development
17. Neostructuralist
18. Syntax, morpheme
19. duos, telegraphic speech
20. overgeneralizations
21. reinforcement
22. language acquisition device, poverty of content
23. infant-directed speech, recasting, scaffolding
24. discourse patterns, gender segregation
25. American Sign Language (ASL)
26. some sort of developmental perspective, Head Start
27. developmentally appropriate practices

Multiple-Choice Self-Test: Factual / Conceptual Questions

1. Choice (b) is correct. Although growth is not as fast as it was in infancy, it does continue in a steady and predictable fashion. Choice (a) is incorrect since growth is rather predictable. Even though growth is slower than in infancy, it is faster than in the middle years, so choice (c) is incorrect, as is choice (d) because growth slows as the preschool years come to an end.

2. Choice (a) is correct. Although the mechanism is not completely understood, children who are apathetic, weak, and have poor relationships with their parents are considered to be socially impaired and show failure to thrive. There is no evidence that failure to thrive is caused by genetic predisposition, choice (b); hormonal imbalances, choice (c); or poor nutrition, choice (d).

3. Choice (c) is correct. Children become more skilled in basic physical actions during the preschool period. Gross motor skills show steady improvement, so choices (a) and (d) are incorrect, and there is no evidence of deterioration or regression, making choice (b) also incorrect.

4. Choice (b) is correct. True running, which involves both feet actually leaving the ground and arm movements, does not occur until the end of the preschool period. Although three-year-olds may appear at times to run, choice (a), the movement is more of a hurried walk without appropriate arm movements for balance. Choices (c) and (d), seven and nine, respectively, are past the time running is established.

5. Choice (c) is correct. Piaget's second stage of development extends from approximately age two to age seven and is called the preoperational stage. Choice (a), concrete operational, is Piaget's third stage, characteristic of the school years. Choice (b), prelogic, is not a term for one of Piaget's stages, and choice (d), primary circular reaction, is the second stage of sensorimotor development, which extends from one to four months of age.

6. Choice (a) is correct. It is the ability to understand that although some features of an object change, its overall identity is constant. Choices (b) and (d), object permanence and sensory integration, respectively, develop during the sensorimotor stage. Choice (c), reversibility, develops during the concrete operational stage.

7. Choice (d) is correct. By definition, functional relationships involve understanding what things seem to go together. However, this does not necessarily imply cause-and-effect relationships, choice (b). Choice (a) is reversibility, while choice (c) relates to properties of objects.

8. Choice (c) is correct. One of the primary reasons preoperational children fail at conservation tasks is because they can't mentally go back to the beginning once an event has taken place. Choice (a), inability to solve mathematical problems, does not typically involve reversibility (although some higher-level problems involve similar concepts); preschoolers actually do have object permanence, so choice (b) is incorrect; choice (d), inability to play games with rules, has to do with understanding more abstract concepts (although games with rules can be played by imitation or rote learning).

9. Choice (c) is correct. Neostructuralists (also sometimes called neo-Piagetians) believe that although the basic descriptions Piaget provided are accurate, the evidence for a large, unified stage is not present and his theory needs to be modified accordingly. Choices (a) and (b), information-processing theorist and behaviorist, respectively, do not see a need for stages at all, while choice (d), Freudian, is not concerned with the same questions as Piaget.

10. Choice (c) is correct. By definition, syntax refers to the rule system or grammar of a language. Choice (a) is pragmatics, choice (b) is semantics, and choice (d) is a morpheme.

Multiple-Choice Self-Test: Application Questions

1. Choice (d) is correct. At this point, bed-wetting is not considered a problem. In fact, about 50 percent of all three-year-olds wet the bed sometimes. It is important to note that one should not create a problem by doing such things as making the child change her sheets, choice (c). If the problem continues and is fairly regular for a year or so, choice (a), seeking medical attention, and, using conditioning techniques, choice (b), may be considered.

2. Choice (d) is correct. Jumping with both feet appears between two and a half to three and a half years of age. Balancing on one foot, choice (a), typically appears at about age five. Catching a large ball, choice (b), and making a representational drawing, choice (c), appear at about age four.

3. Choice (a) is correct. Although there are varying degrees to each of these skills, catching seems to be the most difficult in that children do not really master it until they are at least five years old. Choice (d), throwing a baseball, on the other hand, can be performed fairly efficiently by around four years; choice (b), jumping from a standing point, at around three years; and choice (c), running, at around three to four years.

4. Choice (b) is correct. By definition, scribbling and the drawing of simple shapes are nonrepresentational or prerepresentational drawing. Choices (a), (c), and (d), abstract, associative, and primitive, respectively, are not terms typically used in this context.

5. Choice (c) is correct. The notion that the identity stays the same even though some characteristics may change is identity permanence. Asad knows he will get bigger, but other characteristics may stay the same. Choice (a), conservation, involves the notion that substances stay the same even though certain transformations occur; choice (b), functional relationships, refers to the occurrence of variation in the environment; and choice (d), object permanence, is the notion that an object exists even though it may be out of sight.

6. Choice (d) is correct. Will's behavior involves symbolic play as he pretends that the sticks make an airplane and attributes all the characteristics of airplane to the two sticks. Choice (a), assimilation, is not correct because he is dealing with sticks in a new way; choice (b), false-belief syndrome, does not apply here; and choice (c), functional relationships, refers to the occurrence of variation in the environment.

7. Choice (b) is correct. Although it may look like there is more water in Tanya's pool, she fails to consider the dimensions of the two pools in coming to her conclusion. This shows a lack of conservation skills, which is a characteristic of preschoolers. Choices (c) and (d), lack of identity permanence and lack of symbolic thinking, respectively, are not correct because these are abilities that preschoolers generally possess, and they are not directly related to conservation; choice (a), inability to use classifications, also does not apply.

8. Choice (b) is correct. Cardinality is the idea that the total number of a set corresponds to the last number named when items are counted. Choice (a), ordinality, is incorrect since it involves the idea that there is a particular order to numbers; choice (c), reversibility, is not part of the number concept; and choice (d), one-to-one correspondence, is the notion that a relationship exists between number names and items in a set.

9. Choice (a) is correct. The ability to use language and adjust language to the appropriate context—in this case, a younger listener—is part of pragmatics. Choice (b), semantic anticipation, refers to the understanding and meaning of words, which are also involved here, but they are part of pragmatics. Choice (c), speech recognition, is a more basic skill than is being demonstrated here, and there is no such thing as sibling speech, choice (d).

10. Choice (b) is correct. Studies have found that ASL is a true language and that the learning of the language is very similar to the verbal language learned by hearing children. Thus, Miriam will not be severely impaired or much slower than hearing children, making choices (a) and (d) incorrect; and ASL is considered by most to be a true language, so choice (c) is also incorrect.

CHAPTER 7

Early Childhood: Psychosocial Development

Learning Objectives

1. Discuss the characteristics of play in the preschool years. Identify and compare the three major theoretical approaches to play.

2. Identify the four forms of cognitive play exhibited in the preschool years and describe their developmental patterns.

3. Identify and describe Parten's levels of play and indicate the developmental patterns for each.

4. Describe the factors that contribute to the development of play.

5. Describe the authoritative style of parenting and discuss the probable outcomes for children. Discuss why it is viewed as the most desirable style.

6. Describe the authoritarian style of parenting and discuss the probable outcomes for children.

7. Describe the permissive style of parenting, including the two forms (indulgent and indifferent), and discuss the probable outcomes for children.

8. Describe the nature of the relationship between siblings, especially ones of different ages.

9. Describe the development of friendships during the early childhood years.

10. Define and characterize the changes found in empathy and prosocial behavior during the preschool years.

11. Describe the development of aggression in children, including the various forms aggression takes and developmental changes in aggression. Discuss the impact TV has on aggression.

12. Identify the three steps involved in understanding gender in preschoolers. Describe the characteristics of each step and how the steps progress.

13. Identify and define the various sex-role stereotypes and describe what influences parents, peers, and teachers have on their development.

14. Discuss the various types of child abuse, its causes, and its treatment.

Chapter Overview

Play is the major waking activity of preschoolers. It has several defining characteristics, such as being intrinsically motivated, process oriented, creative, and governed by implicit rules. Psychoanalytic theory emphasizes the mastery and wish fulfillment functions of play. Learning theory stresses the acquisition of social skills through imitation and observation. Cognitive theory emphasizes that play develops in a sequence that generally parallels the major stages of cognitive development. Play can take the form of functional play, constructive play, pretend play, and games with rules. Parten has described play according to levels of its social interaction: unoccupied, solitary, onlooker, parallel, associative, and cooperative. Social participation in different types of play varies with age. A number of factors, such as setting, play materials, physical space, and siblings, influence the play of children.

Authoritative parents show a high degree of control and strong demand for maturity, and high sensitivity and responsiveness to their children's needs and feelings. Their children tend to show greater self-reliance, self-control, and achievement. Authoritarian parents show a high degree of control and strong demand for maturity but low sensitivity and responsiveness to the children's thoughts and feelings. Their children tend to be more distrustful, be unhappy with themselves, and show lower school achievement than other children. Permissive-indulgent parents are warm, caring, and responsive to their children's feelings, but exert little control and make few maturity demands. Their children tend to lack self-reliance and self-control. Permissive-indifferent parents are detached, uninvolved, and inconsistent in their parenting. Their children tend to lack self-reliance and self-control and may be at risk for more severe social and emotional problems. Parents often use mixtures of parenting styles and may change their preferred styles as their children grow older.

Siblings interact differently with each other than with parents. Older siblings serve important functions for younger brothers and sisters. Preschoolers' friendships tend to be unstable, but they become increasingly more stable and involve a greater degree of shared activity. Friendships tend to become more and more based on personal qualities.

Preschoolers commonly exhibit both hostile aggression and instrumental aggression to assert their needs and resolve conflicts. Conflict over possession is the most common cause of anger. As children grow older, verbal methods replace physical ones and overall aggression declines. Temperamental differences, gender, family childrearing practices, peers, and the media all influence the form and frequency of aggressive behavior. Children who cannot control their aggression can be helped to do so with methods such as assertiveness training and social learning theory strategies. Television is a major influence on preschoolers' social development in such areas as aggression, prosocial behavior, and gender stereotyping. Children can be influenced by the highly stereotyped and distorted world it presents. Parents can regulate their children's viewing habits.

During early childhood, children acquire an understanding of gender-typed behaviors and gender identity. A sense of gender constancy, the belief that being male or female is biologically determined and permanent, typically is not achieved until ages seven to nine. Because the development of stereotypes about personal qualities appears to depend on the ability to think abstractly, children do not gain a clear and stable concept of gender until the school years. Influences on gender development include differential expectations and treatment of boys and girls by parents, peers, and the media. The gender schema theory explains how gender roles are learned through social learning and cognitive development. Parents and peers can play important roles in the development of gender. A more flexible approach to gender roles enables children to adopt more androgynous behaviors and attitudes.

There are more than one million cases of child maltreatment reported annually. Maltreatment can take the form of physical, psychological, and sexual abuse. Neglect can be physical or emotional. Causes of maltreatment occur at the levels of the individual parent, the family, the community, and the culture. Consequences of child maltreatment include a range of developmental, adjustment, and emotional problems. Responses to child maltreatment frequently focus on treating the victims and their families with programs targeting "high-risk" families.

Chapter Outline

I. Play in early childhood

    A. The nature of play

        1. Play is intrinsically motivated, because children find it enjoyable and reinforcing.

        2. Children are more interested in the process of playing than in the product of play.

        3. Play is creative and nonliteral; it resembles real-life activities but is not bound by reality.

        4. Play tends to be governed by implicit rules.

        5. Play is spontaneous and self-initiated.

        6. Play is free from major emotional distress.

    B. Theories of play

    All theories of play hold that play activities make a major contribution to the development of important social and emotional skills and understandings.

        1. Psychoanalytic theory

            a. Psychoanalytic theorists emphasize that play provides an opportunity for children to gain mastery over problems.

            b. Play also allows children to use fantasy to gain satisfaction for wishes and desires and may also provide an opportunity for catharsis of upsetting feelings.

            c. Play allows a child to gain increased power over the environment.

        2. Learning theory

            a. Learning theorists view play as an opportunity for children to try out new behaviors and social rules.

            b. Play also exposes the child to adult expectations and practices.

            c. According to learning theory, children learn in three ways: through direct reinforcement for their actions, through vicarious reinforcement, and through cognitive or self-reinforcement.

        3. Cognitive theory

            a. Cognitive theorists identify four major kinds of play.

            b. Play develops sequentially in parallel with major stages of cognitive development.

    C. Cognitive levels of play: Developmental trends

1. **Functional play** involves simple, repeated movements and is most common in the sensorimotor period. It requires no symbolic activity.

2. **Constructive play** involves manipulation of physical objects to build or construct something.

3. **Pretend play** substitutes imaginary situations for real ones and dominates the preoperational period.

    a. Family roles and character roles are most likely to be dramatized by preschool children.

    b. Pretend play grows in frequency and complexity during preschool years, but then decreases in later childhood.

    c. This type of play demonstrates how new forms of experience are assimilated into existing schemes of cognitive understanding.

4. **Games with rules** first appear during the concrete operational period.

    a. The rules for many such games apparently develop out of the more flexible, made-up rules of pretend play.

    b. Games with rules can become traditions handed down.

D. Social levels of play

1. Play varies according to how social it is and can be described as developing in six levels of sociability.

    a. Unoccupied play: The child wanders about and does not become involved in any activity.

    b. Solitary play: The child plays alone, with no awareness of or involvement with other children.

    c. Onlooker play: The child watches others at play without entering into the activities.

    d. Parallel play: Two or more children play with the same toys in much the same way, with an awareness of each other but minimal interaction.

    e. Associative play: Children engage in a common activity and discuss it with one another, but do not assign tasks or roles to individuals.

    f. Cooperative play: Children consciously form into groups to accomplish some activity.

2. Changes in age influence social participation in play.

    a. Parallel play is the most frequent type of preschool play activity.

    b. Parallel play and solitary play decline throughout the preschool period.

      c.   Associative play and cooperative play increase with age.

      d.   As preschoolers get older, play involving coordinated interactions increases, such as imitation and complementary exchanges.

      e.   All forms of play continue to be important to various degrees.

- Working with Javier Hernandez, preschool program coordinator: Play and friendships among preschoolers

    E. Other influences on play

      1.   The composition of children's play is influenced by the range of play opportunities caregivers provide and the types of play they encourage.

      2.   The amount of time for play is important especially as it relates to television watching.

      3.   Economic, cultural, and situational variables also influence the play of children.

      4.   Children use common household objects as props in play.

II. Relationships with others

    A. Relationships with parents

      1.   The child's relationship with his or her parents changes because of verbal and physical development.

      2.   Family rules pose a challenge to preschoolers. Parents are expected to devise their own standards for rearing children.

      3.   Enforcing family rules may be less of a problem in cultures that encourage less individualism and stronger interdependence among people.

      4.   The parent's style of authority is one of the most important aspects of a parent-child relationship.

          a.   **Authoritative** parents exert a high degree of control over their children and demand a lot of them, but they are also responsive, child-centered, and respectful of their children's thoughts, feelings, and participation in decision making. Preschool children of authoritative parents tend to be self-reliant, self-controlled, and able to get along well with peers.

          b.   **Authoritarian** parents also demand a lot from their children and exert high control, but they tend to be less warm and responsive, arbitrary and undemocratic in decision making, and less sensitive to their children's thoughts and feelings. Children of such parents tend to be relatively distrustful of others and have poorer peer relations, poorer adjustment to school, and lower academic achievement than other children do.

          c.   **Permissive** parents show two patterns. **Permissive-indulgent** parents are warm, sensitive, caring, and responsive, but exert low control and make relatively few demands on their children. Their children tend to be less self-reliant and self-controlled and to have lower self-esteem. **Permissive-indifferent** parents are detached and are inconsistent in establishing standards and expectations for their children and in fulfilling their parental responsibilities. Their children tend to be emotionally detached, have a low tolerance for frustration, and experience problems controlling their impulsive and aggressive behavior.

5. Patterns of childrearing also tend to change over time and with changes in family situations; they may be influenced to some degree by particular actions of the child.

- Perspectives: Extended family supports for childrearing

B. Relationships with siblings

1. Most young children are very interested in babies and their repetitions, explanations, and "language practice" speech are very similar to those of adult caregivers.

2. Preschoolers often listen to conversations between their parents and older siblings.

3. Older siblings can be important role models and help young siblings learn social skills and parental expectations.

4. Older siblings may feel burdened by the care of younger siblings.

C. Friendships in early childhood

Children seek intimacy from playing with a familiar friend but also want to play in activities that many different children make possible.

1. The evolution of friendship

   a. Early friendships tend to be somewhat unstable and may change on a weekly or even daily basis. However, children can have sustaining relationships, which is an important step toward forming more lasting relationships later in childhood.

   b. Early friendships may not be as reciprocal or intimate as adult relationships are.

2. Conceptions of friendship

   a. Preschoolers' ideas about friendship are based on activity. A friend, for example, is someone who does certain things with you.

   b. As children near school age, more permanent, personal qualities enter into their conceptions, and crucial features of a friend are more often dispositional, or related to how the friend is likely to behave in the future.

   c. Each child in a friendship is likely to focus primarily on his or her own needs in the relationship.

D. Empathy and prosocial behavior

1. **Empathy** is the ability to experience vicariously the emotions and feelings of another person. Prosocial behavior refers to positive social actions that benefit others. Altruistic behavior is performed with no expectation of reward.

2. In a variety of situations, preschoolers will respond helpfully to another person's distress.

3. Developmental changes

    a. Prosocial behavior is well established by the preschool years and shows up in many behaviors, such as assisting another child, comforting and protecting another child, and warning another child of danger.

    b. Children give increasingly complex reasons for helping and are more strongly influenced by nonaltruistic and altruistic motives.

4. Sources of prosocial behavior

    a. There are many sources of individual differences in prosocial responses. Prosocial behaviors increase due to gains in cognitive functioning, social skills, and moral reasoning.

    b. Differences in temperament affect children's prosocial behavior. Easy children tend to display high levels of prosocial behavior.

    c. Early exposure to prosocial experiences and parental styles influence prosocial behavior.

    d. Both verbal approval for altruistic behavior and an opportunity to discover the benefits of cooperation and helping in play situations have proven successful in increasing altruistic and prosocial behavior among preschoolers.

    e. Preschoolers are more willing to help if adults call attention to other children's distress.

E. Conflict and aggression

Conflict over possessions is the most common cause of anger and physical assault is the second most common cause. Children's use of aggressive revenge and tattling are most frequent when their anger is caused by physical assault.

1. **Aggression** refers to actions that are intended to hurt another person or object and can be divided into two types:

    a. **Instrumental aggression** refers to actions in which one hurts another as a means to achieving a nonaggressive end, often involving conflicts over rights, territory, or objects.

    b. **Hostile aggression** refers to actions in which the goal is hurting another person.

    c. Often aggressive behavior is associated with a child's frustration at being unable to solve a conflict.

2. During the preschool years, the frequency of instrumental aggression declines. The frequency of hostile aggression increases.

3. Influences on the development of aggression have been identified.

a. Temperament differences may contribute to aggression.

b. Throughout preschool, boys show more overall aggressive behavior than girls. Girls are more likely to actively resist by verbal defense; boys are more likely to vent feelings when angered.

c. Styles of childrearing and the quality of the parent-child relationship influence the use of aggression. A number of childrearing characteristics have been found to contribute to aggressiveness in preschoolers. The quality of the parent-child relationship is the most important factor in the development of aggression.

d. Peers contribute to aggression by acting in ways that provoke aggressive retaliation.

e. Watching violence in the media disinhibits, or releases, violent behavior in children already prone to anger and aggression. Most children become desensitized to the pain and hurt that result from aggression. Children have difficulty figuring out the motives of TV characters and the subtleties of plots.

4. Responding to aggressive behavior may be necessary since children who have difficulty controlling their aggression experience considerable problems.

   a. In general, preschoolers conform to parental expectations. Children spanked by loving, thoughtful parents rarely have problems as a result of spanking.

   b. Physical punishment may not be effective in the long term for a number of reasons.

   c. The most successful approaches to aggressive behavior involve working with the entire family to observe what triggers and reinforces the aggressive actions.

   d. The most successful methods of intervention involve reinforcement of positive behaviors, assertiveness training for the child, and increasing the predictability and consistency in the child's daily life.

F. The effects of television on preschoolers' development

   1. Viewing time increases during the preschool years.

   2. The types of programs children prefer watching change with age.

   3. Television watching influences children's social development in aggression, prosocial behavior, consumer behavior, and gender stereotypes.

      a. Television programs designed for both children and adults often convey a highly stereotyped and distorted social world that values being male, youthful, beautiful, and white.

      b. Television is also a very useful educational tool for supporting children's intellectual and social development.

   4. Differences in family circumstances affect television viewing.

5. Parents attempt to regulate their children's television viewing. Families can be divided into four types.

    a. Laissez-faire parents provide low levels of regulation.

    b. Restrictive parents provide high regulation.

    c. Promotive parents have few regulations and high levels of encouragement.

    d. Selective parents highly regulate their children's television watching and encourage specific types of viewing.

III. Gender development

Gender refers to the behaviors and attitudes associated with being male or female. Children go through at least three steps in gender development. Gender identity is beliefs about being one sex or the other. Gender preferences are attitudes about which sex one wishes to be. Gender constancy is the belief that sex is biologically determined, permanent, and unchanging. **Gender role stereotypes** are culturally "appropriate" patterns of gender-related behaviors.

A. Developmental trends during early childhood

    1. From age two onward, preschoolers use gender role stereotypes to guide their behaviors.

    2. Preschool children develop gender stereotypes about personal qualities relatively slowly.

    3. Most children acquire gender identity between ages two and three.

    4. Gender constancy first appears by age four or five.

    5. Gender schema theory proposes that children actively socialize themselves in their gender roles through a process of social learning and cognitive development. A child's gender schema is thought to develop through a series of stages.

        a. First, children learn which objects are associated with each sex.

        b. At about age four to six, children make more indirect and complex associations for their own sex.

        c. At about age eight, children have learned the associations relevant to the opposite sex as well.

B. Influences on gender development

    1. Parents

        a. Parents' actions tend to differ from their expressed beliefs in gender equality. Also, parents support their children for sex-stereotyped activities more than for cross-sex activities.

        b. Chodorow has suggested that the gender differences between girls and boys are related to differences in their experiences of identity formation.

2. Peers

    a. In some ways, peers may shape gender differences more strongly than parents do.

    b. Peer pressures to practice conventional gender roles are both strong and continual, and they occur even if teachers and other adults try to minimize gender-stereotyped play.

C. Androgyny

    1. **Androgyny** refers to a situation in which sex roles are flexible, allowing all individuals to behave in ways that freely integrate behaviors traditionally thought to belong exclusively to one or the other sex.

    2. Bem has suggested that androgynous individuals are more flexible and adaptable because they have not formed organized connections between gender and everyday activities.

    3. How we choose to define gender can affect our understanding of what it means to be male or female.

• A multicultural view: The cultural context of child abuse and neglect

IV. Child maltreatment

Child abuse may be physical, sexual, or emotional; neglect may be physical or emotional.

A. Causes

The causes of child abuse and neglect are best understood within the developmental-ecological contexts in which they occur.

    1. Parent and child characteristics

        a. One explanation is that aggressive and antisocial behavior involved in abuse was previously learned through modeling and direct reinforcement by the parent during his or her childhood.

        b. Internal working models argue that the models of abusive parents are often distorted, unbalanced views of the child.

        c. Personality characteristics may also increase the risk of abuse.

        d. A child who has a difficult temperament, was premature, has a physical disability, is hyperactive, or has other developmental problems may be at risk for child abuse.

    2. Parenting and parent-child interactions

        a. Abusive parents are more likely to use physical punishment and negative control strategies.

        b. Instrumental aggression is transformed into interpersonal violence.

3.   Family, community, and cultural factors

Poverty, unemployment, and other factors can increase the risk of child abuse.

B. Consequences

1.   Abuse and neglect may interfere with children's physical, intellectual, social, and emotional development.

2.   Abused and neglected children may exhibit behavioral problems.

3.   Physical abuse in early childhood is linked to aggressive and violent behaviors in adolescents and adults.

4.   The most common symptoms of sexual abuse include nightmares, posttraumatic stress disorders, and depression.

C. Treatment and prevention

1.   Treatment involves working with parents and children after abuse or the danger of abuse has been discovered. Its goals are to reduce or eliminate the instances of abuse and to provide rehabilitative treatment for the physical and psychological injuries suffered by the child.

2.   Intensive professional help, including family counseling and psychotherapy, is often used. Self-help groups such as Parents Anonymous can be helpful. Parent aides, crisis nurseries, foster care, and short-term residential treatment for family members are among the treatment alternatives.

3.   Early intervention programs target high-risk families and help parents improve their parenting skills, the family climate, and their ability to better cope with stressful life events and conditions.

4.   Social policy efforts include education for parenthood programs and affordable health care.

V. Looking back/looking forward

Key Concepts

Directions: Identify each of the following key concepts discussed in this chapter.

1.   In addition to being intrinsically motivated and spontaneous, play is also _____, _____, and _____.

2.   According to the psychoanalytic view, play is a way to gain _____ over problems. The learning theory of play argues that play is a way to _____ adult social skills.

3.   Play is marked by several cognitive levels. The least complex type of play is thought to be _____, which involves simple, repeated movements that focus on the body. Later _____ involves manipulation of physical objects to build or construct. _____ substitutes make-believe,

imaginary, and dramatic situations for real ones. The play of children entering school years is dominated by _____.

4. Unoccupied play, onlooker play, associative play, and cooperative play are all examples of _____.

5. The availability of _____ and _____ can make a difference in making play a rewarding experience for children.

6. _____ is behavior that involves sharing, cooperating, empathy, and mutual understanding.

7. Baumrind classified parenting styles into three categories based on four dimensions. _____ parents are controlling, demanding of their children's maturity, and lacking in nurturing. _____ parents demonstrate little control over children and place great demands on their children's maturity. _____ parents are controlling, but communicate clearly with children, make reasonable demands on their maturity, and are nurturing. Permissive parents fall into two other subcategories, _____ and _____.

8. Patterns of childrearing can shift due to changes in the _____.

9. Older siblings can help younger siblings by transmitting _____ to them.

10. Early friendships tend to _____. As children develop, their conceptions of friendships involve _____.

11. The ability to vicariously experience the emotions of another person is called _____. Behavior that is performed without anticipation of a reward is called _____.

12. An older child may justify helpfulness in terms of _____. Young children who display _____ levels of prosocial behavior tend to be active, outgoing, and emotionally expressive. Children whose parents are _____ engage in more prosocial, empathic, and compassionate behavior.

13. Firstborn children, who had the most helping experience, tend to be more _____ than lastborn or only children.

14. Two types of _____, or actions that are intended to hurt another person or object, can be seen in children. _____ refers to those actions in which the goal is to hurt, whereas _____ refers to actions in which one child hurts another as a means of achieving a nonaggressive end, involving conflicts over rights, property, or objects.

15. During the preschool years, instrumental aggression _____ and hostile aggression _____. With regard to gender, _____ exhibit more overall aggressive behavior than _____.

16. The parenting styles of _____ and extreme forms of _____ are likely to be associated with higher levels of aggression and lower levels of prosocial behavior.

17. Watching violence _____ violent behavior in children already prone to anger and aggression. Preschoolers have problems understanding the _____ of TV characters.

18. Children ages three to five tend to watch more _____. The amount of TV violence at age eight may be predictive of the seriousness of boys' aggressiveness at age _____. Television communicates a highly stereotyped and distorted social world that values being _____.

19. With regard to regulating television viewing, parents can be classified as being _____, _____, _____, or _____.

20. The behaviors and attitudes we associate with being either male or female refer to _____. Our own belief about being one sex or another is our _____, but our attitudes about what sex we wish to be is our _____. The belief that sex is biologically determined and permanent is a belief in _____. Culturally appropriate patterns of gender-related behavior are called _____.

21. The _____ proposes that children actively socialize themselves in their gender roles through a process of social learning and cognitive development.

22. Preschoolers respond to reinforcement more reliably if it comes from _____.

23. The state of _____ allows all individuals to behave in ways that integrate behaviors traditionally considered exclusive to one sex.

24. Injury to children, termed _____, may be physical, sexual, or emotional. Indifference or negligence of parental responsibility to children, termed _____, also may be physical or emotional.

25. Early intervention programs for child abuse target _____ families. _____ efforts attempt to reduce or eliminate the causes of abuse by changing more general conditions that affect all children and families.

Multiple-Choice Self-Test

Factual / Conceptual Questions

1. The notion that play provides an opportunity to release upsetting feelings that cannot otherwise be expressed is consistent with the _____ theory of play.
   a. cognitive
   b. psychoanalytic
   c. social learning
   d. information-processing

2. Which of the following is considered the most advanced form of cognitive play?
   a. Constructive play
   b. Cooperative play
   c. Games with rules
   d. Pretend play

3. Which of the following forms of social play tends to decrease during the preschool years?
   a. Associative
   b. Cooperative
   c. Parallel
   d. Pretend

4. Sibling conversations tend to be
   a. less aggressive than those with friends.
   b. more reciprocal than those with parents.
   c. more emotional than those with parents.
   d. more task-oriented than those with friends.

5. The most self-reliant and self-controlled children seem to be associated with parents who use the _____ style of parenting.
   a. authoritarian
   b. authoritative
   c. permissive-indifferent
   d. permissive-indulgent

6. Friendships in four-year-olds tend to emphasize
   a. simple discrimination and preference.
   b. shared activities.
   c. shared thoughts and feelings.
   d. status enhancement.

7. The development of prosocial behavior and empathy in the preschool years is related to
   a. a good parent-child relationship and secure attachment during infancy.
   b. infant temperament and other genetic predispositions.
   c. the level of cognitive and metacognitive awareness in the child.
   d. the number of friendships a child experiences.

8. Parents who use excessive permissiveness and inconsistent discipline are likely to produce children who are more _____ than average.
   a. aggressive
   b. androgynous
   c. assertive
   d. empathetic

9. Which of the following concepts seems to emerge during early childhood?
   a. Gender constancy
   b. Gender stereotypes
   c. Gender identity
   d. Gender permanence

10. The internal working model of child abuse indicates that
   a. abusers are genetically predisposed to act violently toward their children.
   b. parents who are too busy and work tend to neglect their children.
   c. parents have an unbalanced and disturbed view of children based on their own experiences.
   d. parents gain satisfaction from having power over children.

Application Questions

1. Which of the following is the best example of play governed by implicit rules?
   a. Playing kickball
   b. Playing school
   c. Playing chess
   d. Playing hide-and-seek

2. When Sarah stacks eight blocks to make a tall tower, her parents cheer her accomplishment. According to learning theorists, Sarah's block playing is being
   a. directly reinforced.
   b. vicariously reinforced.
   c. self-reinforced.
   d. subliminally reinforced.

3. Jean-Claude sits in an empty box and pretends he's a race car driver. His behavior illustrates
   a. constructive play.
   b. dramatic play.
   c. functional play.
   d. parallel play.

4. Josh and Nate sit at the same table in preschool playing with blocks. Josh builds a fort while Nate lines the blocks up to make a train. Although they are using the same set of blocks, they don't seem to be sharing or communicating with one another. Their play would best be described as
   a. associative.
   b. cooperative.
   c. solitary.
   d. parallel.

5. Rudy and Chandra tend to tell their children what to do, seldom seek their input in family decisions, and generally seem somewhat distant from them. Their style of parenting would most likely be classified as
   a. authoritarian.
   b. authoritative.
   c. permissive-indifferent.
   d. permissive-indulgent.

6. Brandy's parents tend to be permissive-indifferent. She is likely to show
   a. a moderate sense of autonomy.
   b. highly aggressive behavior.
   c. emotional problems.
   d. moderate levels of self-esteem.

7. When eight-year-old Kara saw that a younger boy, whom she did not know, had dropped his candy bar in the mud and was crying, she immediately offered to give him half of hers. Kara's behavior is best termed
   a. altruistic.
   b. egocentric.
   c. prosocial.
   d. reciprocal.

8. After Leroy took Bernie's toy in preschool, Bernie got his tricycle and peddled right into Leroy, hitting him in the leg. Bernie's action can be described as
   a, hostile aggression.
   b. instrumental aggression.
   c. operant aggression.
   d. passive aggression.

9. Larry is not a very aggressive child but does tend to watch a considerable amount of violent TV. The most likely effect is that he will become
   a. a violent and aggressive child.
   b. desensitized to the effects of violence.
   c. more hyperactive.
   d. very depressed.

10. Carlos has been sexually abused by his mother. He is likely to show all of the following except
    a. aggression.
    b. bed-wetting.
    c. emotional withdrawal.
    d. nightmares.

Answer Key

Key Concepts

1. process oriented, creative, governed by implicit rules
2. mastery, learn
3. functional play, constructive play, Pretend play, games with rules
4. social levels of play
5. physical space, play materials
6. Prosocial behavior
7. Authoritarian, Permissive, Authoritative, permissive-indulgent, permissive-indifferent
8. family situation
9. customs and traditions
10. unstable, personal qualities
11. empathy, altruistic
12. gaining approval from peers, high, authoritative
13. prosocial
14. aggression, Hostile aggression, instrumental aggression
15. declines, increases, boys, girls
16. permissive-indifferent, authoritarian
17. disinhibits, motives
18. cartoons, nineteen, male, (youthful, beautiful, and white)
19. laissez-faire, restrictive, promotive, selective
20. gender, gender identity, gender preference, gender constancy, gender-role stereotypes
21. gender schema theory
22. a child of their own sex
23. androgyny
24. child abuse, neglect
25. high-risk, Social policy

Multiple-Choice Self-Test: Factual / Conceptual Questions

1. Choice (b) is correct. The notion that play is an emotional release is consistent with the psychoanalytic view. Choice (a), cognitive, indicates that play is based on problem solving and thinking. Choice (c), social learning, indicates that play is used to test new behaviors and social roles. Information processing, choice (d), does not specifically deal with play.

2. Choice (c) is correct. Games with rules are a more formalized form of cognitive play than the others, and this type of play tends to emerge last. Choice (a), constructive play, is the second level of cognitive play; choice (b), cooperative play, is the highest form of social play; and choice (d), pretend play, is the second highest level of cognitive play.

3. Choice (c) is correct. Parallel play tends to be characteristic of young preschoolers' play and decreases throughout the preschool period. Choices (a) and (b), associative and cooperative, respectively, are considered more social/interactive forms of play and tend to increase during

the preschool period. Choice (d), pretend play, grows in frequency and complexity during the preschool years, although it decreases later in childhood.

4. Choice (b) is correct. Sibling conversations, especially when there is an age difference, tend to have a give-and-take nature. In fact the older sibling will often adjust his or her speaking style to meet the needs of the younger sibling. There do not appear to be differences in terms of aggression, choice (a); emotionality, choice (c); or the degree of task orientation, choice (d).

5. Choice (b) is correct. The authoritative style provides for input by the child and fosters the development of autonomy primarily through the use of reasoning in the parent-child interaction. Choice (a), authoritarian, tends to foster distrust, unhappiness, and lower levels of achievement. Choices (c) and (d), permissive-indifferent and permissive-indulgent, respectively, tend to foster a lack of self-reliance and self-control.

6. Choice (b) is correct. Preschoolers' friends are often determined by what they are doing together as opposed to dispositional or personality factors. Choice (a), simple discrimination and preference, is very primitive and may be found in toddlers. Choice (c), shared thoughts and feelings, is more sophisticated and found in school-age children; preschoolers tend not to share thoughts or feelings. Choice (d), status enhancement, is not a strong determinant of friendships in children of any age.

7. Choice (a) is correct. Early developments in attachment and other aspects of the parent-child relationship (including parenting style) in infancy set the stage for preschool empathy and prosocial behavior. Studies have not found choices (b), (c), or (d) to be related to preschool levels of prosocial behavior and empathy.

8. Choice (a) is correct. Aggression has been associated with permissive parents, particularly if they are indifferent to the needs of the child with respect to limit setting and emotional support. Excessively permissive parents tend to produce children who are less assertive, so choice (c) is incorrect, and less empathetic, so choice (d) is also incorrect. Androgyny, choice (b), does not seem to appear until later.

9. Choice (c) is correct. Gender identity (recognition of one's sex) appears to emerge first, by about two years of age. Choices (a) and (d), gender constancy and gender permanence, respectively, develop around seven years of age, and choice (b), gender stereotypes, develops sometime after gender identity is established (around age three).

10. Choice (c) is correct. The internal working model is a schema-based theory that attempts to explain abuse in terms of inappropriate conceptions of how children should be raised. This schema develops from the individual's own experiences of being raised; thus it explains why abusers may often have been abused themselves. The other potential explanations, choices (a), (b), and (d), have little or no support.

Multiple-Choice Self-Test: Application Questions

1. Choice (b) is correct. Implicit rules are generally transmitted by simply observing what others are doing and are generally not verbalized. Playing school is a good example of an activity that is learned through observation or by simply joining in. Younger children, who may never have attended school, pick up what to do by watching what older kids do. Kickball, chess, and hike and seek, choices (a), (c), and (d), respectively, all have rules that can be and often are communicated. Hide-and-seek has the fewest explicit rules, while chess has the most.

2. Choice (a) is correct. This is a clear example of the use of reinforcement—praise and approval—to increase a behavior. Choices (b) and (c), vicariously reinforced and self-

reinforced, respectively, reflect more subtle forms of indirect reinforcement, while choice (d), subliminally reinforced, is a nonexistent form of reinforcement.

3. Choice (b) is correct. Jean-Claude is involved in make-believe and role-playing activity using certain objects to represent other things. Choice (a), constructive play, involves the manipulation of objects to build or create something; choice (c), functional play, involves repeated motions that focus on one's own body; and choice (d), parallel play, is a form of social play void of true interaction.

4. Choice (d) is correct. Parallel play involves two children seemingly playing together (at least physically) but each doing quite different things and not monitoring what the other is doing. Thus although they are playing together physically and may be sharing the same toys, they are not interacting in the sense of cooperation and mutuality. Choice (c), solitary, is when a child simply plays alone with his or her own set of exclusive toys; choices (a) and (b), associative and cooperative, respectively, have varying levels of true interaction.

5. Choice (a) is correct. Authoritarian parents tend not to seek input from their children and are power- or punishment-oriented. Choice (b), authoritative, tends to involve the children in decision making but maintains the right of final approval. Choices (c) and (d), permissive-indifferent and permissive-indulgent, respectively, tend to be low in control, high in communication, and low in maturity and nurturance.

6. Choice (c) is correct. Brandy's parents are low in nurturance and low in control; actually, they would be classified as neglectful. These characteristics have been associated with low levels of self-esteem and self-reliance as well as emotional problems so choices (a) and (d) are incorrect. The permissive-indifferent parenting style is sometimes associated with moderate levels of aggression, choice (b), but aggression is more often found in the children of authoritarian parents.

7. Choice (a) is correct. Kara's behavior is unselfish and aimed at helping someone. What makes her behavior altruistic as opposed to prosocial, choice (c), is that she does this deed without any expectation of having the favor returned in any way (mainly because the young boy is a stranger). Had this been a friend, her behavior may have been considered only prosocial, since there would be underlying expectations based on the friendship relationship. Choice (b), egocentric, is a self-centered behavior, and choice (d), reciprocal, implies expectation of some return or mutuality.

8. Choice (a) is correct. There are two main types of direct aggression, hostile and instrumental. Hostile aggression occurs when the intent is to hurt, while instrumental aggression, choice (b), occurs when hurt is inflicted but not intentionally. Bernie's actions in this case are intentional. Choice (c), operant aggression, is not a form of aggression, while choice (d), passive aggression, is an indirect form of aggression.

9. Choice (b) is correct. Studies show that children who are already aggressive increase their level of aggression from watching violent TV (choice [a]), while children who are not aggressive tend to become desensitized to the violence they see on TV (choice [b]). Larry would fall into the second category. Consistent results have not been found for choices (c) and (d), becoming hyperactive and becoming depressed, respectively.

10. Choice (b) is correct. There is a long list of symptoms associated with abuse, including depression, aggression, regression, nightmares, general posttraumatic stress syndrome, emotional withdrawal, and anxiety disorders. Bed-wetting, however, has not been specifically identified.

CHAPTER 8

Middle Childhood: Physical and Cognitive Development

Learning Objectives

1. Describe the physical growth characteristics of the middle childhood years and compare them with the preschool years.

2. Discuss the social and psychological consequences of obesity during the school years.

3. Discuss the role of athletics in the development of physical and social skills. Identify gender differences in athletic activity during the middle childhood years.

4. Describe the general state of health in schoolchildren compared to preschoolers and other groups.

5. Distinguish between acute and chronic illnesses in children during the school years. Describe the effect of socioeconomic status on illness.

6. Identify and discuss the characteristics of hyperactivity and attention-deficit hyperactivity disorders (ADHD). Discuss treatment methods for ADHD.

7. Name the main characteristics of Piaget's concrete operational stage and contrast it with the preoperational stage.

8. Describe Piaget's concept of conservation and discuss the results of training studies on conservation. Differentiate between the classic Piagetian view and other views.

9. Describe the changes in short-term and long-term memory during the school years.

10. Discuss learning disabilities during the school years, including their likely causes and what can be done to help alleviate the problems.

11. Describe the development and use of metaphor in the school-age child.

12. Discuss bilingual children, including the cognitive consequences of bilingualism.

13. Define what psychologists generally mean by intelligence; describe how it is measured and identify potential problems.

14. Discuss the potential biases and misinterpretations associated with intelligence tests.

15. Describe how the information-processing approach has changed the way we view intelligence, with particular emphasis on the triarchic theory of intelligence.

16. Describe the sociocultural approach to intelligence.

Chapter Overview

Although the rate of physical growth slows in middle childhood, there are significant differences in height and weight among children of any single age. Toward the end of the elementary school years, girls tend to grow taller than boys. Girls tend to experience a growth spurt before the growth of breasts and pubic hair. The growth spurt in boys tends to follow other physical changes in adolescence. Those children who weigh significantly more than average often experience social rejection and risk medical problems. Children develop the ability to play games with rules, and their improvements in coordination and timing enhance their performance in sports. Gender differences in athletic skills appear during middle childhood, probably because of social expectations. Children are usually relatively healthy, with low rates of mortality. Most common childhood illnesses are acute and are viral, although compared to preschoolers, school-age children catch fewer of these illnesses. Family socioeconomic and parental beliefs about illness affect how much children actually stay at home as a result of getting sick. Children with attention-deficit hyperactivity disorder (ADHD) are extremely and active and have considerable concentration problems. ADHD may be caused by a combination of genetic, physical, and social factors. About 5 to 10 percent of school-age children are seriously overactive. Ritalin is a drug used to stimulate the child's nervous system, which can reduce the immediate symptoms of ADHD. Behavior modification has also been used to eliminate or reduce the inappropriate behavior.

Piaget argued that during middle childhood, children become skilled at concrete operations, or reasoning that focuses on real, tangible objects. A very important skill is conservation, the belief that certain properties, such as size and length, remain constant despite perceptual changes in the objects. Efforts to train children in conservation have had moderate success. Concrete operational children also acquire new skills in seriation, temporal relations, and spatial relations. Although Piaget never intended his research to serve as a theory of education, his constructivist approach and stage theory have influenced teaching methods.

According to the information-processing approach, thinking can be divided into several components including short-term memory, long-term memory, recognition memory, and recall memory. Both short-term and long-term memory improve with age, in part because of other cognitive developments, such as growing skill in using learning strategies. Improvements in logical reasoning sometimes improve long-term-memory functioning. Some children have difficulty in basic information processing that interferes with their understanding or use of language. It has been proposed that minimal brain damage, or the way the child organizes and processes information, can cause learning disabilities. After careful diagnosis to identify what steps in information processing are affected, an individual instructional plan can be developed.

Language continues to develop in middle childhood, as reflected in the child's ability to understand metaphors. Being bilingual can benefit a child's cognitive development if both languages are equally learned and respected by people in the child's environment. There are social biases that create negative attitudes and stereotypes about language. Additive bilingual programs may help children by developing both languages. Black English is a complex language that is different from standard English in several ways.

Intelligence can be described as the ability to learn from experience. Intelligence can be studied from the psychometric approach, but newer perspectives based on information-processing theory and on sociocultural principles have challenged this perspective. The psychometric approach uses achievement and aptitude tests to assess intelligence. Sternberg's triarchic theory of intelligence contends that there are three realms of cognition that contribute to intelligence (i.e., componential, experiential, contextual). Gardner's theory of multiple intelligences argues that general ability consists of six factors or skills: language, kinesthetic, logical, spatial, interpersonal and intrapersonal, and musical. The sociocultural perspective argues that the important aspect of intelligence is the interaction of a person and the environment. Vygotsky's zone of proximal development is a key concept of this approach to intelligence.

Chapter Outline

I. Physical development

Physical growth slows during middle childhood, and practice and instruction help children acquire skills.

II. Trends and variations in height and weight

A. During the middle years, variations in growth among children increase dramatically.

B. Girls tend to become significantly taller than boys of the same age. For boys, a spurt in height tends to follow the other physical changes of adolescence. For girls, a spurt in height usually occurs before the growth of secondary sex characteristics.

C. At least one American child in ten suffers from obesity—weighing more than 130 percent of the normal weight for his or her height and bone size.

D. The dilemma is particularly acute for girls, since cultural norms emphasize physical appearance, especially thinness.

E. Children who continue to be obese into adulthood run more risk of a variety of minor illnesses, as well as of a few major ones such as heart disease and diabetes.

F. Children must have the full support of parents and siblings to diet and exercise, which may be difficult to sustain over long periods of time.

- A multicultural view: Dieting in cross-cultural perspective

III. Motor development and athletics in the middle years

A. Fundamental motor skills continue to improve during the school years and gradually become specialized in response to children's particular interests, physical aptitudes, life experiences, and the expectations of others.

B. Children develop the ability to play games with both formal and informal rules. At the same time, their improvements in coordination and timing make performance better in all sports.

C. There may be some risks as well as benefits associated with early athletics.

D. In North America, girls seem especially likely to drop out of athletic activity late in their middle years, for cultural rather than physiological reasons.

1. Throughout childhood, girls compare well with boys in strength, endurance, and motor skill, but at about age twelve, the girls begin to do less well than boys. This may result from social expectations about gender.

2. Some boys and girls begin to emphasize nonathletic interests, losing the benefits of physical activity.

3. Since sex-role standards may be shifting, athletic activity has become more attractive.

IV. Health and illness in middle childhood

   A. During the middle years, children usually are relatively healthy, rarely experiencing serious illnesses or accidents with medical consequences.

   B. There is a low **mortality** rate among schoolchildren.

   C. Most common childhood diseases are **acute illnesses**, meaning they have a distinct beginning, middle, and end. Most acute illnesses develop from viruses, complex protein molecules that come alive only when they infect a host tissue.

   D. Some children develop **chronic illnesses** that persist for many months without significant improvement. The most common chronic illnesses in developed countries are lung and breathing disorders.

   E. The seriousness and frequency of illnesses vary according to children's social and economic circumstances.

      1. Low-income families lack money for doctors' visits and access to special child care when the child is sick, and they cannot take time away from work to tend to sick children.

      2. Because of a lack of money, visits to the doctor may occur only when there is a serious illness.

      3. Race and sex are important variables with regard to illness.

   F. Attention-deficit hyperactivity disorders

      1. **Hyperactivity, or attention-deficit hyperactivity disorder (ADHD),** makes children extremely active and causes them to have considerable trouble concentrating on any one activity for long.

      2. Most children show excessive activity some of the time.

      3. There are five criteria for deciding when an activity is a problem.

      4. Causes of ADHD

         a. ADHD in individual children has different biological causes, such as oxygen deprivation at birth, exposure to toxic substances, artificial additives in food, and head injuries.

         b. The research is unclear as to whether certain parents or teachers can cause hyperactivity in individual children.

         c. Parents and teachers probably do not cause hyperactivity directly, but they may unintentionally aggravate it by responding inappropriately to active children.

5. Helping children with ADHD and their families

    a. Although no single strategy exists for treating or dealing with hyperactivity, a group of strategies has proven helpful.

    b. To reduce immediate symptoms, stimulant medication such as Ritalin quiets behavior by making the central nervous system more alert.

    c. **Behavior modification** is a psychotherapeutic technique that identifies unwanted behaviors and uses specific methods for eliminating or reducing them.

    d. Consistency and predictability are important in behavior modification.

V. Cognitive development

VI. Piaget's theory: Concrete operational skills

A. During the middle years, children become skilled at **concrete operations**, mental activities focused on real objects and events.

B. Concrete operations have three interrelated qualities.

    1. Decentration means attending to more than one feature of a problem at a time.

    2. Sensitivity to transformations combines different perceptions of the same object in logical ways.

    3. Reversibility of thought means understanding that certain logical operations can be reversed by others.

C. **Conservation** refers to the belief that properties of an object remain the same despite changes in the object's appearance. Piaget found that after about age seven, most children can conserve quantity in the water glass experiment.

D. Conservation training

    1. Piaget argued that biological maturation and extensive experience with physical objects having conservation properties lead to the ability to conserve.

    2. Many psychologists have tried to teach conservation and have had some success. But children trained in conservation often do not maintain conservation concepts.

E. Other concrete operational skills

    1. Piaget described other forms of knowledge that appear during the middle years.

    2. Seriation refers to the ability to put items in sequence according to a specific dimension.

    3. Schoolchildren's understanding of the nature of time is much better than that of preschoolers.

    4. Spatial relations improve during the school years, allowing children to make maps and models of familiar places.

F.   Piaget's influence on education

His ideas and approach have significantly influenced educators. The assumption that children develop their own concepts through active engagement with the environment is called constructivist philosophy.

VII.   Information-processing skills

During the middle years, children show important changes in how they organize and remember information.

A.   Memory capacity

1.   Some tasks rely primarily on short-term memory (STM), a feature of thinking that holds information only for short periods. On tasks that emphasize short-term recognition memory, school-age children perform less well than adults do.

2.   **Recognition memory** involves comparing an external stimulus or cue with preexisting experiences or knowledge. **Recall memory** involves trying to remember information in the absence of external cues.

3.   Long-term memory (LTM) is the feature of thinking that holds information for very long periods. This capacity develops slowly, relying on complex storage and retrieval processes.

4.   Young children may remember less because they have fewer memorable events, or they use fewer methods of deliberately remembering information and experiences.

5.   Children make fewer inferences than adults.

6.   A child's memory may affect learning during the school years. Teachers may need to help children see connections among material learned in school.

B.   Difficulties with information processing: Learning disabilities

1.   About 5 percent of children develop **learning disabilities**, disorders in basic information processing that interfere with understanding or using language, either written or spoken.

2.   Learning disabilities can take many forms, such as dyslexia. There is a diversity of symptoms.

a.   In word blindness, the child can read letters singly but not in combinations that make words.

b.   Some dyslexic children can read words but fail to comprehend them.

c.   Some children with dyslexia can read combinations of digits that make large numbers, but cannot separate out the individual numbers.

3.   Causes of learning disabilities

a.   Many learning disabilities may reflect undetected minimal brain damage that occurred during or before birth.

b.   Learning disabilities may result from subtle differences in how the mind organizes and processes information.

c.   Some children with dyslexia show strong perceptual masking.

4.   Helping children with learning disabilities

a.   Help consists of a careful diagnosis of which steps in thinking cause difficulty followed by individual instructional plans to strengthen those particular steps.

b.   Adults can help children who are self-conscious about failing to learn.

• Working with Terry Wharton, special education teacher: Giving children a second chance to learn

VIII.   Language development in middle childhood

Although language continues to develop in terms of an expanding vocabulary and increases in complexity and subtlety, children have not necessarily mastered syntax.

A.   Understanding metaphor

1.   A **metaphor** is a figure of speech in which a word or expression ordinarily used for one thing is used for another.

2.   Children can understand a variety of metaphors even in the preschool years. Not until about age ten, however, do children reliably interpret a metaphor in conceptual or relational terms.

B.   Bilingualism and its effects

A majority of children around the world are bilingual. When children are **balanced bilinguals**, meaning they acquire both languages equally well and the languages are treated with respect by others, their skill benefits their cognitive development.

1.   Cognitive effects of bilingualism

a.   Balanced bilingual children show greater cognitive flexibility than children fluent in only one language do.

b.   Such flexibility shows **metalinguistic awareness**, the knowledge that language can be an object of thought.

c.   Unbalanced bilingualism has mixed effects on children's thinking skills.

2.   Social effects of bilingualism

a.   When children acquire two languages, one language usually has more prestige than the other.

b.   Negative attitudes toward non-English languages reduce school performance by making children less willing to use their first language in public and reducing their self-confidence about linguistic skills in general.

    c. Additive bilingual education programs allow the child to develop skills in both of his or her languages.

C. Black English

    1. In the United States, some African Americans use a dialect of English called **Black English**, which differs in several ways from standard English.

    2. Studies of Black English find it just as complex as other languages and equally capable of expressing the full range of human thought and emotion. Unfortunately, society's attitudes toward it remain rather negative.

IX. Defining and measuring intelligence

A. **Intelligence** refers to adaptability or a general ability to learn from experience.

B. **Psychometric approach to intelligence**

Psychometric definitions of intelligence have derived from standardized tests, all of which share three important features. They always contain clearly stated questions with relatively specific answers. They always include clear, standardized procedures for administration and scoring. They allow for comparative evaluation of the performances of particular groups or individuals.

    1. Kinds of standardized tests

        a. Standardized tests can be grouped into **achievement tests**, which measure previously learned skills or knowledge, and **aptitude tests**, which measure ability or try to predict future performance.

        b. Standardized tests, especially achievement tests, can help educators know how well schools or classrooms are functioning.

        c. Standardized tests can help educators to identify students with special academic needs.

    2. Biases of intelligence and general ability tests

        a. Tests often contain biases, such as favoring children who have a good command of language. Intelligence tests measure academic ability better than any other skill.

        b. Tests show their cultural assumptions and biases by including questions that often demand knowledge that can be attained only through immersion in White, middle-class society.

        c. Tests show their cultural assumptions and biases by including conversations that emphasize abstract or general propositions.

• Perspectives: Gifted students: Victims or elite?

C. Information-processing approaches to intelligence

1. An approach that draws explicitly on information-processing principles is Sternberg's **triarchic theory of intelligence**. This theory proposes three realms of cognition that contribute to general intelligence: components of thinking, experiences, and context of thinking.

   a. Components of thinking refer to the basic elements of the information-processing model such as coding, representing, and higher-order skills.

   b. Experiences refer to skills with new experiences.

   c. Context of thinking refers to the extent to which a person can adapt to, select, or alter environments relevant to and supportive of his or her abilities.

2. Gardner's theory of **multiple intelligences** proposes that general ability consists of several factors defined in terms of the culture or society of which an individual is a part. These several intelligences include the following skills: language, musical, logical, spatial, kinesthetic, interpersonal and intrapersonal.

D. Sociocultural approaches to intelligence

1. In the **sociocultural perspective**, intelligence is not actually "in" individuals but in the interactions and activities among individuals. Therefore, it is not the individual who adapts to, learns, and modifies knowledge but the person and the environment in combination.

2. A key concept in the sociocultural view is Vygotsky's zone of proximal development, or the level of problem solving at which a child cannot solve a problem alone but is able to with the assistance of an adult or a more competent peer.

3. This approach assumes that the issue of cultural bias on psychometric tests is an outcome to be expected rather than a problem.

X. The changing child: Physical, cognitive, and social

Key Concepts

Directions: Identify each of the following key concepts discussed in this chapter.

1. For boys, the spurt in height tends to _____ other physical changes of adolescence. For girls, the spurt in height tends to _____ other physical changes of adolescence.

2. The term used to mean a child's weight is more than 130 percent of the normal weight for his or her height and bone size is _____.

3. Girls tend to drop out of athletic activity because of _____.

4. The proportion of persons dying at a given age is called _____.

5. Most childhood illness can be termed _____ since it has a distinct beginning, middle, and end. _____ is that type of illness that persists for long periods without significant improvement. Most acute illness can be attributed to a particular _____ that infects the child.

6. _____ also known as _____ makes children seem extremely active and have considerable trouble concentrating on any one activity for very long.

7. _____ is a drug used to reduce the immediate symptoms of ADHD. A technique used to identify and reduce unwanted behaviors that accompany this disorder is _____.

8. During the middle years, children become skilled at _____, which are mental activities focused on real objects and events. These mental processes have three interrelated qualities: _____, or attending to more than one feature of a problem at once; _____, or solving problems by going back to their beginning; and _____, which means having different perceptions of the same object and combining them in logical ways.

9. One of the main accomplishments during the middle years, in terms of cognitive ability, is _____, or the belief that properties of an object remain the same regardless of changes in its appearance.

10. Other concrete operational skills that emerge during middle childhood are _____, understanding _____, and representing _____.

11. The assumption that children develop their own concepts through active engagement with the environment is called _____.

12. The type of memory in which a person compares an external stimulus with preexisting experience or knowledge is called _____. The type of memory that involves remembering information without the assistance of external cues is known as _____.

13. Disorders that involve problems in basic information processing that interfere with understanding or using language are known as _____. If you perceive one set of features but no others, _____ is occurring.

14. A(n) _____ is a figure of speech in which a word or expression ordinarily used for one thing can be used for another. Preschoolers can understand some of these figures of speech, but not when expressed in _____ or _____ terms.

15. A child who has acquired two languages equally well is called a(n) _____.

16. Cognitive flexibility reflects _____, or the knowledge that language can be an object of thought. _____ consists of programs where language skills in both a child's languages are developed.

17. A dialect used by some African American people in the United States is termed _____. It differs from standard English in some sounds, certain grammatical forms, and some words and expressions.

18. A general ability to learn from experience, or adaptability, is termed _____. Proponents of the _____ to intelligence have derived their definition of the term from standardized tests measuring abilities and achievement quantitatively.

19. The two types of standardized test are _____ and _____ tests.

20. Many intelligence tests are biased because questions assume that the child is from the _____.

21. Sternberg has proposed the _____ theory, which incorporates three realms of cognition that contribute to general intelligence: components of thinking, experience, and _____ of thinking.

22. Gardner proposed a theory of _____.

23. _____ view intelligence not simply as belonging to an individual, but as a result of interactions and activities among individuals and their environments.

24. Vygotsky's concept of the _____ is important to the sociocultural view of knowledge.

Multiple-Choice Self-Test

Factual / Conceptual Questions

1. During the middle years, physical growth tends to
   a. fluctuate considerably in males as compared with females.
   b. increase sharply.
   c. remain remarkably stable.
   d. slow down as compared with growth in the preschool years.

2. Between ages six and twelve, the average child will grow _____ inches taller.
   a. six
   b. fourteen
   c. twenty-two
   d. thirty-four

3. Data from the middle years indicate that
   a. accidental deaths are at their highest level.
   b. chronic illness increases sharply.
   c. it is one of the healthiest times of life.
   d. mortality rates remain relatively stable.

4. Most acute illnesses
   a. are caused by bacterial infection.
   b. can be treated with antibiotics.
   c. are treated with simple bed rest.
   d. affect sensory organs.

5. Attention-deficit hyperactivity disorder is most closely associated with
   a. dyslexia.
   b. hyperactivity.
   c. hyposensitivity.
   d. minimal brain damage.

6. Studies that attempt to teach conservation have generally
   a. been successful.
   b. been successful, and the conservation skills that are taught are exactly like the naturally occurring skills.
   c. been successful although the ability is not identical to conservation ability that is not taught.
   d. been successful only if the child is beyond age twelve.

7. In which form of memory are external cues compared with preexisting knowledge?
    a. Long-term memory
    b. Metamemory
    c. Recall memory
    d. Recognition memory

8. In general, recall memory
    a. is a short-term memory process.
    b. is more difficult to access than recognition memory.
    c. occurs only in adults and adolescents.
    d. stores information temporally.

9. In comparison with children who are fluent in one language only, children who learn two languages equally well during childhood can be all of the following *except*
    a. more aware of language.
    b. more cognitively flexible.
    c. lacking in confidence about linguistic skills if there is a social bias against the primary language.
    d. higher in average IQ.

10. An aptitude test measures
    a. expected future performance.
    b. intelligence.
    c. learned skills or knowledge.
    d. motor skills.

Application Questions

1. Amanda is six years old and weighs about forty-five pounds. By the time she is twelve, Amanda 's weight should increase by about _____ pounds.
    a. twenty to twenty-five
    b. thirty-five to forty
    c. fifty to fifty-five
    d. sixty-five to seventy

2. Eight-year-old Indira just moved to the United States from India. As compared to the other girls in her class, Indira should be
    a. much taller.
    b. just slightly taller.
    c. the same height.
    d. shorter.

3. Elisa and Bryant, both of whom are average children, are exactly the same age. Elisa should be
    a. shorter than Bryant throughout the school years.
    b. taller than Bryant throughout the preschool years and shorter during the school years.
    c. taller than Bryant toward the end of elementary school.
    d. taller than Bryant throughout the school years.

4. Raymond should weigh seventy pounds, given his height and bone size, but he actually weighs one hundred pounds. Raymond would most likely be considered
    a. obese.
    b. physically advanced for his developmental level.
    c. slightly overweight.
    d. within the normal weight range.

5. Eight-year-old Tyrone has been taking Ritalin for about a year. Chances are Tyrone has been diagnosed as
   a. having asthma.
   b. having AIDS.
   c. being HIV+.
   d. being hyperactive.

6. Marilyn has just attained the concrete operational stage. Her new abilities should include
   a. abstract reasoning.
   b. functional relationships.
   c. identity permanence.
   d. reversibility.

7. Eleven-year-old David is able to tell you the entire starting lineup for the Chicago Cubs. His ability illustrates
   a. functional memory.
   b. short-term memory.
   c. recall memory.
   d. recognition memory.

8. Manuel sees a triangular sign with the letters Y-I-E-L-D. Although he knows all the letters, he is incapable of putting them together to form the word. Manuel is probably
   a. bilingual.
   b. mentally retarded.
   c. dyslexic.
   d. severely brain damaged in the Broca's area.

9. At what age would a child first understand the meaning of a phrase like "a sea of troubles"?
   a. About age five
   b. About age eight
   c. About age ten
   d. About age thirteen

10. After having been a very successful art major in college, Elena uses her art skills in a new job as a feature editor at a small newspaper. Elena's ability to make successful adjustments probably indicates that she is high in Sternberg's _____ intelligence.
    a. componential
    b. contextual
    c. experiential
    d. general

Answer Key

Key Concepts

1. follow, precede
2. obese
3. social expectations about gender
4. mortality
5. acute illness, Chronic illness, virus
6. Hyperactivity, attention-deficit hyperactivity disorder (ADHD)
7. Ritalin, behavior modification

8. concrete operations, decentration, reversibility, sensitivity to transformations
9. conservation
10. seriation, temporal relations, spatial relations
11. constructivist philosophy
12. recognition memory, recall memory
13. learning disabilities, perceptual masking
14. metaphor, conceptual, relational
15. balanced bilingual
16. metalinguistic awareness, Additive bilingual education
17. Black English
18. intelligence, psychometric approach
19. achievement, aptitude
20. White middle-class
21. triarchic, context
22. multiple intelligences
23. Sociocultural perspectives
24. zone of proximal development

Multiple-Choice Self-Test: Factual / Conceptual Questions

1. Choice (d) is correct. From ages six to twelve, the middle years, physical growth slows down even more than during early childhood. Although there are greater individual variations, they are not related to sex, choice (a). Choices (b) and (c), increase sharply and remain remarkably stable, respectively, are incorrect because a definite decline in growth rate is observed.

2. Choice (b) is correct. The average six-year-old is forty-six inches and the average twelve-year-old is sixty inches, which is a difference of fourteen inches. Thus, choices (a), (c), and (d) are incorrect.

3. Choice (c) is correct. During the middle years, children rarely experience serious illness or accidents that have medical consequences. At this stage of life, most illnesses are due to colds or minor viral infections. Accidental deaths, choice (a), are much more common in adolescence. Chronic illness, choice (b), actually decreases. Mortality rates, choice (d), decrease during the school years.

4. Choice (c) is correct. Acute illnesses have a definite beginning, middle, and end and generally need to run their course. Many are caused by viruses, not bacteria, which makes choice (a) incorrect. Since antibiotics are ineffective against viruses, choice (b) is also incorrect. Acute illnesses tend to be such things as colds and flu and are not related to sensory organs, so choice (d) is also incorrect.

5. Choice (b) is correct. Children who are extremely active and have difficulty concentrating on one activity have been termed ADHD, or hyperactive. Choice (a), dyslexia, refers to reading problems. Choice (c), hypersensitivity, is actually a low level of sensitivity to stimulation. Choice (d), minimal brain damage, refers to a possible cause of various learning disabilities or other cognitive-based disorders.

6. Choice (c) is correct. Although it does appear that conservation can be taught, studies have shown that trained conservers are more likely to be swayed from their beliefs than are natural conservers. Thus, choices (a), (b), and (d) are inaccurate statements.

7. Choice (d) is correct. In recognition, the retrieval process is minimized because the cues are present; for example, this multiple-choice question uses recognition, while an essay test requires you to generate the cues and recall the information, choice (c). Long-term memory, choice (a), is where we hold the information that is either recognized or recalled, whereas choice (b), metamemory, refers to our knowledge of our memory abilities.

8. Choice (b) is correct. Recall memory is more difficult to access than recognition memory because relatively few cues are used to bring information back into awareness. Choice (a) is incorrect because recall is a long-term memory process. Choice (c) is incorrect because recall has been observed in school-age children and younger children. Choice (d) is incorrect because recall represents a use of information rather than a store of information.

9. Choice (d) is correct. There does not seem to be a connection between intelligence and being bilingual. However, the cognitive effects of bilingualism include greater metalinguistic awareness, choice (a), and greater cognitive flexibility, choice (b). If there is a bias against the primary language, children may lack confidence in their linguistic ability, choice (c).

10. Choice (a) is correct. Aptitude tests are used to predict future performance. An intelligence test, choice (b), is a form of aptitude test, but not all aptitude tests are intelligence tests. Choice (c) would be measured by an achievement test, and choice (d) would most likely be assessed with an ability test.

Multiple-Choice Self-Test: Application Questions

1. Choice (b) is correct. The average twelve-year-old weighs about eighty to eighty-five pounds, which is a thirty-five to forty pound weight gain.

2. Choice (d) is correct. The average height of eight-year-old girls in the United States is about 48.5 inches, while the average height of eight-year-old girls in India is 45.5 inches, a three-inch difference. Therefore, Indira should be shorter.

3. Choice (c) is correct. Since Elisa and Bryant represent average children, Elisa should be taller toward the end of elementary school because girls tend to begin their growth spurt before boys. During the early school years, boys and girls are approximately the same height, so choice (a) is incorrect. Toward the end of the elementary school years, when the growth spurt begins, girls temporarily surpass boys in height, so choices (b) and (d) are also incorrect.

4. Choice (a) is correct. Raymond weighs about 145 percent of the normal weight for his height and bone size. Weights over 130 percent are considered obese; therefore, Raymond would be considered obese. Excess weight is not viewed as a sign of being physically advanced, so choice (b) is incorrect. Raymond is considered neither slightly overweight, choice (c), nor within a normal range, choice (d).

5. Choice (d) is correct. The most common drug prescribed for ADHD (hyperactivity) is Ritalin.

6. Choice (d) is correct. During the middle years, children develop the ability to mentally undo something by going back to the beginning. This ability is called reversibility. Choice (a), abstract reasoning, is a formal operational ability, which does not develop until early adolescence. Choices (b) and (c), functional relationships and identity permanence, respectively, are preoperational abilities, which develop in the early childhood years.

7. Choice (c) is correct. Getting information out of long-term memory without the use of external cues is recall. Thus, memorizing something and then repeating it is recall. Choice (d),

recognition memory, would involve the use of cues; choice (b), short-term memory, is a temporary memory storage where information can be manipulated. Functional memory, choice (a), is not a term used in this context.

8. Choice (c) is correct. Dyslexia is an inability to read; more specifically, it is an inability to put the letters together to form words. Although choice (b), mentally retarded, might also be correct, there would be other clues than simply this problem, including an inability to recognize the letters (depending on the severity of the condition). Brain damage is also a possibility, but not in Broca's area, choice (d). Choice (a), bilingual, is unlikely, since that is being able to understand two languages.

9. Choice (c) is correct. Children first begin to understand and reliably interpret metaphors in conceptual or relational terms at about age ten. Children ages five, choice (a), and eight, choice (b), have not developed this understanding, while in thirteen-year-olds, choice (d), it is fairly well established.

10. Choice (b) is correct. A person high in contextual intelligence is able to utilize information in one context and apply it to another. This seems to be what Elena is doing. Sternberg's other two forms of intelligence are choices (a) and (c), componential and experiential, respectively, while choice (d), general, refers to a more global concept of intelligence.

CHAPTER 9
Middle Childhood: Psychosocial Development

Learning Objectives

1. Identify and describe the basic psychosocial challenges of the middle years.

2. Define and describe the development of the self throughout the middle years.

3. Describe Freud's and Erikson's views of middle childhood. Discuss the basic issues of development according to these two theories and show how they differ.

4. Describe the development of achievement motivation during middle childhood. Distinguish between the two forms of achievement motivation and indicate how they develop.

5. Describe Sullivan's views on the functions of peers.

6. Describe the role of peers in development during the middle childhood years.

7. Discuss how age, gender, and race affect peer group membership during the school years. In particular, describe how these variables affect attitudes and behavior.

8. Describe the characteristics and psychosocial outcomes of a popular and an unpopular child.

9. Describe the development of friendships and peer conformity in the middle years.

10. Examine the role of the child within the family and the changing relationships that occur during middle childhood.

11. Discuss the impact of the special circumstances of modern families, including divorce, stepparents, and blended families.

12. Discuss the concepts of death, loss, and grieving in children.

13. Describe the impact of parental employment on children, including issues of maternal employment and after-school care.

14. Describe the roles school and teachers play during middle childhood.

Chapter Overview

During middle childhood, children face challenges concerning the development of an identity, or a sense of self, achievement, peer relationships, family relationships, and school. A child develops a sense of self that can grow out of social experiences with others. Children also acquire a sense of self-constancy and learn to distinguish their thoughts and feelings from those of others. According to some psychodynamic theorists, schoolchildren repress their earlier romantic attachments to their parents and focus instead on developing a sense of industry. During middle childhood, children shift their achievement orientation from an exclusive focus on learning, or a task orientation, to a performance orientation that includes others' responses to the achievements. Achievement motivation is defined as the tendency to show initiative and persistence in attaining goals and increasing competence by meeting standards of excellence. Children may show a learning orientation or a performance orientation. Children become more performance oriented in middle years than in earlier years. A number of factors, such as family, environmental, and cultural variables, affect motivational orientation.

Peers become increasingly more influential in the life of the child. According to Piaget, peers help children overcome their egocentrism by challenging them to deal with perspectives other than their own. Sullivan argued that peers help children develop democratic ways of interacting and also offer the first opportunity to form close or intimate relationships with others. Peers serve unique functions by creating voluntary relationships of equality among children. Most children prefer to play with others of approximately the same age and of the same gender. Playmate selection is influenced by sharing gender-based play activities. Groups of peers vary in membership and behavior in terms of age, gender, and race or ethnic group. Peer groups tend to segregate themselves by gender, race, and socioeconomic status. Popular children are viewed by peers as being confident, good-natured, kind, outgoing, and energetic; unpopular children are seen as unpleasant, disruptive, selfish, and having few positive characteristics. As children mature, equality and reciprocity become key elements in friendships. In addition, peer groups can exert negative and positive influence.

Families are experiencing change, with an increasing number of mothers working outside the home and a high percentage of marriages ending in divorce. Divorce usually creates stress for all members of the family, although girls and boys react differently. Divorce is especially hard for children during middle childhood. Relationships between parents and children frequently deteriorate during and immediately after a divorce. Blended families are especially hard on preadolescent girls.

Between ages five and seven, most children come to understand that death is an irreversible, nonfunctional, and universal state. When confronted with the death of someone, children pass through three stages of the grieving process. Maternal employment generally does not seem to have any negative effects on children. When fathers are unemployed, both they and their families experience significant stress. Providing good after-school supervision is a concern for many working parents. Formal after-school care arrangements can have positive effects on children. Children can get emotional support from siblings, other adults, grandparents, and pets.

Children are influenced by their school's culture. This influence is more likely to be positive if the school's culture and the child's familial culture are compatible. The child is influenced by the school's formal and informal curriculum. Teachers can unintentionally communicate negative expectations of students. Children often experience learning environments that are not positive. Open classrooms and cooperative learning can contribute to greater student involvement and learning.

Chapter Outline

I. Psychosocial challenges of middle childhood

During the middle years, children's psychosocial development involves five **major** challenges: (1) the challenge of **knowing who you are**, (2) the challenge to achieve, (3) the challenge of **peers**, (4) the challenge of family relationships, and (5) the challenge of school.

II. The sense of self

Throughout their development, children actively develop a **sense of self**, a structure that helps them organize and understand who they are based on others' views, their own experiences, and cultural categories such as gender and race.

A. The development of self in childhood

1. **Self-constancy**, a belief that identity remains permanently fixed, does not become firm until the early school years.

2. The first beliefs in psychological traits

    a. Up to age five or six, children tend to define self in terms of observable features and behaviors.

    b. Around age eight, some children form a more stable sense of self by including psychological traits in their self-descriptions. At first these traits have no reference to others. Often they are contradictory.

    c. By the end of the middle years, fuller integration of contradictory traits occurs, making a more stable sense of self possible. But the middle-years child's consciousness of inner traits still lacks the subtlety and flexibility found in adolescents and adults.

    d. Significant cultural differences exist in how the concept of self is constructed.

B. Processes in constructing a self

1. Children in middle childhood develop a sense of identity by developing a social self, which involves awareness of the relationships with others in their lives.

2. They construct their identities by distinguishing their thoughts and feelings from those expressed by others.

3. School-age children distinguish between their own emotions and those of others, an accomplishment necessary to develop a mature sense of self.

III. The age of industry and achievement

The years from six to twelve are important to the development of competence.

A. Latency and the crisis of industry

1. Psychodynamic theories explain children's behavior in terms of emotional relationships in early childhood.

2. Freud emphasized the emotional hardship of preschoolers' disappointment and their consequent repression of their wishes toward their parents.

3. Because the child's earlier feelings have gone underground, Freud terms this period **latency**.

4. Erikson went beyond Freud's account to stress the positive functions of skill building. Becoming competent helps children be more like adults through identification and recognition from others.

5. Erikson called this process the crisis of **industry versus inferiority**, since children are concerned with the capacity to do good work. Children who do not convince themselves and others of this capacity suffer from feelings of inferiority, or poor self-esteem.

B. Achievement motivation

1. **Achievement motivation** is the tendency to show initiative and persistence in goal attainment and increasing competence by successfully meeting standards of excellence.

2. Differences in achievement motivation

   a. **Learning orientation** is one type of achievement motivation; it is focused on competence and is intrinsically motivated.

   b. **Performance orientation** is extrinsically motivated and may be related to the child's trying to please or satisfy others.

   c. Higher levels of intrinsic motivation have been found to be related to an internal sense of control, feelings of enjoyment, and other mastery-related characteristics, including higher academic performance and learning.

3. Achievement motivation in middle childhood

   a. During their middle years, children become more performance oriented than in earlier years.

   b. A child's belief in his or her ability to achieve depends partly on whether others give him or her credit for having that ability; this belief lies at the core of performance orientation.

   c. Successful achievement becomes more complicated in the middle years.

   d. Environmental factors, family factors, and cultural and ethnic backgrounds can also influence achievement orientation.

   e. Children shift toward a performance orientation and become more similar to adults in their achievement orientation.

IV. Peer relationships

A. What theorists say about peer relationships

   1. Piaget

a. Piaget argued that peers help children overcome their egocentrism—their tendency to assume that everyone views the world the same way they do.

b. Piaget claimed that parents and other authority figures have limited influence since they cannot behave as true equals with children.

2. Sullivan

a. Sullivan also believed peer relationships are fundamentally different than a child's relationships with adults.

b. Peers provide a life for children outside their families and thus help correct emotional biases (i.e., warps) imposed on children by their families.

c. This form of learning occurs in the **juvenile period**, from about ages five to ten.

d. As children near the end of the elementary years, they supposedly focus interest on a few select same-sex friends, or chums.

• A multicultural view: Parental expectations and academic achievement

B. Functions of peers

1. Peers probably serve several purposes.

a. Peers provide a context for sociability, enhancement of relationships, and sense of belongingness.

b. Peers promote concern for achievements and a reliable and integrated sense of identity.

c. Peers provide opportunities for instruction and learning.

2. Children's reliance on peers rather than parents seems to increase with age.

3. Although children's relationships with peers show considerable similarities to those with adults, there are several unique features.

a. Peer relationships are horizontal and symmetrical.

b. The child must act in a way that explicitly supports the relationships.

• Perspectives: The psychological functions of preadolescent peer activities

C. Influences on peer group membership

Peer group formation is influenced by several factors, particularly age, gender, and race or ethnic background.

1. Age

a. Children play with others of approximately their own age and prefer agemates as friends.

       b.   Mixed-age groups have special qualities.

       c.   Same-age groups encourage the opposite qualities.

   2.   Gender

       a.   Although mixed-sex play occurs in elementary school, even before school age and as children approach grade five, groups and preferred play partners become increasingly characterized by a single gender.

       b.   As children approach middle school and adolescence, the trend reverses.

       c.   Gender-based separation emerges primarily in social situations and varies with the gender composition of the groups involved.

       d.   Girls' long-term friendships more often tend toward exclusive intimacy than those of boys.

       e.   One study found that girls made mutually exclusive choices (dyads, or two-person relationships) more often than boys did. Boys more frequently formed patterns in which no choice was reciprocated.

       f.   Girls' styles may put them at a disadvantage as children enter adolescence.

       g.   Peers exert pressure toward conformity with same-gender friendship patterns.

   3.   Race and ethnic background

       a.   Prejudice is an attitude toward an individual based solely on the person's membership in a particular group.

       b.   Prejudices are often based on stereotypes, or patterns of rigid, overly simplified, and generally inaccurate ideas about another group of people.

       c.   More research is needed to explore prejudice in middle childhood.

       d.   Racial and ethnic prejudice may be reduced by fostering peer interactions, cooperative learning experiences, and multicultural competence.

- Working with Lisa Truong, fourth-grade teacher: Reducing gender role stereotyping in play

  D. Popularity, social acceptance, and rejection

   1.   Children are generally classified as popular, rejected, controversial, or neglected.

   2.   The popular child

       a.   Easily noticed characteristics are quite important to acceptance in early grades. As children get older, they choose their friends increasingly on the basis of personal qualities such as honesty, kindness, humor, and creativity.

       b.   Peers view popular children as confident, good-natured, kind, outgoing, and energetic. Popular children are well liked, easily initiate and maintain social interactions, understand social situations, possess a high degree of interpersonal skills, and behave in ways that are prosocial, cooperative, and in tune with group norms.

    c.   Assets such as peer competence and athletic ability remain valuable to children as they move into adolescence.

    d.   Because of the importance of peer relationships during the school years, the interpersonal competencies associated with peer acceptance and popularity are likely to have a positive impact not only on a child's current adjustment but on his or her psychological well-being as well.

3.   The unpopular child

    a.   Peers describe unpopular children as unpleasant, disruptive, selfish, and having few positive characteristics.

    b.   Such children are likely to exhibit socially inappropriate aggression, hyperactivity, inattention or immaturity, and experience behavioral and academic problems in school.

4.   Aggression

    a.   The highest level of aggression is displayed by unpopular-rejected children and is influenced by social context.

    b.   Children who are exposed to ongoing violence suffer from emotional distress, learning problems, sleep disturbances, and preoccupation with safety.

    c.   Emotional withdrawal may cause problems when these children become parents themselves.

    d.   School-based intervention programs help reduce aggression and foster prosocial behavior.

5.   Friends

    a.   During the early middle years, children base friendships on shared interests and activities, exchanges of possessions, and concrete supportive behaviors.

    b.   As children move into later childhood and preadolescence, equality and reciprocity become key elements of friendships.

    c.   Children increasingly see themselves as others view them.

    d.   By second or third grade, children become better able to live with differing perspectives within their friendships and feel less pressure to choose between one or the other.

    e.   There are implications of having friends, the identity of one's friends, and friendship quality. Friends provide social scaffolding.

E. Conformity to peers

1. Because peer groups involve social equals, they give children unique opportunities to develop their own beliefs without having parents or older siblings dominate or dismiss them.

2. Peer groups demand conformity to group expectations in return for continued acceptance and prestige.

3. Pressures to conform sometimes lead children to violate personal values or needs or those of parents and other adult authorities. Peer groups can exert positive pressures, too, such as encouraging athletic achievement above and beyond what physical education teachers can produce, and they can create commitments to fairness and reciprocity.

4. Whether pressures are positive or negative, peer groups offer a key setting for acquiring social skills, evaluating and managing personal relationships, and handling competition and cooperation.

V. Family relationships

   A. The quality of parent-child relationships in middle childhood

      1. Children gradually learn more about parental attitudes and motivations and the reasons behind family rules, becoming better able to control their own behavior.

      2. Parents continue to monitor children's efforts to take care of themselves, but in more indirect ways.

      3. If children have become securely attached during the preschool years, they and their parents often enjoy each other's company more than ever during the middle years.

   B. The changing nature of modern families

      1. Mothers are working outside the home in increasing numbers.

      2. Because approximately two-thirds of divorced parents remarry, it is expected that most children of divorce will live in reconstituted families, consisting of a parent, stepparent, siblings, and stepsiblings.

   C. Divorce and its effects on children

      1. Most divorcing parents must make adjustments that deeply affect their children.

      2. Many divorced mothers must take on new or additional employment, and their standard of living frequently declines. Both custodial and noncustodial fathers are more likely to maintain or improve their standard of living following divorce.

      3. The psychological pressures of divorce involve learning to manage a household alone and experiencing isolation from relatives or friends.

      4. Even before actual separation and divorce, many families experience long periods of distress, tension, and discord that continue for two or three years following separation.

5. Children face problems of divided loyalties and inconsistent discipline due to poor communication between parents.

6. A study found that ten years following the divorce, children experienced fear of disappointment in love relationships, lowered expectations, and a sense of powerlessness.

7. Divorce has differing effects on boys and girls.

   a. Boys tend to express their distress in externalizing ways, such as being more aggressive and willful, and are more frequently victims of power struggles and inconsistencies in matters of discipline.

   b. Some studies suggest that girls become less aggressive after a divorce, tend to worry more about schoolwork, and often take on more household responsibilities. They may be internalizing their stress by acting more responsibly than usual.

   c. Other research suggests that daughters of divorced parents develop a preoccupation with relationships with males.

   d. Certain factors can help reduce the negative effects of divorce, including parental efforts to reduce conflict and appropriate use of professional help.

8. Custody arrangements

   a. Relationships between parents and children frequently deteriorate during and immediately after a divorce.

   b. Parents without physical custody of children do not face the same daily hassles custodial parents do, but they report feeling rootless, dissatisfied, and unfairly cut off from their children.

   c. Fathers often increase time spent with children immediately following divorce, but soon decrease that time to well below what it was before the divorce.

   d. Sometimes joint custody can alleviate some of these problems.

9. Remarriage and blended families

   a. Most divorced parents remarry within a few years, creating reconstituted or **blended families**.

   b. Younger children appear better able than young adolescents to accept a stepparent in a parenting role.

   c. Daughters, especially those approaching adolescence, appear to have a more intense and sustained negative psychological reaction to their mothers' remarriage and more difficulty accepting and interacting with their new stepfathers.

   d. Stepmothers are more emotionally involved and take a more active role in discipline than stepfathers do.

D. Death, loss, and grieving during the school years

1. Experiences with death can have a developmental impact throughout the lifespan.

2. Children between five and seven years old come to understand death as an irreversible, nonfunctional, and universal state. Younger children think death is reversible and think that some people will not die.

3. Loss is being separated from someone to whom one was emotionally attached. Grieving is the emotional, cognitive, and perceptual reactions and experiences that accompany the loss.

4. Bereaved children go through three phases of the grieving process.

   a. Early-phase tasks involve understanding that someone has died, the implications of death, and protecting oneself and family from physical and emotional harm.

   b. Middle-phase tasks consist of grieving, accepting and emotionally acknowledging the reality of loss, exploring one's relationship to the person who died, and experiencing psychological pain.

   c. Late-phase tasks require the child to consolidate a new sense of personal identity that includes the loss as well as identification with the deceased person.

5. Children are faced with the question of why the deceased person had to die and leave.

6. The developmental impact of death is dependent on a number of factors.

7. Joining a support group can help children understand and process a death; children in these groups participate in stories, drawings, role playing, and discussion.

E. The effects of work on families

1. Effects of maternal employment

   a. Research suggests that maternal employment does no developmental harm to children; what does matter is the woman's choice of whether to work or not.

   b. Families with working mothers divide household responsibilities and child care more evenly than other families do. Children are often expected to help with household chores and caring for younger siblings.

   c. The blend of housework and earning money seems to create less stereotyped attitudes in the children of working mothers about the proper roles of mothers and fathers.

   d. Many working mothers compensate for possible negative effects of their working through more frequent shared activities with their children.

2. Involuntary paternal unemployment can create significant economic, social, and psychological disruptions for children and their families.

3. Finding after-school supervision is a concern for many parents.

a. One study found that children attending a formal after-school program had better grades, conduct in schools, emotional adjustment, and peer relations.

b. Formal after-school programs may be less important for children who live in communities that provide safe and constructive after-school experiences.

F. Other sources of social support

1. Siblings can also provide social support. They can help with companionship, friendship, social support, and mentoring.

2. Siblings can transmit customs and family expectations and provide challenges that lead their young sibling to new learning.

3. Young school-age children confer a unique role on their older siblings.

4. Siblings tend to be less domineering and more nurturant in families in which children feel secure and parents get along well together.

5. Additional sources of support include other adults, grandparents, and even family pets.

6. Children use hobbies to unwind, have special secret hideaways, and seek out peers for activities when they need an emotional lift.

7. This broadening of social support enables them to better manage stresses inside and outside of their families.

VI. School influences

Next to the family, school is probably the single most important developmental influence during middle childhood.

A. School culture

1. Each school has its own culture, which includes the values, beliefs, traditions, and customary ways of thinking and behaving that make it unique and distinguish it from other schools and institutions.

2. The closer the fit between the school culture and children's values and expectations, the more likely it is that the school's developmental impact will be positive.

B. The informal curriculum

1. Schools influence children through two curricula.

2. The **formal curriculum** emphasizes academic knowledge and skills.

3. The **informal curriculum** incorporates the implicit norms, expectations, and rewards for certain ways of thinking and acting that are conveyed by schools' social and authority relationships.

C. Teacher influences

1. With the exception of their parents, most elementary-school children spend more time with their teachers than with any other adults.

2. Effective teachers are able to establish learning environments that are calm, predictable, and engaging; to provide smooth transitions; and to stay on top of the classroom situation.

3. Teacher beliefs and expectations can affect students' performance and overall school adjustment by changing students' behavior in the anticipated direction and thereby serving as a self-fulfilling prophecy.

4. Teacher expectations

   a. Teachers treat students for whom they have high expectations differently than they do students for whom they do not.

   b. Teachers may also unintentionally communicate negative expectations of students, particularly if they do not fit the teachers' own expectations.

   c. Different groups within the same classroom receive different treatment.

D. The student's experience

   1. In traditional, teacher-centered classrooms students typically experience delay, denial of their desires, distractions, and social disruptions. As a result, many classrooms are organized to minimize these difficulties.

   2. The open classroom approach encourages children to take an active role in learning.

   3. Cooperative learning techniques support children of varying ability in working together to achieve both individual and shared learning goals.

   4. Effective schools provide an environment with clear rules and expectations, effective control, open communication, high nurturance, and respectful relationships. Teacher-student relationships in these schools tend to be authoritative.

VII. Looking back/looking forward

Key Concepts

Directions: Identify each of the following key concepts discussed in this chapter.

1. During the elementary school years, children must learn to get along with others of their age, or their _____.

2. Children continue to develop their _____, a growing structure that helps them organize who they are based on others' views, experiences, cultural categories to which they belong, and expectations. A very important part of this developmental process is children's development of a(n) _____, or how they feel about themselves, also based on these factors. The belief that one's identity remains permanently fixed, called _____, does not become firm until the middle years.

3. With regard to a child's sense of self, by the end of the middle years, fuller integration of _____ traits occurs.

4. _____ described the _____ period as a time when the Oedipus and Electra conflicts are pushed out of awareness. Since he believed these feelings go underground, he termed this period _____.

5. Erikson called this period the crisis of _____, since children must be _____ and work hard on school tasks so they will not suffer from failure to do good work and subsequent feelings of _____, or poor self-esteem.

6. The tendency to show initiative and persistence in attaining goals is termed _____. This tendency can manifest itself as _____, which is focused on competence and reflects intrinsic motivation. Achievement motivation also can demonstrate itself as _____ in those who are extrinsically motivated.

7. With regard to achievement motivation, during the middle years, children become more _____ than they were at earlier ages.

8. Peers, by providing a life for other children outside their families, help compensate for what Sullivan termed the emotional _____, or the biases that families inevitably give their children. This learning occurs during the time of life Sullivan called the _____.

9. Children play mostly with others of approximately the same _____. First-graders generally name children of their own _____ as best friends.

10. Girls' long-term friendships more often tend toward _____ than boys' do.

11. Middle childhood children, like the rest of society, often demonstrate attitudes toward others based solely on the others' group membership. These attitudes reflect _____ toward others.

12. When peers are asked to evaluate each other's likability, children are generally classified as _____, _____, _____, or _____.

13. Boys are more likely to attack peers through _____, whereas girls are more likely to display _____.

14. Only _____ of families fit the model of a traditional family.

15. Girls often respond to divorce by taking on more household responsibility and showing increased concern over schoolwork. These changes could indicate that girls are _____, or holding inside, stresses they may feel about their parents' divorce by trying to be more helpful and responsible.

16. In responding to divorce, boys express their distress in _____.

17. In _____ arrangements following a divorce, children often spend half their time with one parent and half with the other.

18. When remarriage occurs following divorce, a(n) _____ can occur, made up of a parent, a stepparent, and the children of one or both adults in the new relationship.

19. _____ appear to have a more intense and sustained negative psychological reaction to their mothers' remarriage.

20. _____ refers to being separated from someone to whom one was emotionally attached, and _____ refers to the complex emotional, cognitive, and perceptual reactions and experiences that accompany it.

21. Women who are _____ to work report more stressful relations with their children.

22. Schools have two curricula, a(n) _____, which teaches academic knowledge and skills, and a(n) _____, which includes the norms, expectations, and rewards for certain ways of thinking and acting that are conveyed by the school's social and authority relationships.

23. Often, teachers' beliefs and expectations for children affect school performance and adjustment by changing children's behavior to meet these beliefs and expectations. This phenomenon is called a(n) _____.

Multiple-Choice Self-Test

Factual / Conceptual Questions

1. Which of the following is *not* considered a major developmental challenge of the middle years?
    a. Achievement
    b. Peer relationships
    c. Family relationships
    d. Individuation

2. Self-constancy becomes firmly developed
    a. by age two.
    b. between ages two and five.
    c. between ages six and twelve.
    d. after age twelve.

3. Freud believed that during the latency stage a child attempts to deal with previous feelings through
    a. direct expression.
    b. regression.
    c. repression.
    d. sublimation.

4. Achievement motivation is defined as the
    a. tendency to strive for enhanced competence in some area of skill or knowledge.
    b. ability to do well on complex, age-related tasks.
    c. conscious attempt to finish a task once it has been initiated.
    d. unconscious motivation to strive for prestige and power.

5. Achievement motivation during the middle years becomes more _____ oriented.
    a. learning
    b. performance
    c. power
    d. socially

6. Piaget believed that peers are more effective than parents in helping children overcome their egocentrism because parents
   a. are formal operational.
   b. cannot act as true equals.
   c. do not interact with school-age children.
   d. themselves are egocentric.

7. Peer relations differ from parental relations in that the child
   a. gets relief from anxiety-provoking situations from parents.
   b. learns social skills from parents.
   c. must act in ways that explicitly support the peer relationship.
   d. all of the above.

8. Which of the following is *not* a characteristic of a male peer group compared to a female group during the school years?
   a. More active
   b. More intense and intimate
   c. More outdoor oriented
   d. Larger than the female group

9. Six- and seven-year-olds tend to base their friendships on
   a. mutual support.
   b. physical characteristics.
   c. practical behaviors.
   d. psychological qualities.

10. Which of the following is *not* part of the informal curriculum of a school?
    a. Study habits
    b. Conformity to school norms
    c. Standard achievement test performance
    d. Social interactions

Application Questions

1. After Joseph and his mother watched a bagpiper dressed in a kilt play his bagpipes, Joseph's mother asked him if he would like to learn to play the bagpipes when he got older. "No," Joseph replied, "because then I'd be a girl." His answer reflects
   a. egocentric thinking.
   b. lack of object permanence.
   c. lack of self-constancy.
   d. undeveloped self-concept.

2. Seven-year-old Mariel at times believes she's a great artist; at other times she says her drawings are terrible. These mixed feelings are indicative of
   a. a negative self-concept.
   b. self-deception.
   c. lack of self-constancy.
   d. normal development.

3. Chris feels that he is a poor reader and speller even though his performance indicates that he is slightly above average. Erikson would say that Chris lacks a sense of
   a. autonomy.
   b. integrity.
   c. industry.
   d. identity.

4. Jerry has learned how to play the guitar so that he can impress his girlfriend. His achievement motivation is primarily
   a. learning oriented.
   b. performance oriented.
   c. power oriented.
   d. social oriented.

5. Tariq interacts with a mixed-age group most of the time. As compared to a same-age group, he should experience _____ in the group.
   a. being dominated by younger children
   b. less helpfulness
   c. less sociability
   d. more aggression

6. Who is more likely to have someone of a different race as one of his or her best friends?
   a. Four-year-old Brandy
   b. Six-year-old Bobby
   c. Eight-year-old Bruce
   d. Ten-year-old Brianna

7. None of Jordan's classmates list him among the top three or the bottom three children they would like to play with. Jordan's popularity classification would most likely be
   a. controversial.
   b. neglected.
   c. neutral.
   d. rejected.

8. As compared to when she was younger, the qualities that eleven-year-old Alice emphasizes in her friendships are
   a. activities.
   b. exchange of favors.
   c. physical appearance.
   d. psychological.

9. Bette's parents recently divorced. Bette is likely to express her distress about the divorce through
   a. aggression.
   b. being disobedient.
   c. taking on more household responsibilities.
   d. verbal arguments with both parents.

10. Jason has just found out that he is adopted and is struggling to answer the question "How could my parents give me up?" His reaction to this will probably be similar to a child who experiences
   a. attachment formation.
   b. the death of a parent.
   c. identity development.
   d. the first day at a new school.

Answer Key

Key Concepts

1. peers
2. sense of self, self-concept, self-constancy
3. contradictory
4. Freud, latency, repression
5. industry versus inferiority, industrious, inferiority
6. achievement motivation, learning orientation, performance orientation
7. performance oriented
8. warp, juvenile period
9. age, gender
10. exclusive intimacy
11. prejudice
12. popular, rejected, controversial, neglected
13. overt aggression, relational aggression
14. 7 percent
15. internalizing
16. externalizing ways
17. joint custody
18. blended family
19. Girls
20. Loss, grieving
21. forced
22. formal curriculum, informal curriculum
23. self-fulfilling prophecy

Multiple-Choice Self-Test: Factual / Conceptual Questions

1. Choice (d) is correct. The need to achieve, choice (a), and the development of relationships with peers and with the family, choices (b) and (c), present challenges for six- to twelve-year-olds. Individuation, choice (d), is the process involved in forming the identity found in adolescence.

2. Choice (c) is correct. Self-constancy, the belief that identity remains permanently fixed, becomes firm sometime after age six but before adolescence. Thus, the other age ranges, choices (a), (b), and (d), are incorrect.

3. Choice (c) is correct. Freud believed that beginning at about age six, children repress feelings of intimacy for the opposite-sex parent and competition with the same-sex parent. Choice (a), direct expression, would just create more anxiety; choice (b), regression, would represent a return to previous immature behaviors; and choice (d), sublimation, would involve redirecting the anxieties into socially acceptable activities.

4. Choice (a) is correct. Achievement motivation involves the tendency to show initiative and persistence in attaining certain goals and enhancing competency. Choice (b) relates more to success as opposed to motivation; choice (c) only partially covers achievement motivation by defining persistence; and choice (d) refers to motivation for power.

5. Choice (b) is correct. Studies indicate that emphasis shifts from learning-oriented achievement motivation, choice (a), to actually demonstrating those abilities, as indicated by performance-

oriented achievement motivation. Choices (c) and (d), power and socially, respectively, are not forms of achievement motivation.

6. Choice (b) is correct. According to Piaget, children's release from egocentrism comes through interaction on an equal basis because it promotes discussion and negotiation, which allow alternative views to develop. Choice (a), parents are formal operational, is not critical; interactions (not cognitive level) are important. Parents do interact with school-age children, so choice (c) is incorrect. Parents are typically beyond egocentrism, so choice (d) is incorrect.

7. Choice (c) is correct. Peer relationships, unlike parental relationships, are voluntary and involve comparable equals; thus, the individual must act in ways to preserve the relationship. Relief from anxiety, choice (a), can be obtained from either parents or peers. Many social skills are learned from peers rather than from parents, so choice (b) is incorrect.

8. Choice (b) is correct. As compared to female peer groups, male peer groups are more active, choice (a); tend to have more outdoor activities, choice (c); and are larger, choice (d). However, their levels of intensity and intimacy tend to be less.

9. Choice (c) is correct. Six- and seven-year-olds tend to base friendships on shared activities, interests, and concrete behaviors. Nine-, ten-, and eleven-year-olds tend to base friendships on mutual support, choice (a), and psychological qualities, choice (d). For preschoolers, physical characteristics, choice (b), may be a factor that influences friendship.

10. Choice (c) is correct. Standard test scores are part of the formal curriculum. Study habits, choice (a); the ability to conform to school norms, choice (b); and social interactions, choice (d), are all part of the informal curriculum.

Multiple-Choice Self-Test: Application Questions

1. Choice (c) is correct. Joseph is apparently still using physical dress to determine sexual identity and fails to realize that even though changes occur in some dimensions, other dimensions remain constant. This notion of self-constancy develops in the middle-school years. His answer does not reflect egocentric thinking, choice (a); nor does it show a lack of understanding about objects' permanence, choice (b). Although it is true that Joseph probably has an undeveloped self-concept, choice (d), his comment does not address that issue directly.

2. Choice (d) is correct. It is not unusual for children's feelings about themselves to fluctuate wildly at this age as they try to understand themselves and their abilities. Mariel's variable feelings do not indicate a problem with her self-concept, choice (a); or deception of self, choice (b); or lack of self-constancy, choice (c).

3. Choice (c) is correct. According to Erikson, school-aged children are dealing with the issue of industry versus inferiority, which is not determined by actual performance as much as it is by perceived performance. The other choices—autonomy, choice (a); integrity, choice (b); and identity, choice (d)—reflect outcomes of Erikson's other stages.

4. Choice (b) is correct. Jerry's reason for playing the guitar is to receive external reinforcement from his girlfriend. Choice (a), learning oriented, would involve an internal source of motivation. Choices (c) and (d), power oriented and social oriented, respectively, are not forms of achievement motivation.

5. Choice (c) is correct. Mixed-age groups tend to have less chatting or friendly conversations than same-age groups. In mixed-age groups, younger children show more dependency rather than

domination, choice (a); tend to be more helpful and nurturant rather than less helpful, choice (b); and actually have fewer fights or arguments rather than more aggression, choice (d).

6. Choice (a) is correct. The younger the individual, the less likely he or she will use race as a factor in determining friendships.

7. Choice (b) is correct. Since no one has listed him among either their top three or bottom three choices, Jordan probably doesn't have any friends but is not disruptive and therefore is not rejected by others, choices (d) and (a). Essentially, Jordan is ignored by most. Choice (c) is not a popularity classification, but the concept of being neutral certainly applies here.

8. Choice (d) is correct. By age eleven, children begin to look at dispositional or personality factors as being more important than physical appearance, choice (c); activities, choice (a); and even exchange of favors, choice (b).

9. Choice (c) is correct. Girls tend to internalize while boys tend to externalize in response to divorce. Thus, choices (a), (b), and (d)—aggression, being disobedient, and verbal arguments, respectively—are all things boys tend to do. Girls, on the other hand, tend to withdraw a bit, hold their emotions inside, and rechannel their feelings by helping more around the house.

10. Choice (b) is correct. Adoption, divorce, and the death of a parent can all produce a grief response as children try to understand why this is happening to them. Choices (a), (c), and (d)—attachment formation, identity development, and first day of school, respectively—typically do not produce the same kind of reaction, which includes understanding the loss, emotional separation, and ultimate acceptance.

CHAPTER 10

Adolescence: Physical and Cognitive Development

Learning Objectives

1. Describe the concept of adolescence, explain how it has changed, and cite the factors that have influenced those changes. Discuss the two major theoretical views of the adolescent period.

2. Discuss the adolescent growth spurt. Describe the characteristic height and weight changes that occur during adolescence.

3. Define and identify the primary and secondary sex characteristics and indicate how they change during adolescence.

4. Discuss the role of hormones in puberty. Identify and discuss the functions of the major sex hormones.

5. Describe the effects of early versus late maturing in males and females, including information concerning long-term effects.

6. Characterize the health of the adolescent and describe the major health problems of adolescence, including sexually transmitted diseases.

7. Discuss drug, alcohol, and other problems in adolescence.

8. Identify the adolescent eating disorders, including symptoms and treatment.

9. Describe Piaget's stage of formal operational thought; characterize reasoning beyond the formal operational level—in particular, reasoning for everyday or real-life problems.

10. Discuss the information-processing view of adolescent thinking; describe the characteristics of an expert and explain how an individual develops expertise in a particular area.

11. Define what is meant by critical thinking and discuss ways in which adolescents can develop this skill.

12. Describe the development of social cognition and adolescent egocentrism.

13. Describe morality and Kohlberg's six stages of moral judgment.

14. Discuss Gilligan's alternative to Kohlberg and describe her emphasis on the ethics of care.

Chapter Overview

Adolescence begins around age ten and lasts until about age twenty-two. The idea of adolescence is a new one to modern industrial society; it has been described as a time of storm and stress, but in fact, most individuals adapt well to the changes. One of the more visible signs of puberty is the growth spurt. Boys typically start this spurt about two years later than girls. In addition to the growth spurt, a larger pattern of changes occur that leads to full physical and sexual maturity or puberty. Primary sexual maturation among boys includes rapid growth of the penis and scrotum and the production of fertile sperm. Menarche is a complex biological process that signals the beginning of sexual maturity for girls. Maturation of secondary sex characteristics includes enlargement and development of the breasts, growth of body hair, deepening of the voice, and increased production of sex-related hormones. During puberty, boys experience significantly greater increases in muscle tissue than girls do. Girls experience a somewhat greater increase in body fat than boys do. Most adolescents are preoccupied with their physical appearance. Early maturation in boys seems to be positive in the short run, but somewhat negative in the long run. Late maturation appears to have the reverse effects. Early maturing girls may feel awkward and have less peer support, but they tend to benefit in the long run. Late maturation appears to have the reverse effects.

There is considerable continuity between childhood and adolescent patterns of illness and health care. Both are influenced by individual and family attitudes and resources. The leading causes of death typically are related to risky lifestyles and adolescents' belief that they are invulnerable. Sexually transmitted diseases, alcohol, tobacco, and drug abuse are all significant health problems for adolescents. Many adolescents receive inadequate nutrition, which can affect their ability to concentrate. Some adolescents experience anorexia nervosa and bulimia.

During adolescence, teenagers develop formal operational thought, or the ability to reason about ideas regardless of their content. Formal operational thinking is characterized by an ability to consider possibilities, to reason in scientific and systematic ways, to combine ideas in logical ways, and to solve problems using hypothesis testing. Adolescents use these abilities inconsistently, however. Information-processing skills continue to improve during adolescence. Adolescents accumulate greater expertise in specific domains of knowledge or skill. One important development is the ability to think critically. This refers to the ability to reflect or think about complex issues to make a decision or take action. Educational programs that foster critical thinking tend to share a number of characteristics, such as teaching critical thinking directly and explicitly.

The social cognition of adolescents is characterized by a form of self-centeredness called adolescent egocentrism. Adolescents may feel as if they are performing for an "imaginary audience." In addition, there is a belief in a personal fable, which is the idea that an adolescent's own life is unique and special. Adolescents develop two forms of morality at the same time, one oriented toward justice and one oriented toward caring. Kohlberg's theory of moral thought consists of six stages in the development of moral judgments oriented toward justice. A number of issues have not been resolved about Kohlberg's theory, including the role of form versus content of moral beliefs, the difference between conventions and morality, and the possibility of gender differences in morality. Gilligan proposes a theory of moral development oriented toward personal caring; on average, it may be slightly more characteristic of females than males, though many exceptions exist.

Chapter Outline

I. The concept of adolescence

Adolescence is the stage of development that leads from childhood to adulthood. It ranges from about age ten to about age twenty-two. Every society uses ceremonies and rituals to signify the transition to adulthood.

A. Adolescence: From idea to social fact

1. The concept of adolescence as a stage of life developed largely as a response to social changes that accompanied U.S. industrial development in the nineteenth century.

2. Some researchers have proposed that adolescence was defined as a separate stage to prolong the years of childhood.

3. Compulsory education, child labor laws, and special legal procedures for juveniles all played a role in making adolescence a social reality.

B. Theoretical views of adolescence

1. One idea holds that adolescence is a time of "storm and stress" when children experience crisis and conflict.

2. Systematic observation and research suggest that as they pass through adolescence, most individuals adapt quite well to the changes in themselves and to the changing demands and expectations of parents and society.

3. How negative or positive adolescent changes are depends on the degree of fit between adolescents' developing needs and the opportunities afforded them by their social environments, particularly school and home. The adolescent's subjective construction of his or her environment is also an important variable.

II. Physical development

III. Growth in height and weight

A. Rapid change in height and weight is due to a dramatic **growth spurt** preceded and followed by years of comparatively little increase.

1. The reason for males' greater average height is that boys start their growth spurt two years later than girls do and thus undergo two additional years of childhood growing.

2. Weight is more easily influenced by diet, exercise, and lifestyle than height is, and therefore weight changes are less predictable.

B. Growth patterns and height during childhood are better predictors of adult height than growth patterns and height during adolescence are.

IV. Puberty

Rapid increases in height and weight are only one part of the pattern of changes, called **puberty**, that lead to full physical and sexual maturity. **Primary sex characteristics** make reproduction possible. A number of changes in **secondary sex characteristics** also occur.

A. Primary sexual maturation

1. The most significant sign of sexual maturation in boys is rapid growth of the penis and scrotum.

a. Enough live sperm are produced during adolescence to allow reproduction.

b. Boys' first ejaculation of semen occurs around age twelve.

      c.   Nocturnal emissions, which frequently accompany erotic dreams, usually are experienced one or two years before puberty.

  2. For girls, **menarche**, the appearance of the first menstrual period, signals sexual maturity. Menarche is preceded by other physical changes, including enlargement of the breasts.

B. Maturation of secondary sexual characteristics

  1. Breasts

     a. Girls first develop breast "buds" at the beginning of puberty.

     b. Breast development is a potential source of concern for girls.

     c. Boys also have a small amount of breast development.

  2. Hair

     a. Both boys and girls acquire more body hair.

     b. **Pubic hair** darkens and becomes coarser, and underarm, or **axillary, hair** also becomes dark and coarse.

  3. Voice

     a. In both sexes, the voice deepens near the end of puberty and becomes richer in overtones, making it more adultlike.

     b. Fluctuations in voice qualities can be a cause of embarrassment.

C. Hormonal changes and their physical consequences

  1. Hormones are chemicals produced by the endocrine glands. They are secreted into the bloodstream and carried to various organs.

  2. **Testosterone** (male sex hormone), a type of androgen, and **estrogen** (female sex hormone) are two important sex hormones.

  3. Hormones are also responsible for the typical differences in overall body build between the sexes.

  4. Testosterone stimulates muscle and bone growth in both sexes.

  5. Sex differences in muscle growth may also result from gender-specific life experiences.

  6. Estrogen stimulates the increased deposits of subcutaneous fat.

  7. Boys tend to keep most of their fat deposits in adolescence, but girls develop significant new subcutaneous fat deposits.

V. Psychological effects of physical growth in adolescence

The timing of puberty can make a lasting difference in the psychological development of an adolescent.

A. Although early-maturing boys are perceived as more mature, self-confident, and competent than others, they often are more somber, less creative, and less spontaneous due to their need to live up to expectations of them.

B. Late-maturing boys still resemble children physically, sometimes as late as age sixteen, and are judged impulsive, immature, lacking in self-confidence, and socially inferior. Their physical immaturity may protect them from increasing pressures and allow them freedom to develop their own unique identities.

C. Early-maturing girls often feel less attractive and more concerned about their physical appearance, are more awkward in social situations, experience less peer support, and have poorer self-concept.

   1. Because early-maturing girls may be more shapely and sexually mature, they may encounter dating and sexual difficulties that they are not psychologically ready to handle.

   2. After successfully coping with these challenges, early-maturing girls are likely to experience positive effects of maturing early, such as increased status and popularity.

D. Late-maturing girls often experience social advantages, being viewed as attractive and good leaders.

E. On-time-maturing boys tend to feel less attractive than do early-maturing boys but more attractive than late-maturing boys. On-time-maturing girls have more positive body images and greater feelings of social attractiveness.

VI. Health in adolescence

Adolescents experience greater health risks than either younger children or adults do.

A. Continuity with health in childhood

   1. The health and health-care patterns of most individuals show considerable consistency and continuity from early childhood through adolescence.

   2. Factors such as social class and the quality and accessibility of services play a major role in adolescent patterns of use of health and mental health services and their own health-related behaviors.

   3. Poverty and lack of accessible and developmentally responsive health care may be the most important factor in determining whether adolescents receive adequate care.

   4. Adolescents' understanding of the relationship between behavior and health may be inadequate.

   5. Programs to encourage self-care have had significant success, especially when they are based in junior and senior high schools and offer comprehensive health care and family planning to teenagers.

B. Causes of death among adolescents

1. The death rate during adolescence is one of the highest for all age groups. Risky environments, risk-taking behavior, and adolescents' belief in invulnerability undoubtedly contribute to this fact.

2. Males are significantly more at risk than females.

3. Leading causes of deaths are motor vehicle accidents, homicides and other intentional violence, and suicide.

C. Adolescent health problems

1. Sexually transmitted diseases are a major problem for adolescents. Risk factors include the increased acceptability of early sexual activity and inadequate use of contraceptives.

2. AIDS (acquired immune deficiency syndrome) is the best-known and most feared sexually transmitted disease.

    a. AIDS is spreading among teenagers.

    b. AIDS destroys the body's ability to maintain its normal immunity to diseases. It is transmitted through introduction of the HIV virus through the body fluids of an infected person.

    c. Formal instruction about AIDS is now given to a growing number of teenagers. The use of condoms has not increased as rapidly as teenagers' knowledge.

    d. Some sexual practices and behaviors are safer than others.

3. Drug abuse and alcohol abuse are typical of adolescence and represent a rite of passage. On the other hand, they are associated with leading causes of death and injury among adolescents.

    a. Prolonged or chronic drug abuse is destructive to developmental processes.

    b. Problem drug use often is a symptom rather than a cause of personal and social maladjustment.

4. Alcohol abuse can lead to severe health problems; alcohol is readily available and is very popular among adolescents. Tobacco use has been advertised to be a sign of adulthood.

    a. Patterns of drinking and smoking are strongly influenced by lifestyles of family members and peers and the environment.

    b. Prevention efforts are directed at adolescents and include life skills training, increasing knowledge, and improving confidence and social competence.

5. Nutritional problems occur more often in adolescents than among all other age groups.

    a. Inadequate nutrition can interfere with a teenager's ability to concentrate at school and work and to actively engage in activities with peers.

    b. Obesity can affect both a teenager's sense of himself or herself as a physically attractive person and his or her overall identity development.

    c. The dominant cultural standard for feminine beauty is a lean body, leading to **anorexia nervosa** and **bulimia** in many adolescent females who desire to achieve this standard.

- Perspectives: Two serious eating disorders: Anorexia nervosa and bulimia

VII. Cognitive development

Cognitive development allows an adolescent to imagine situations and events that he or she has not experienced concretely and to speculate on what might have been. The ability to plan ahead and set goals further develops. Logical thought and thinking about thoughts are evident in the adolescent.

VIII. The cognitive developmental viewpoint: Formal thought

Adolescents acquire **formal operational thought**, which differs in three ways from concrete operational thought.

A. Possibilities versus realities

The adolescent can consider possibilities rather than only actual realities.

B. Scientific reasoning

Problems can be reasoned through in a systematic way.

C. Logical combination of ideas

    1. Several ideas can be kept in mind and combined or integrated in logical ways.

    2. Formal operational thinkers can qualify their opinions better than preformal operational thinkers.

D. Cognitive development beyond formal thought

    1. Formal or abstract thought may not be the final cognitive achievement.

    2. Adolescents may overrate their formal reasoning, failing to notice the limits of their logic.

    3. Less systematic reasoning serves as well or better for solving daily problems.

    4. For older adolescents, the cognitive challenge consists of converting formal reasoning from a goal in itself to a tool used for broader purposes and tailored to the problems at hand.

E. Implications of the cognitive development viewpoint

    1. A majority of adolescents (and adults) use formal thinking inconsistently or even fail to use it at all.

2.   Adolescents tend to use formal operational thought only partially or intermittently.

IX. Information-processing features of adolescent thought

When cognition is viewed from the information-processing perspective, development consists largely of overcoming the bottlenecks in processing information, especially those caused by the limited capacity of the executive and of short-term memory.

A. Improved capacity to process information

An adolescent can process more information than a child can.

B. Expertise in specific domains of knowledge

1.   By adolescence, many individuals have become comparative experts in specific domains of knowledge or skill.

2.   Much of such expertise may depend not on generalized development of cognitive structures but on the long, slow acquisition of large amounts of specific knowledge, along with a greater capacity to organize that knowledge.

C. Implications of the information-processing viewpoint

Psychologists who have tried to identify developmental trends in information processing have emphasized specific sequences within particular domains of thinking.

X.   Supporting adolescents' cognitive development

A. The nature of critical thinking

1.   **Critical thinking** refers to reflection or thought about complex issues, usually to make decisions or take actions.

2.   Critical thinking consists of several elements.

a .   Basic operations of reasoning

b.   Domain-specific knowledge

c.   Metacognitive knowledge

d.   Values, beliefs, and dispositions

•   A multicultural view: Cross-cultural misunderstandings in the classroom

B . Programs to foster critical thinking

1.   Programs can differ in a number of ways.

2.   There are several general principles that enhance the quality of critical thinking programs.

a .   Teaching thinking is best done directly and explicitly.

b. Programs offer a lot of practice in solving actual problems.

c. Successful programs create an environment explicitly conducive to critical thinking.

3. Critical thinking programs are based on Piagetian theory, information-processing theory, and the human context of cognitive development in adolescence.

XI. The development of social cognition

Most developmental psychologists agree that the new cognitive skills of adolescents have important effects on their **social cognition**, or their knowledge and beliefs about interpersonal and social matters. A special form of self-centeredness, **adolescent egocentrism**, affects teenagers' reactions to others and their beliefs about themselves.

A. Adolescents often become overly impressed with the ability to reason abstractly, making them idealistic and keeping them from appreciating the practical limits of logic.

B. Often teenagers act as though they are performing for an **imaginary audience**, one that is as concerned with their appearance and behavior as they are themselves.

C. Teenagers also reveal concern with an imaginary audience through strategic interactions with their peers—encounters that aim to reveal or to conceal personal information directly. Telephoning often serves as a strategic interaction.

D. As a result of their egocentrism, teenagers often believe in a **personal fable**, or the notion that their own lives embody a special story that is heroic and completely unique. Because of this, adolescents fail to realize how other individuals feel about them and still have only limited empathy.

E. The relative balance between an accurate awareness of others' opinions about oneself and self-conscious preoccupation with others' opinions depends, among other things, on the supportiveness of parent-adolescent relationships.

• Working with Carole Castleton, psychiatric group worker: Cognitive strategies for social problems

XII. Moral development: Beliefs about justice and care

As adolescents gradually overcome egocentrism, they develop their personal **morality,** or sensitivity to and knowledge of what is right and wrong.

A. Kohlberg's six stages of moral judgment

Kohlberg proposed a six-stage process of developing moral judgment. The stages were developed by presenting children with moral dilemmas.

1. Earlier stages (1 through 4) represent more egocentric and concrete thinking than do later stages.

a. Stage 1: children accept the perspectives of authorities.

b. Stage 2: children begin to show some ethical reasoning.

    c.   Stage 3: children are concerned chiefly with the opinions of peers.

    d.   Stage 4: children focus on the opinions of community and society.

2.   When thinking about justice, teenagers' ethical judgments are less opportunistic than children's.

3.   Adolescents base their evaluations of situations either on principles expressed by peers and relatives or on socially sanctioned rules and principles.

4.   A few teenagers develop **postconventional moral judgment**, meaning that ethical reasoning goes beyond the judgments society conventionally makes about right and wrong.

B. Enduring issues about the development of moral judgment

1.   Kohlberg's stages describe only the form of thinking, not its content. Studies suggest that ethical thinking probably is not separate from content.

2.   Kohlberg's theory does not fully distinguish between social conventions and morality. **Social conventions** are the arbitrary customs and agreements about behavior that members of society use; morality refers to matters of justice and of right and wrong.

3.   Kohlberg's theory may be gender biased.

C. Gilligan's ethics of care

1.   According to Gilligan, boys and girls tend to view moral problems differently.

2.   Boys learn to think more often in terms of general ethical principles that they can apply to specific moral situations. The principles tend to emphasize independence, autonomy, and rights of others.

3.   Girls tend to adopt an ethics of care—a view that integrates principles with the contexts in which judgments must be made. This view grows out of a general concern for the needs of others more than for their own independence.

4.   Gilligan argues that Kohlberg's theory underrates the moral development of females.

5.   When faced with hypothetical dilemmas, girls show as much capacity as boys to reason in terms of abstract ethical principles. But when faced with real-life dilemmas, girls make different choices.

D. The ethics of care during adolescence

1.   Adolescents develop somewhat conventional ethical attitudes about caring for others.

2.   Egocentrism remains in that teenagers often fail to distinguish between actions that please others and actions that are right in a deeper, ethical sense.

3.   A few individuals move beyond the conventional pleasing of others toward integrated care, when they realize that pleasing everyone is not always possible but balancing one's own needs and the needs of others is important.

Key Concepts

Directions: Identify each of the following key concepts discussed in this chapter.

1. The stage of development that leads from childhood to adulthood and comprises ages ten to twenty-two is termed _____. This period of life was often described as a time of "_____ and _____."

2. Teenagers experience rapid changes in height and weight, termed _____, which are preceded and followed by periods of relatively little increase.

3. Boys start their growth spurt _____ than girls.

4. The pattern of changes that leads to full physical and sexual maturity is called _____.

5. The _____ make sexual reproduction possible. Enlargement of the breasts, growth of body hair, and deepening of the voice are all examples of _____.

6. A sticky fluid produced by the prostate gland that carries sperm is called _____. "Wet dreams" are also known as _____.

7. In females, sexual maturation is marked by _____, the onset of menstruation.

8. Both sexes acquire more body hair during puberty. _____ becomes darker and coarser, as does _____, or underarm hair. Other _____, such as the development of breasts, occur in both sexes. Males, however, have less breast development than females.

9. The onset of puberty brings an increase in the levels of all sex _____ in the blood. The male sex hormone is also known as _____, while _____ is a female sex hormone.

10. Early-maturing boys experience positive effects _____. Early-maturing girls experience positive effects _____.

11. Adolescents experience _____ health risks than either younger children or adults do.

12. Syphilis, gonorrhea, genital warts, genital herpes, chlamydia, and AIDS are all examples of _____.

13. Some sexual practices and behaviors are _____ than others in that they significantly reduce the risk of contracting AIDS.

14. Two eating disorders that seem to occur more in females than males are _____ and _____. The prevalence of these disorders may be partially due to the prevailing cultural standards for female beauty.

15. Adolescents achieve the stage of _____ in their cognitive development. This allows adolescents to consider _____ versus realities, do _____ reasoning, and to _____ combine ideas.

16. According to information-processing theory, development is seen as overcoming _____ in processing information.

17. When a person reflects or thinks about complex issues to make decisions or take action, he or she is engaging in _____.

18. Knowledge and beliefs about interpersonal and social matters are known as _____. A new form of self-centeredness, _____, affects adolescents' reactions to others and beliefs about themselves.

19. Often adolescents act as if they are performing for a(n) _____. Sometimes they believe in a(n) _____, the idea that their lives are both heroic and unique.

20. As adolescents gradually overcome their egocentrism, they begin to develop a personal _____, or a sensitivity to the difference between right and wrong.

21. Kohlberg used hypothetical stories that contained _____ to study moral development. According to Kohlberg, the stage of _____ means that ethical reasoning goes beyond the judgments society conventionally makes about right and wrong.

22. Arbitrary customs and agreements about behavior that members of the society use are called _____.

23. Gilligan argues that morality in girls is guided by the ethics of _____. The stage of the ethics of care where the person realizes that pleasing everyone is not always possible, but that it is important to balance everyone's needs is called _____.

Multiple-Choice Self-Test

Factual / Conceptual Questions

1. Physical development in height and weight during adolescence can best be characterized as
   a. irregular and uneven.
   b. slow and steady.
   c. dramatically accelerating and increasing.
   d. trivial.

2. As a result of the adolescent growth spurt, boys grow about _____ inches.
   a. three or four
   b. six or seven
   c. nine or ten
   d. twelve or thirteen

3. Physical features that make reproduction possible are termed
   a. gonads.
   b. primary sex characteristics.
   c. secondary sex characteristics.
   d. secular trends.

4. The first sign of puberty in males is
   a. breast enlargement.
   b. appearance of pubic hair.
   c. enlargement of testes and penis.
   d. a growth spurt.

5. Which groups seem to have the most disadvantages during the adolescent period?
   a. Early-maturing males and females
   b. Early-maturing males and late-maturing females
   c. Late-maturing males and early-maturing females
   d. Late-maturing males and females

6. Which of the following is a characteristic of adolescent thinking?
   a. It functions primarily in the realm of reality rather than possibility.
   b. It is incapable of abstract problem solving.
   c. It increasingly uses imagination.
   d. It tends to use postconventional moral reasoning.

7. The formal operational skill required to solve tasks like the bending rods problem is
   a. reversibility.
   b. logical combination of ideas.
   c. symbolic representation.
   d. the ability to distinguish reality from possibility.

8. A formal operational thinker does all of the following *except*
   a. hold several ideas in her mind at once.
   b. make careful and systematic observations.
   c. go beyond concrete representations of ideas.
   d. easily solve real-life problems.

9. Egocentrism in adolescence
   a. results from the confusion of one's thoughts with the thoughts of others.
   b. is identical to egocentrism in childhood.
   c. is a concrete operational skill.
   d. occurs in individuals who had imaginary playmates as children.

10. Most adolescents function at the _____ level of moral and ethical development.
    a. postconventional
    b. preconventional
    c. conventional
    d. egocentric

Application Questions

1. Troy has larger bones and muscles than his sixteen-year-old twin sister, Helen. The most likely cause of this is Troy
   a. exercises more than his sister.
   b. is maturing faster than his sister.
   c. has more testosterone than his sister.
   d. eats more than his sister.

2. Barry has syphilis. If left untreated, it could result in
   a. acute liver infection.
   b. abdominal discomfort.
   c. central nervous system damage.
   d. increased risk of prostate cancer.

3. Ron has contracted the AIDS virus. Which of the following is *not* a likely means by which he got the virus?
   a. Blood transfusion
   b. Food sharing
   c. Unprotected heterosexual sex
   d. Dirty needle from a drug addict

4. Jeremy is a typical adolescent. By the time he's a high school senior he is most likely to have tried
   a. alcohol.
   b. cigarettes.
   c. cocaine.
   d. marijuana.

5. Rose looks like a "walking skeleton" even though she thinks she weighs too much. Most of the time she refuses to eat at all, but once in a while she eats massive quantities of food and then induces vomiting to get rid of it. Rose seems to have
   a. anorexia nervosa.
   b. bulimia.
   c. anemia.
   d. both anorexia nervosa and bulimia.

6. Of the following, which kind of problem is the formal operational individual *least* capable of solving?
   a. How much weight a suspension bridge can potentially hold
   b. Who would make the best president of the country
   c. How much income tax to pay
   d. What the best driving route from Boston to Chicago is

7. Pierre is an expert in mechanical engineering. He probably also
   a. is very good at chemistry.
   b. uses heuristics.
   c. has an IQ over 140.
   d. functions at the concrete operational level.

8. Which of the following tasks requires the *least* critical thinking skills?
   a. Balancing the checkbook
   b. Deciding on a menu for a dinner party with sixteen guests
   c. Fixing a lawn mower that won't start
   d. Settling a dispute between two friends

9. Gayle is considered a critical thinker; this means that she does all of the following *except*
   a. use basic reasoning skills.
   b. try to be objective.
   c. tend to focus her perspective.
   d. use metacognitive skills.

10. Bess believes that she is headed for fame and fortune. Her diary reveals her thoughts about what will happen once Nashville discovers her voice. Bess's behavior reflects the adolescent characteristic of
    a. imaginary audience.
    b. personal fable.
    c. strategic interaction.
    d. self-deception.

Answer Key

Key Concepts

1. adolescence, storm, stress
2. growth spurts
3. two years later
4. puberty
5. primary sex characteristics, secondary sex characteristics
6. semen, nocturnal emissions
7. menarche
8. Pubic hair, axillary hair, secondary sex characteristics
9. hormones, testosterone, estrogen
10. initially, later
11. greater
12. sexually transmitted diseases
13. safer
14. anorexia nervosa, bulimia
15. formal operational thought, possibilities, scientific, logically
16. bottlenecks
17. critical thinking
18. social cognition, adolescent egocentrism
19. imaginary audience, personal fable
20. morality
21. moral dilemmas, postconventional moral judgment
22. social conventions
23. care, integrated care

Multiple-Choice Self-Test: Factual / Conceptual Questions

1. Choice (a) is correct. Because of variations in growth spurts, changes in height and weight during adolescence are irregular and uneven. Choices (b) and (d), slow and steady and trivial, respectively, do not describe changes in the growth spurt. Although growth accelerates during part of adolescence, choice (c), it slows as the growth spurt ends.

2. Choice (c) is correct. On the average, boys add nine to ten inches to their height during the adolescent growth spurt. The drama of the spurt comes from the fact that height almost levels off prior to this and that increases of as much as four inches in one year occur at the peak.

3. Choice (b) is correct. By definition, primary sex characteristics make sexual reproduction possible. The gonads, choice (a), are one of the primary sex characteristics. Choice (c), secondary sex characteristics, refers to changes that are not directly related to reproduction but are associated with puberty. Choice (d), secular trends, refers to the trends of increases in size and earlier onset of puberty in recent generations.

4. Choice (c) is correct. Growth in the testes and penis is the earliest sign, followed by the appearance of pubic hair, choice (b), and then the growth spurt, choice (d). Most males do not show significant breast enlargement, choice (a).

5. Choice (c) is correct. Late-maturing males tend to be regarded as socially inferior and immature, and they tend to lack self-confidence. Early-maturing females appear to be awkward in social situations and more stressed. Early-maturing males, choices (a) and (b), and late-maturing females, choice (d), are often viewed quite positively by their peers and teachers.

6. Choice (c) is correct. Adolescents are capable of hypothetical reasoning, which, in turn, leads to speculation and imaginative thinking. Adolescents are capable of functioning in the realm of possibility, so choice (a) is incorrect, as well as abstract problem solving, so choice (b) is also incorrect. But they still tend to use conventional moral reasoning, so choice (d) is incorrect.

7. Choice (b) is the best answer, since the use of logical combinations of ideas involves the ability to hold several ideas in the mind at the same time, which would greatly aid solving this task of manipulating variables. Choice (a), reversibility, is a concrete, not formal, skill (even though it is still present in formal operational individuals); choice (c), symbolic representation, is a preoperational skill; and choice (d), ability to distinguish reality from possibility, is a formal operational skill but not really directly relevant to the bending rods task.

8. Choice (d) is correct. Formal operational thinkers can logically combine ideas, choice (a); use scientific reasoning, choice (b); and deal with the realm of possibility, choice (c). However, it takes skills beyond formal operations to solve real-life problems, which require many of the same problem-solving skills, but they need to be applied to situations that may not have solutions.

9. Choice (a) is correct. The adolescent realizes that others can have thoughts about him or her. Thus, there is confusion between what the adolescent thinks is occurring and what is actually occurring. Egocentrism in childhood, choice (b), involves concrete problems; adolescent egocentrism concerns abstract problems. Adolescent egocentrism represents a formal skill, not a concrete operational skill, choice (c), because of the abstract abilities. It is unrelated to imaginary playmates, choice (d).

10. Choice (c) is correct. Adolescents' reasoning is consistent with Kohlberg's third and fourth stages. Adolescents tend to follow personal and social conventions. Only a few adolescents tend to use postconventional reasoning, choice (a). Most have advanced beyond preconventional levels, choice (b). Choice (d) is not a level of moral or ethical development.

Multiple-Choice Self-Test: Application Questions

1. Choice (c) is correct. The action of testosterone is the primary reason for the greater bone and muscle development. However, choices (a) and (d), more exercise and more eating, respectively, may also be true, though they don't contribute as much as testosterone. It is unlikely that choice (b), maturing faster, is occurring.

2. Choice (c) is correct. If left unchecked, the syphilis virus ultimately invades the brain, causing severe damage. Hepatitis has been associated with choice (a), acute liver infection. Syphilis is not known for causing abdominal discomfort, so choice (b) is inaccurate. Chlamydia has been associated with choice (d), increased risk of prostate cancer.

3. Choice (b) is correct. Since the AIDS virus cannot survive in air or water, getting AIDS from sharing food, even with an individual who has AIDS, has never occurred. Choices (a), (c), and (d), blood transfusion, unprotected heterosexual sex, and dirty needle, respectively, are all common ways in which the virus can be transmitted.

4. Choice (a) is correct. Eighty-eight percent of all seniors have tried alcohol at least once; 63 percent have smoked cigarettes, choice (b); 37 percent have tried marijuana, choice (d); and 8 percent have used cocaine, choice (c).

5. Choice (d) is correct. Many individuals with anorexia nervosa also have bulimia (or at least bulimic symptoms). Although the primary diagnosis would be anorexia, the other is clearly present, and the behaviors described in the question are typical of both. Rose could also have anemia, choice (c), as a byproduct of the anorexia, but the symptoms of anemia are not described in the question.

6. Choice (b) is correct. The choice of a president represents a real-life problem in which there are many unknown variables and a considerable amount of uncertainty. Although a formal operational person can make a decision on such an issue, there is no real objective solution. Choice (a) is a straightforward physics/engineering question that has a definite answer and can be solved easily with formal operational skills. Choices (c) and (d) are a bit more like real-life problems, but have somewhat objective solutions, as compared to choice (b).

7. Choice (b) is correct. Experts often use general strategies to solve certain classes of problems (heuristics); this way they do not need to get bogged down in the basics, like most novices. Experts are not necessarily smarter, choice (c); nor good in other fields, choice (a); but most experts, especially mechanical engineers, would function beyond the concrete level, choice (d).

8. Choice (a) is correct. Balancing a checkbook requires some mathematical and organization knowledge, but beyond that it does not require reflective thinking (unless you are really into creative financing). On the other hand, choice (b), deciding on a menu for a dinner party, requires you to juggle a number of variables and make important decisions in which cost versus the impression you want to make come into play. Choice (c), fixing a lawn mower, requires some problem solving, some elimination of certain variables. Choice (d), settling a dispute between two friends, also requires skills in dealing with people and being objective and reflective.

9. Choice (c) is correct. A critical thinker does need skills in basic reasoning, choice (a); needs to be aware of his or her own abilities, choice (d); and needs to be objective so as not to interject bias, choice (b). A critical thinker, however, needs to take a broad perspective (at least initially) to be sure he or she is considering all the options and has not overlooked anything.

10. Choice (b) is correct. Adolescents often see themselves as being very successful because of their uniqueness. As such, they construct a personal fable that they may attempt to live out. Bess's would be a common scenario. This personal fable is not self-deception, choice (d), because it is something that the adolescent strives for, and it motivates her. Fable making reflects a part of adolescent egocentrism, which includes the concepts in choice (a), imaginary audience, and choice (c), strategic interaction.

CHAPTER 11

Adolescence: Psychosocial Development

Learning Objectives

1. Discuss the process of identity development from the standpoint of individuation. Describe the four major phases of this process.

2. Describe how Erikson viewed the process of identity development in adolescence.

3. Identify and describe Marcia's four identity statuses. Compare his approach with Erikson's.

4. Discuss the nature of adolescents' social relationships, especially with their parents.

5. Identify and describe the various parenting styles and indicate their effect on adolescent development.

6. Discuss the impact of divorce, remarriage, and stepfamilies on the adolescent.

7. Describe the nature of adolescent friendships. Discuss the developmental changes in friendships and describe sex differences in peer relations.

8. Describe the development of the peer group during the adolescent period. Indicate the relevant variables that determine peer group participation.

9. Discuss the role schools and the school environment play in adolescent development. Describe the impact of dropping out on adolescent development.

10. Discuss the nature of sexuality during adolescence, including dating, sexual behavior, and sexual preferences.

11. Describe the impact of dating on adolescent sexuality, including date rape and nonheterosexual orientation.

12. Describe the problem of teenage pregnancy and the likely psychosocial outcomes.

13. Describe the characteristics of teenage depression and suicide.

14. Describe the characteristics of juvenile delinquency and gang involvement during adolescence.

Chapter Overview

The process of individuation, or becoming a separate and independent person, appears to follow a fairly predictable pattern: differentiation, practice and experimentation, rapprochement, and consolidation of self. A key task of adolescence is successful resolution of the psychosocial crisis of identity versus role confusion. Identity formation involves selectively keeping and integrating certain aspects of one's earlier childhood identity and discarding others. Successful resolution of identity conflicts depends in part on having adequate opportunities to experiment with different identities and roles. Erikson refers to a psychological moratorium, in which the individual is free to suspend or delay taking on adult commitments and to explore new social roles. Marcia has extended Erikson's work by suggesting four categories of identity status: identity-achieved, identity-diffused, moratorium, and foreclosure.

A significant consequence of developing an identity is relationships with others. Even though the relationship may seem slightly unstable, parents and their teenage children get along fairly well together. Teenagers appear to feel most positive about authoritative parenting styles and most negative about parents who are authoritarian. Parents continue to have influence over their children in basic attitudes and values that guide long-term life choices. Parenting styles can influence the type of parent-teenager relationship. There are also social-class effects on the development of the adolescent. An increasing number of adolescents have encountered the stresses of growing up in a family that has experienced divorce, remarriage, or single parenthood. Divorce can be especially difficult for teenagers as they develop their own identity and seek independence.

Friendships are very important to adolescents; friends provide acceptance and support. Friendships that are increasingly based on mutual respect, trust, intimacy, and prosocial behavior are likely to help adolescents cope with stress in the family and in school. Peer groups play a significant part in the lives of adolescents and can take the form of a clique or crowd. Each contributes positive and potentially negative effects to the individual. School plays a central role in the adolescents' development through both its formal and its informal curriculum. Employment can provide the adolescent several advantages if the hours worked are kept under about ten per week. Students who work more than ten hours per week tend to experience more problems.

Adolescents' sexual needs are closely tied to their need to establish a secure identity and to achieve both intimacy and independence. Masturbation and sexual fantasies play a significant role in adolescents' sexual development. Girls and boys differ in their reasons for their first experience of sexual intercourse and in their attitudes toward sexual activities. Dating has tended to begin earlier, with most adolescent girls beginning to date at twelve and boys at thirteen. Date rape, when a girl is forced to have sex with the person she is dating, may occur. The prejudice and discrimination regarding nonheterosexual orientations still exist and make identity development more difficult for nonheterosexual adolescents. It remains unclear what variables lead to the development of nonheterosexual orientation. Most cases of teenage pregnancy are caused by inadequate or no contraception. Teenage mothers are less likely to finish high school, find a stable paying job, enter secure marriages, or achieve equal job status or income in their lifetimes. They are also more likely than older women to experience complications during pregnancy and labor. Their children are also more at risk.

About 7 percent of adolescents suffer from depression so severe that treatment is required. Suicide is the third leading cause of death among children ages fifteen to nineteen. The development of juvenile delinquency tends to follow a sequence of experiences. Gangs provide adolescents opportunities for support and a sense of identity. Programs designed for children and adolescents who are at risk for delinquency can reduce the high school dropout rate, illiteracy, and the number of arrests for delinquency.

Chapter Outline

I. Theories of identity development

    A. Josselson: Individuation and identity development

        1. **Individuation** is the process by which an adolescent develops a unique personal identity or sense of self, distinct and separate from all others. It consists of four distinct, overlapping stages.

            a. During differentiation, the early adolescent recognizes being psychologically different from his or her parents.

            b. In practice and experimentation, the adolescent believes she or he knows it all and can do no wrong.

            c. Rapprochement, which occurs during middle adolescence, is the time when the teenager has achieved a fair degree of separateness from parents and partially but conditionally reaccepts parental authority.

            d. During consolidation of self, the adolescent develops a sense of personal identity.

    B. Erikson: The crisis of identity versus role confusion

        1. Erikson believed the crisis of **identity versus role confusion** occurs during adolescence.

        2. During this time, teenagers selectively accept or reject the many different aspects of self that were acquired during childhood and form a more coherent sense of identity.

        3. Changes in an adolescent's increasing capacity for abstract thought and self-understanding play a central role in identity development.

        4. According to Erikson, a number of identity outcomes are possible.

            a. **Psychosocial moratorium** is a period during which the individual is free to suspend or delay taking on adult commitments and to explore new social roles.

            b. **Identity diffusion**, or a failure to achieve a relatively coherent, integrated, and stable identity, takes a number of forms, such as avoidance of closeness with others, diffusion of time perspective, diffusion of industry, and **negative identity**.

        5. Successful resolution of the crisis of identity versus role confusion prepares the adolescent for the crisis of intimacy versus isolation.

        6. Marcia classified students into four categories of **identity status** based on whether they had gone through an identity crisis and the degree to which they were now committed to an occupational choice and to a set of religious and political values and beliefs.

            a. Identity-achieved individuals successfully resolve crises concerning values and life choices and are able to commit to an occupation and to a religious and political ideology.

    b. Identity-diffusal individuals, whether or not they have experienced a crisis, show little concern or commitment regarding occupational choice and religious and political beliefs.

    c. Moratorium individuals are presently in crisis, actively making commitments and preoccupied with achieving successful compromises among their parents' wishes, societal demands, and their own capabilities.

    d. Foreclosure individuals prematurely commit to important aspects of identity without experiencing significant conflict or crisis.

    e. Both genders are equally represented among the four identity statuses and seem to develop in similar ways.

II. Social relationships during adolescence

  A. Relationships with parents

    1. Most parent-teenager relationships are likely to be slightly unstable.

    2. Separation from parents consists of four important accomplishments.

      a. Functional independence is the ability to manage one's own personal and practical affairs with minimal help from one's parents.

      b. Attitudinal independence is a view of oneself as unique and separate from one's parents.

      c. Emotional independence is freedom from being overly dependent on parents for approval, intimacy, and emotional support.

      d. Conflictual independence is freedom from conflict and other negative emotional states.

    3. Leaving home, at least in a psychological sense, is part of becoming self-reliant and achieving an identity. Parents and teenagers often have a different understanding of and reaction to leaving home, which may lead to conflicts.

    4. The overall quality of adolescent-parent relationships often improves for adolescents who have successfully left home and are living on their own.

    5. The majority of adolescents and parents continue to get along rather well together. Parents and adolescents most often disagree about matters concerning social life and behavior.

    6. Parents have more influence than peers in basic attitudes and values that guide long-term life choices. During adolescence, a fine line exists between sensitive, respectful parental involvement and intrusive overinvolvement that does not adequately respect adolescents' need for separateness and independence.

    7. Parent-child relationships that are hostile and uncooperative frequently result in conflict and failure. Parents and adolescents get along best when decision making is consistent and collaborative, decisions are viewed as fair rather than arbitrary, and the developmental needs and sensitivities of all family members are respected.

8. Adolescents' relationships with their parents may also influence their relationships with peers.

9. A major series of studies of families revealed some important socioeconomic differences affecting adolescents' development.

    a. Differences between the values, childrearing practices, and expectations of middle-class parents and those of working- and lower-class parents closely paralleled differences in the nature of their day-to-day work experiences with respect to degree of autonomy versus control.

    b. Adolescents in middle-class families were encouraged to be independent and to control their own behavior.

    c. Working-class parents were more authoritarian than middle-class parents in their childrearing patterns and were less likely to support their children's attempts to be independent and to participate in decision making.

B. Divorce, remarriage, and single parenthood

    1. The impact of separation and divorce on the adolescent depends on a number of factors.

    2. Adolescents tend to be sensitive about being "normal" and insecure about their identities, making divorce especially hard for them.

    3. Divorce often makes it difficult for adolescents to achieve realistic hopes about their own love relationships.

    4. The quality of postdivorce relationships is a major factor in the success of negotiating the tasks of later adolescence and young adulthood.

    5. Living with a stepparent can be particularly hard for an adolescent because of the lack of commonly accepted roles and the teenager's need to be independent of adult control and authority.

C. Friendship

    1. Friends offer easier and more immediate acceptance than most adults do.

    2. They offer reassurance, understanding and advice, and emotional and social support in stressful situations.

    3. Friends promote independence by providing knowledge of a world beyond the family.

    4. Qualities of adolescent friendships

        a. There is a trend toward greater mutuality through increased loyalty and intimacy.

        b. There is a recognition of complementary relationships, in which two people with different strengths and abilities cooperate for mutual benefit.

    c.   Teenagers gain intimacy in friendship through self-revelation, confidence, and exclusivity.

5.   Gender differences

    a.   Friendships formed by boys have lower levels of intimacy than those of girls.

    b.   Girls tend to develop more intimacy with members of the opposite sex than boys do.

    c.   Gender differences may be products of sex-role stereotyping or due to the fact that girls tend to have fewer but closer friends than boys, who have many, less intimate acquaintances. Also, adolescent males may equate intimacy exclusively with heterosexual friendships.

6.   Interethnic friendships

    a.   Friendships between teenagers from different ethnic groups tend to be the exception.

    b.   The social contexts in which interactions occur seem to make an important difference in the development of friendships across ethnic groups.

D. Peer groups

1.   Peer groups play an even greater role in the lives of adolescents than they do in younger children.

2.   Adolescent peer groups frequently include individuals from a relatively wide age range and are much less likely to be all one gender.

3.   Peer groups provide a support base outside of the family from which the teenager can more freely try on different identity roles.

4.   Adolescent peer groups generally are of two types.

    a.   A **clique** is a small, closely knit group of two or more members who are intimately involved in shared purposes and activities and exclude those who are not involved.

    b.   A **crowd** is a larger, less cohesive group of between fifteen to thirty adolescents and is composed of from two to four cliques.

5.   Advantages of clique membership include security, feelings of importance, and acquisition of socially acceptable behaviors that conform to group norms. However, cliques can suppress individuality, promote snobbishness, intolerance, and other negative values and behaviors, and possibly contribute to adjustment problems.

6.   Advantages of crowd membership are opportunities to interact with those from a broad range of backgrounds and experiences. However, crowds can promote snobbishness and can pose real or imagined threats to parental and teacher authority.

7.   Parents can help adolescents with their friendships and relationships.

- Perspectives: Can parents influence their adolescent's choice of peer groups?

    E. The influence of school and work

        1. School plays a central role in adolescents' development.

        2. Schools serve two primary functions.

            a. The formal curriculum provides basic knowledge and skills.

            b. The informal curriculum provides role models for achievement, motivation to learn, and skill mastery.

        3. The transition to middle school or junior high school may be a period of increased social and emotional stress and be particularly difficult for poor urban youth.

        4. Critics argue that middle or junior high school should be more like elementary school, and that transitions should be more gradual.

        5. School failure and dropping out

            a. About 25 percent of all students drop out of high school.

            b. Students leave school for different reasons.

            c. Students who have recently immigrated sometimes experience disillusionment and cultural vertigo.

        6. Work during adolescence serves three functions.

            a. It facilitates transition from school to work.

            b. It provides structure for involvement in family- and school-related activities.

            c. It provides an arena in which adolescents can have an independent life with peers.

        7. Students who work more than ten hours per week do more poorly academically and report more psychological and physical problems.

        8. Working more hours can interfere with academic achievement, expose adolescents to negative role models, and limit the amount of monitoring and supervision.

        9. Working fewer than ten hours per week generally appears to have no negative effects on adolescents.

- A multicultural view: Adaptive strategies of families of minority youth

III. Sexuality during adolescence

During adolescence, the expression of sexual urges interacts closely with the need for security, freedom from anxiety, and the need for intimacy.

    A. Sexual fantasies and masturbation

1. Sexual fantasies about real or imaginary situations often accompany masturbation.

2. Sexually experienced adolescents tend to masturbate more than those who are less experienced.

3. Boys tend to give up masturbation when involved in an ongoing sexual relationship, whereas girls tend to masturbate more often.

B. Heterosexuality

   1. Sexual experience

     a. Sexual activity among college-age adolescents has significantly increased, particularly among females.

     b. The percent of college-age adolescents who have had sex with only one person and who believe in having sex only with someone they are deeply involved with emotionally has also increased.

     c. Timing of first sexual intercourse is related to several factors.

   2. Sexual attitudes

     a. Boys tend to be more sexually active and to have more sexual encounters than girls.

     b. Girls are more likely to emphasize intimacy and love as necessary parts of sexual activity and less likely to engage in sex merely as a physically pleasurable activity.

     c. Males and females differ in reasons and reactions to first intercourse.

   3. Dating

     a. Currently, many adolescent girls begin dating at age twelve and boys at age thirteen.

     b. Date rape refers to a situation in which a person, usually a female, is forced to have sex with a person she is dating. It typically involves individuals who know each other fairly well.

     c. It is likely that cultural expectations and the tendency to place blame on the victim contribute to this problem.

C. Nonheterosexual orientations

   1. Public acceptance of homosexuality has increased significantly during the past several decades, acknowledging the right of individuals to freely practice their own sexual orientations and lifestyles and to be protected from discrimination.

   2. **Homophobia,** the fear or dislike of homosexuals, remains strong among adolescents.

   3. Homosexual adolescents are likely to experience feelings of attraction for the same sex for several years before publicly acknowledging their sexual orientation.

4. There is no agreement on the specific pattern of factors that leads to the development of homosexuality.

5. A growing number of researchers are exploring the possibility of biological and genetic predispositions to the development of nonheterosexual orientations.

6. Although achieving a secure sexual identity is a challenging task for most adolescents, it is considerably more difficult for many homosexual adolescents, who may be rejected by parents, peers, schools, churches, and other community institutions.

D. Sex and everyday life

Sexuality does not necessarily dominate the lives of adolescents.

IV. Special problems of adolescence

A. Adolescent pregnancy and parenthood

1. Unsound contraceptive practices

a. The great majority of teenage pregnancies are the result of inadequate or no contraception.

b. Birth control pills are not reliable during the first month of use. Only foam and condoms or a diaphragm and contraceptive jelly are really effective for first intercourse.

c. Irregular use of contraception is correlated with economic disadvantage, poor communication with parents, lack of knowledge about parental contraceptive experience, experiences of friends who became parents, low educational achievements and aspirations, high levels of anxiety, low self-esteem, and feelings of fatalism, powerlessness, and alienation.

2. Choosing between abortion and parenthood

a. More than 50 percent of teenage mothers who decide to have their babies become increasingly committed to motherhood during the course of the pregnancy.

b. Reactions to an unplanned pregnancy are influenced by feelings about school, relationship with the baby's father, relationship with parents, perceived family support for keeping the child, number of peers who have become parents, and sense of self-esteem.

c. The experience of abortion is psychologically stressful for teenagers.

d. Socioeconomic status, ethnicity, and culture influence teenagers' feelings and attitudes about abortion.

3. Consequences of teenage parenthood

a. Many teenage mothers see having a baby as a way to gain identity and a way to have a relationship with another person.

b. Teenage mothers are less likely to finish high school, find a stable paying job, enter a secure marriage, and achieve equal job status or income in their lifetime.

c. Teenage mothers are more likely to experience complications during pregnancy.

d. Children of teenage mothers are also more likely to suffer developmentally, displaying poorer cognitive and social functioning in preschool and elementary school and a higher rate of learning and social adjustment problems as adolescents than are children born to older mothers. Also, they are more likely to become teenage parents themselves.

4. Prevention and support programs

a. Prevention programs have taken four approaches: educating teenagers about sexuality and contraception, changing attitudes about early sexual involvement, providing contraceptive and family-planning services, and increasing girls' self-esteem.

b. Most programs have had only moderate success. Prenatal care programs are the most successful of the services provided.

c. Different prevention approaches may be needed for different types of at-risk teenagers.

• Working with Janet Whalen, nurse practitioner: Helping pregnant teenagers

B. Teenage depression and suicide

1. About 20 to 25 percent of adolescents report experiencing a depressed mood during the last six months.

2. About 7 percent of adolescents suffer from a **clinical depression**, meaning their depression is severe enough to be diagnosed as an emotional disorder requiring treatment.

3. Suicide is the third leading cause of death for children ages fifteen to nineteen.

4. Studies have found that many teenagers who attempt suicide have experienced serious family difficulties, and depression often is a factor.

5. Suicide attempts almost always represent cries for help.

6. Suicide prevention includes early detection and intervention in family and personal crises, school-based education about depression and suicide risk factors, training in problem-solving and coping skills, crisis counseling, and emergency hotlines.

C. Juvenile delinquency

1. **Juvenile delinquency** refers to a pattern of destructive or antisocial activities and lawbreaking offenses committed by adolescents.

2. The route to chronic delinquency may follow a predictable developmental sequence of experiences.

a. The first step involves ineffective parenting and problematic family interaction processes.

b. The second step involves conduct-disordered behaviors that lead to academic failure and peer rejection.

c. The third step is increased risk for depression and involvement in a deviant peer group.

3. A number of factors are associated with delinquency, such as a parent-child relationship characterized by hostility, lack of affection, underinvolvement, and lack of parental supervision.

4. Many delinquents belong to gangs, which are highly structured and focused on antisocial activities. Gangs provide acceptance and social support lacking in families or schools.

5. Gangs identify with or claim control over territory in the community and engage in violence.

6. Typically, gangs are formed by individuals from poor and racial or ethnic minority and immigrant backgrounds.

7. Gangs provide alternative economic opportunities and social support.

8. Adolescents who are at risk for delinquency can be helped by programs that provide support and opportunities.

9. Early childhood intervention programs for at-risk preschool children and their families have achieved significant success in reducing delinquency.

V. Looking back/looking forward

Key Concepts

Directions: Identify each of the following key concepts discussed in this chapter.

1. _____ is the process by which an adolescent develops a unique personal identity, or sense of self.

2. During _____, adolescents realize they are different from their parents, and in _____, adolescents feel they know all. During middle adolescence and _____, the teenager achieves enough separation from his or her parents to be able to accept some parental authority. A sense of personal identity is achieved in _____.

3. Erikson believed that the adolescent integrates many childhood identifications during the crisis of _____. At this time of life, according to Erikson, the young adult can experience _____, or a suspension of taking on adult commitments and responsibilities. _____ reflects the adolescent's failure to achieve a stable identity. The choice of a(n) _____ results in the teenager's rejection of roles offered by family and community.

4. Successful resolution of the crisis of identity versus role confusion prepares the adolescent for the crisis of _____.

5. Marcia classified students into four categories of _____, which are based on the degree to which adolescents are committed to occupation, religious beliefs, and political ideology. In _____, life choice crises are successfully resolved, whereas in _____, adolescents have little concern or commitment toward making these choices. In _____, teenagers are still actively making choices, and in _____, they prematurely commit to choices similar to those of their parents.

6. Most parent-teenager relationships are likely to feel slightly _____.

7. Leaving home can give the adolescents four types of independence. _____ is the ability to manage one's own personal and practical affairs with minimal help from one's parents. _____ is a view of oneself as unique and separate from one's parents. _____ is freedom from being overly dependent on parents for approval, intimacy, and emotional support. _____ is freedom from conflict and other negative emotional states.

8. Most of the conflict between parents and teenage children is about the teenager's _____ and _____.

9. Adolescents whose families have a(n) _____ parenting style have better relationships at home.

10. _____ is determined by parents' level of education, cultural values, lifestyle, income, and type of work.

11. Adolescents report that _____ and _____ are important in defining close friendships and how they are initiated, maintained, and ended.

12. Social relationships of adolescents extend beyond the family to include the _____, or agemates who have common interests with the teenager. A small, exclusive, close-knit group of two or more peers is considered a(n) _____, whereas a(n) _____ is a larger, less cohesive group composed of several cliques.

13. The _____ of a school provides students with basic knowledge and skills. Adolescents are exposed to role models for academic achievement and motivation to learn in the school's _____.

14. Students who work more than _____ hours per week experience negative effects.

15. When it comes to sexual attitudes, girls tend to be more _____ than boys. Girls are more likely to emphasize _____ and _____ as necessary parts of sexual activity.

16. _____ occurs when a person, usually a female, is forced to have sex with a person she is dating.

17. A dislike and fear of homosexuals is called _____. Public acknowledging sexual orientation is called _____.

18. The great majority of teenage pregnancies are the result of _____ or _____.

19. Depression that is severe enough to be diagnosed as an emotional disorder that requires treatment is called _____. _____ is the leading cause of death among children ages fifteen to

nineteen. The majority of teenagers who attempt suicide have experienced serious _____ problems.

20. A pattern of destructive or antisocial activities and lawbreaking offenses committed by adolescents is termed _____.

Multiple-Choice Self-Test

Factual / Conceptual Questions

1. In which phase of individuation does the adolescent feel he or she knows it all and can do no wrong?
   a. Consolidation
   b. Differentiation
   c. Practice and experimentation
   d. Rapprochement

2. Erikson viewed the development of identity as
   a. a product of learning experiences during the school years.
   b. the creation of an entirely new self.
   c. the integration of childhood identities.
   d. the loss of egocentric thinking.

3. Which of Marcia's identity statuses involves no crisis and no commitment?
   a. Foreclosure
   b. Identity diffusion
   c. Identity achievement
   d. Moratorium

4. In what area do we find the most foreclosure in adolescence?
   a. Political philosophy
   b. Religious belief
   c. Sex-role preference
   d. Vocational choice

5. Lower-middle- or working-class adolescents tend to have parents who are
   a. authoritative.
   b. authoritarian.
   c. democratic.
   d. permissive.

6. What are the two main dimensions of friendship in adolescence?
   a. Activities and companionship
   b. Independence and flexibility
   c. Mutual understanding and intimacy
   d. Socializing and sex

7. Females tend to _____ intimacy during adolescence and express it in _____ friendships.
   a. increase, opposite-sex
   b. increase, same-sex
   c. increase, opposite- and same-sex
   d. decrease, same-sex

8. The major activity of a clique is _____; a crowd involves _____.
   a. sexual, social activities
   b. small parties, sports
   c. talking, organized social functions
   d. weekend events, weekday events

9. The percentage of teenagers who use contraceptive devices or other birth-control methods the first time they have sex is approximately
   a. 10 percent.
   b. 30 percent.
   c. 50 percent.
   d. 70 percent.

10. As compared to adolescent females, adolescent males are _____ as likely to successfully commit suicide.
    a. half
    b. just
    c. three times
    d. nine times

Application Questions

1. Sean is beginning to reconsider some of the things his parents said about going to college and pursuing a business degree, which he flatly rejected just six months ago. He seems to be in the _____ phase of individuation.
   a. consolidation
   b. differentiation
   c. practice and experimentation
   d. rapprochement

2. Suzy, who ran away at sixteen, is on her way to Las Vegas to be a high-priced prostitute. Erikson would say that she
   a. is identity-achieved.
   b. has a negative identity.
   c. is in moratorium.
   d. is identity-diffused.

3. Cynthia has always wanted to be a physician because both her parents are physicians, and it was expected of her. She's currently preparing for medical school and has surrounded herself with other premed friends. She avoids other areas of study except what she absolutely has to take to graduate. Cynthia's identity is
   a. foreclosed.
   b. identity-achieved.
   c. identity-diffused.
   d. in moratorium.

4. Which category of activity takes up the most of sixteen-year-old Alexei's day?
   a. Productive work
   b. Maintenance
   c. Leisure
   d. Eating

5. Parents tend to exert more influence on their adolescent children than do peers in issues concerning
   a. career goals.
   b. dating.
   c. music.
   d. dress.

6. April's parents tend to watch over her like a hawk because they fear that she will wind up pregnant. Their parenting style is most likely
   a. authoritative.
   b. authoritarian.
   c. neglectful.
   d. permissive.

7. Thirteen-year-olds Blair, David, Mike, and Tyler spend a considerable amount of time together talking about various things and playing video games. Rarely does anyone else join them. These four would most likely be considered a
   a. chum.
   b. clique.
   c. gang.
   d. pack.

8. Who is most likely to drop out of high school in America?
   a. Jay, an Asian American
   b. Brock, an American Indian
   c. Jose, a Hispanic
   d. Jesse, an African American

9. What is the likelihood that Sidney, a high school senior, has never been on a date?
   a. About 10 percent
   b. About 20 percent
   c. About 30 percent
   d. About 40 percent

10. Deirdre is irritable most of the day, doesn't participate in activities with others, seems to feel worthless, and has difficulty sleeping. She is showing symptoms of
    a. anorexia.
    b. bulimia.
    c. clinical depression.
    d. delinquency.

Answer Key

Key Concepts

1. Individuation
2. differentiation, practice and experimentation, rapprochement, consolidation of self
3. identity versus role confusion, psychosocial moratorium, Identity diffusion, negative identity
4. intimacy versus isolation
5. identity status, identity achievement, identity diffusion, moratorium, foreclosure
6. unstable

7. Functional independence, Attitudinal independence, Emotional independence, Conflictual independence
8. social life, behavior
9. authoritative
10. Social class
11. mutual understanding, intimacy
12. peer group, clique, crowd
13. formal curriculum, informal curriculum
14. ten
15. conservative, intimacy, love
16. Date rape
17. homophobia, coming out
18. inadequate contraception, no contraception
19. clinical depression, Suicide, family
20. juvenile delinquency

Multiple-Choice Self-Test: Factual / Conceptual Questions

1. Choice (c) is correct. During the practice and experimentation phase, the adolescent denies any need for caution or advice and actively challenges his or her parents. Choice (a), consolidation, involves the development of a personal identity of a more realistic nature; choice (b), differentiation, involves the realization that the adolescent is different from his or her parents; and choice (d), rapprochement, involves a cooperative and conciliatory view of others.

2. Choice (c) is correct. Erikson viewed identity development as the selection of an identity based on previous experiences, thus integrating all the possibilities into a final identity. Erikson did not limit experience to the school years, choice (a), but rather looked at the entire lifespan. The child does not form a new self, choice (b), but rather takes aspects of the existing self and integrates them. Erikson did not deal with egocentric thinking, choice (d).

3. Choice (b) is correct. Marcia uses two dimensions, crisis and commitment, to form his four identity statuses. The absence of both of these is seen in identity diffusion, while the presence of both is seen in choice (c), identity achievement. Choice (a), foreclosure, has commitment but no crisis and choice (d), moratorium, has crisis but no commitment.

4. Choice (c) is correct. Foreclosure involves acceptance or adoption of some set of values without having a crisis or exploring the area fully. Most individuals simply accept their sex-role preference without question, and therefore that area shows the most foreclosure. Choice (a), political philosophy, tends to show more diffusion, while choices (b) and (d), religious belief and vocational choice, respectively, tend to show both achievement and moratorium.

5. Choice (b) is correct. The authoritarian parental style tends to emphasize conformity to extrinsic expectations and is more punishment oriented. Choices (a), (c), and (d) are the other parental styles typically used and are not the norm for lower-middle- or working-class parents.

6. Choice (c) is correct. Studies have found that mutual understanding and intimacy help foster complementary relationships in adolescence. Activities and companionship, choice (a); independence and flexibility, choice (b); and socializing and sex, choice (d), have varying degrees of importance. But they are not the main dimensions of friendship in adolescence.

7. Choice (c) is correct. Intimacy in friendships increases during adolescence. For females, this is expressed toward both males and females, while males show increased intimacy only toward females. Thus, choices (a), (b), and (d) are incorrect.

8. Choice (c) is correct. Cliques tend to be small, same-sex groups based on shared purposes and activities. Their major activity tends to be talking. Crowds are larger groups, often made up of several cliques. Their main purpose involves social functions. Choices (a), (b), and (d) are not primary functions of cliques and crowds, respectively.

9. Choice (c) is correct. About half of all teenagers fail to use any method of birth control the first time they have sexual intercourse.

10. Choice (c) is correct. Although adolescent females attempt suicide three to nine times more than adolescent males, males are three times as likely to be successful since they tend to choose more violent methods. Thus, choices (a), (b), and (d) are inaccurate.

Multiple-Choice Self-Test: Application Questions

1. Choice (d) is correct. In the rapprochement phase, adolescents reconsider their parents' viewpoint, which they previously rejected in the differentiation phase, choice (b). After rapprochement, Sean should progress to practice and experimentation, choice (c), and then finally to consolidation, choice (a).

2. Choice (b) is correct. Erikson believed that when a person selects an identity that goes counter to what is acceptable in society, he or she forms a negative identity. Suzy seems to be doing this. She does not seem to be in moratorium, choice (c), since there does not seem to be an ongoing crisis, only a decision. Choice (d), identity-diffused, is possible, but she's made a firm commitment to a course of action and is following through with her plans. She has achieved *an* identity, choice (a), but it is a negative one.

3. Choice (a) is correct. Having no crisis but having made a commitment is what Marcia describes as foreclosed identity. It is clear that Cynthia has simply adopted her parents' expectations, and she seems to avoid everything that might alter her choice. Choice (b), identity-achieved, is a person who has had a crisis and made a commitment; choice (c), identity-diffused, has neither had a crisis nor made a commitment; and choice (d), moratorium, indicates crisis with no commitment.

4. Choice (c) is correct. In a recent study of adolescents' daily activities, researchers found that 40 percent of the day was spent in leisure activities; 31 percent in maintenance, choice (b); 29 percent in productive work, choice (a); and 5.6 percent was spent eating, choice (d).

5. Choice (a) is correct. Parents tend to have more influence in issues that have long-range consequences as opposed to issues touching on current social life and behavior. Choices (b), (c), and (d)—dating, music, and dress, respectively—would be considered issues of current social life or behavior over which parents have less influence.

6. Choice (b) is correct. Although the information is limited, it seems that the parents are exerting considerable control and basically don't trust their daughter. This is consistent with an authoritarian style. If they were actively seeking April's input in the matter, then choice (a), authoritative, would be correct. Their parenting style is not neglectful, choice (c), or permissive, choice (d), since these exert little or no control.

7. Choice (b) is correct. By definition, a close-knit group like this that centers primarily around talking is classified as a clique.

8. Choice (b) is correct. American Indians have the highest dropout rate, 22.7 percent, followed by choice (c), Hispanics, at 18.7 percent; choice (d), African Americans, at 16.8 percent; and Asian Americans, choice (a), at 4.8 percent.

9. Choice (a) is correct. In a recent survey, only 10 percent of the seniors surveyed indicated that they had never been on a date.

10. Choice (c) is correct. Moodiness and negative affect, withdrawal from others, and disruption of sleep are all signs. Choices (a) and (b), anorexia and bulimia, respectively, are eating disorders that involve self-starvation, faulty body image, and, in the case of bulimia, binge eating and purging. Choice (d), delinquency, would involve acting out, status offenses, and other criminal activities.

CHAPTER 12
Early Adulthood: Physical and Cognitive Development

Learning Objectives

1. Describe the changes in physical growth during the early adulthood period, including changes in strength.

2. Describe the age-related changes in the major body systems and characterize the health of the young adult.

3. Describe the effects of diet, exercise, and weight control on early adulthood.

4. Discuss the effects of health-compromising behaviors, including smoking, alcohol, drug abuse, and unsafe sex.

5. Identify the different forms of stress and describe Selye's general adaptation syndrome. Explain how young adults should cope with stressful situations.

6. Describe the five stages of the sexual response cycle.

7. Discuss sexual attitudes and behavior during the young adulthood period.

8. Identify and describe the common sexual dysfunctions found in young adults. Discuss the causes and treatment of infertility.

9. Describe the characteristics of postformal thought, including the various theories of adult cognition.

10. Identify and describe Schaie's stages of adult thinking.

11. Describe Perry's contextual approach to adult cognition.

12. Discuss adult moral reasoning. In particular, describe the alternatives to and expansions of Kohlberg's theory.

13. Discuss the effect of college on intellectual development. Describe the demographics of college students today.

14. Discuss the role of work and the development of careers during the young adulthood period. Describe the differences based on gender, race, and socioeconomic status.

Chapter Overview

Early adulthood is a time of assuming responsibility for the adult tasks of earning a living and establishing a household. It is also a time of peak physical ability and functioning. Although age-related changes begin in early adulthood, the declines are gradual. By age forty, the cardiovascular and respiratory systems show the most noticeable changes. Young adults are generally healthy and even if disease is present, it is likely to be unsymptomatic. Unhealthy environments and health-compromising behaviors can cause pathological aging, however, leading to many of the losses in functioning. There are many things an individual can do to set the stage for healthy aging.

Stress can influence health in multiple ways by wearing down the physiological system. Selye developed the general adaptation syndrome to describe the pattern of physical response to stress. It includes the alarm stage, the resistance stage, and the exhaustion stage. The experience of stress is a two-step process, according to Lazarus, consisting of primary and secondary appraisal.

The sexual response cycle has five stages—desire, excitement, plateau, orgasm, and resolution—that are very similar for men and women. Both sexes experience sexual dysfunction. Common dysfunctions include low sexual desire, orgasmic problems, ejaculatory problems, and erectile dysfunction. In the United States, about 10 to 15 percent of couples are infertile. Infertility can cause psychological reactions of grief, anger, and guilt.

With regard to cognitive development, Piaget proposed formal operations as the most mature mode of reasoning. Other cognitive theorists have proposed a fifth postformal stage of adult thought that is characterized as relative and nonabsolute, accepting and synthesizing contradiction.

Schaie's theory of intellectual development includes three or four stages that go beyond Piaget's formal operations and reflect the goal-directed and contextual nature of adult thinking. Mature thinking depends on the context of the event and the framework of the knower. Perry's work describes how college students' thinking changes from basic dualism to contextual relativism. Studies of adult moral reasoning indicate that the content or situation of the problem may be more important than gender in influencing whether a justice or a care orientation is used.

The college experience fosters intellectual development. Although different types of schools provide different benefits, the biggest difference in cognitive growth occurs between adults who attend college and those who do not. Today's college student body is diverse in terms of age, gender, and race/ethnicity. Work is a major social role of adult life and forms a critical part of one's identity. Work starts early and continues throughout life, but with different emphases or stages. Gender, race, and socioeconomic status affect which jobs people are likely to attain.

Chapter Outline

I. Physical development

II. Physical functioning

Young adults are at the peak of their physical abilities. Their organs have reached maturity and are at their strongest by the mid-twenties.

A. Growth in height and weight

1. Virtually all people reach their full height by their mid-twenties as a result of ossification.

2. Considerable variables in cessation of growth occur for both women and men.

3. Exercise and good nutrition produce a reservoir of bone and calcium that can alleviate the bone loss associated with aging in later stages of adulthood.

4.   Women and men experience weight increases during early adulthood. Increases in percent of body fat occur as the body continues to fill out.

5.   Social factors also contribute to adult patterns of weight gain. Society stresses physical attractiveness and slimness.

B.   Strength

1.   Strength continues to increase after full height is reached and peaks in the early thirties.

2.   **Organ reserve** is the extra capacity each body organ has for responding to very intense or prolonged effort or stress. This extra capacity declines with age after the peak in the thirties.

C. Age-related changes

Appearance changes relatively little during early adulthood, although some individuals may have a few facial creases or a few gray hairs by their late twenties.

1.   The cardiovascular system undergoes a steady decline in functioning throughout the adult years.

2.   Gradual decreases in respiratory efficiency start at about age twenty-five, and noticeable decreases appear by age forty, although it is difficult to distinguish between normal aging of the lungs and aging due to damage caused by environmental factors.

3.   Peak central nervous system functioning occurs in early adulthood.

a.   The senses vary in the degree of age-related changes.

b.   The changing in senses are slight and usually do not concern young adults.

III. Health in early adulthood

Typically, young adults are healthy and even when ill do not experience symptoms. Young adults with poor health habits are not yet likely to suffer from the negative effects, although damage is occurring in their bodies.

A. Health behaviors

Adopting healthy behaviors and avoiding health-compromising behaviors promote better health, and young adults are in the best situation to prevent illness from developing.

1.   Many of the losses in functioning associated with aging are the result of illness, abnormality, genetic factors, or exposure to unhealthy environments. This is called **pathological aging**.

2.   **Health-compromising behaviors** can lead to pathological aging as well as to illness.

3.   Diet plays a significant role in cardiovascular disease and contributes to the development of cancer.

    a. A diet low in cholesterol, fats, calories, and additives and high in fiber, fruits, and vegetables is healthy.

    b. This diet is not typical of most Americans. Poor eating habits are often acquired in childhood.

    c. Attitudes can influence one's diet.

4. Physical activity is associated with staying healthy.

    a. Exercise is beneficial to the cardiovascular system. It reduces or controls hypertension and improves cholesterol levels.

    b. Exercise can also improve mood and self-esteem and reduce the chance of engaging in health-compromising behaviors.

5. Obesity is a major health problem and is associated with a number of medical problems such as heart disease.

    a. More than one-third of the adult population is overweight or obese, and the percentage has been increasing over the last twenty years.

    b. There are several factors that increase the risk of obesity: genetic predisposition, childhood patterns of eating and exercise, and socioeconomic status.

    c. The best strategies for weight loss are exercise and a healthy diet.

B. Health-compromising behaviors

Many of the behaviors that put individuals at risk in adolescence persist among young adults.

1. Smoking is responsible for more preventable illnesses and deaths than any other single health-compromising behavior.

    a. Passive smoking increases the health risks to nonsmokers who are subjected to air contaminated by smokers.

    b. Smoking-related illnesses take years to develop. This allows smokers to deny or ignore the threat to their health.

    c. Smoking is influenced if parents, older siblings, best friends, or peers smoke; socioeconomic status also plays a role.

    d. There are racial/ethnic differences in smoking patterns and attitudes.

    e. People who suffer from multiple addictions report that smoking is harder to stop than taking drugs or drinking alcohol.

    f. Smoking prevention is particularly important because nicotine may serve as an entry-level drug that makes one more likely to use other drugs in the future.

2. Alcohol consumption can affect health in many ways, such as increasing the risk of some cancers and cirrhosis of the liver.

a. For some, one or two drinks a day may be too much.

b. Alcohol abuse can damage nearly every organ and function of the body.

c. Problem drinking and alcoholism can result from heavy drinking.

d. Drinking and heavy drinking are more common among younger adults than older adults.

3. Unsafe sex creates risk for STDs and HIV infection.

a. Adolescents and young adults are at greater risk than other age groups because they have more sex partners.

b. AIDS is the most feared sexually transmitted disease because it is fatal.

c. Young adults often do not consider the consequences of unsafe sex, forget about them when under the influence of alcohol or drugs, or protect themselves from AIDS but not from other STDs.

d. The risk for AIDS has been greatest for homosexual men, intravenous drug users, and minority populations, but the number of affected women is growing.

• Working with Daniel Longram, care manager: Helping families cope with AIDS

IV. Stress

Stress is the arousal of the mind and body in response to demands made on them by unsettling conditions or experiences. Stress can be positive (eustress) or negative (distress). Selye developed the **general adaptation syndrome** to describe the pattern of physical response to stress; the syndrome consists of three stages: alarm, resistance, and exhaustion.

A. Stress and health

1. Stress can have a direct effect by increasing wear and tear on the physiological system and causing physical changes that can lead to illness.

2. Some people have personalities or health conditions that predispose them to stress. People with negative affectivity may be prone to disease.

B. The experience of stress

1. Lazarus identified a two-step process that people go through when faced with a stressor.

a. In primary appraisal, the person determines if the stressor is positive, neutral, or negative. If negative, the person assesses its potential for harm, threat, or challenge.

b. The person's assessment of whether he or she has sufficient coping strategies to the negative stressor is called secondary appraisal.

c. Negative, uncontrollable, ambiguous, or overwhelming events are perceived as more stressful than positive, controllable, clear-cut, or manageable ones.

2. **Posttraumatic stress disorder** describes the physical and psychological symptoms of a person who has been the victim of a highly stressful event.

V. Sexuality

  A. The sexual response cycle

   1. Masters and Johnson studied women's and men's physiological response in sexual activity.

     a. Healthy individuals go through the same physiological processes.

     b. Male and female sexual responses are much more similar than different.

   2. There are four physiological stages in the human sexual response cycle.

     a. In the desire stage, physiology and emotion contribute to sexual arousal.

     b. The first sign of arousal occurs in the excitement stage and includes vasocongestion.

     c. When the changes of the excitement stage reach a high state and then level off, the plateau stage has been reached.

     d. Orgasm releases the buildup of muscular tension and vasocongestion and involves involuntary, rhythmic contractions of the muscles of the pelvis.

     e. The resolution stage is characterized by the body's return to a nonaroused state.

• Perspectives: How does stress relate to women's employment?

  B. Sexual attitudes fall into three broad categories—traditional, relational, and recreational.

   1. For traditional people, their religious beliefs serve as a guide for sexual behavior.

   2. Relational people say that sex is a part of a loving relationship but is not limited to marriage.

   3. Sex and love are not necessarily related for recreational people.

   4. There is a relationship between attitudinal groups and behavior.

  C. **Sexual dysfunction** is an inability to function adequately in or enjoy sexual activities and has been experienced by 77 percent of wives and 50 percent of husbands in one study of married couples.

   1. Low sexual desire is a common complaint of women and men and can be caused by a variety of physical factors.

   2. Orgasmic problems in females can take the form of primary orgasmic dysfunction, where a woman never experiences an orgasm, and it may be related to psychological and physiological problems.

3. The most common male sexual dysfunction is premature ejaculation.

4. Erectile dysfunction is when a man is generally unable to get or keep a firm enough erection to have intercourse.

VI. Infertility

Infertility refers to a couple's inability to conceive a pregnancy after one year of sexual relations without contraception. Between 10 and 15 percent of married couples in the United States are believed to be infertile. Infertility has become a more frequent problem in the last twenty-five years. There are several suspected causes, including sexually transmitted diseases, environmental hazards, and limited access to medical care.

A. The two major causes of female infertility are failure to ovulate and blockage of the fallopian tubes.

B. Male infertility may be due to low sperm count, low sperm mobility, poor semen quality, or blockage of the ducts of the reproductive tract.

C. Psychological reactions to infertility include five common emotional responses, and people often initially respond to the diagnosis of infertility with shock or denial.

D. Many new reproductive technologies have been developed, but they can be expensive and are not always successful.

VII. Adult choices

Major life decisions are made during early adulthood, and they can have significant implications for development.

VIII. Cognitive development

Some cognitive theorists believe that we reach higher levels of cognitive development than described by Piaget.

IX. Postformal thought

Formal operations is the final Piagetian stage of cognitive development; it represents a generalized orientation toward problem solving.

A. Critiques of formal operations

Several researchers have criticized formal operations and suggest **postformal thought**.

1. Postformal thinkers understand that knowledge is relative and nonabsolute.

2. Postformal thinkers accept contradiction as a basic aspect of reality.

3. Postformal thinkers can synthesize contradictions into coherent wholes.

B. Is there a fifth stage?

1. **Problem finding** involves generating new questions about oneself, one's work, or one's surroundings.

2. Some researchers have proposed a **fifth stage of cognitive development** and include problem finding, dialectical postformal thought, metasystematic operations, intrasystemic thought, intersystemic thought, and autonomous thought.

X. Development of contextual thinking

Schaie conducted longitudinal research and proposes three or four stages of adult thought.

A. Schaie's stages of adult thinking

1. Childhood and adolescence constitute the **period of acquisition**, when a person builds basic skills and abilities.

2. Young adults are in the **achieving stage** and move toward specific goals while considering contexts and consequences.

3. In middle adulthood, people enter the **responsible stage** and strive to meet personal goals and consider their responsibilities to others.

4. Some middle-aged people who have more complex responsibilities are in the **executive stage**, requiring the application of postformal thinking to practical problems.

5. People in late adulthood are in the **reintegrative stage**, when they have fewer long-range plans and fewer responsibilities to job and family.

B. Contextual relativism

Perry studied how students at Harvard University progressed through the college years.

1. Freshmen had a **basic dualism** perspective: they saw things in terms of right or wrong, good or bad.

2. In the **contextual relativism stage**, students began to see truth as relative—that meaning depended on context and who was trying to understand the event.

3. Perry's sample did not represent all adults or even all college students, and no female responses were used.

4. Perry's work has been broadened by Belenky et al. in their interview of 135 women. Their study revealed other responses:

a. Silent knowing involves seeing authorities as all-powerful.

b. Received knowing consists of receiving the truth from others.

c. Individuals in subjective knowing are less concerned about persuading others; they distrust logic, analysis, and abstraction, and use inward listening and watching to learn.

d. Procedural knowing is based on abstract reasoning and is a shift from subjective opinions to reasoned arguments.

e. Constructed knowing consists of integrating subjective and objective knowing.

XI. Adult moral reasoning

Kohlberg's theory focused on the abstract ethic of justice, while Gilligan's argued that empathy is a primary motivator for moral reasoning and ethical behavior.

A. Context and moral orientation

Research has shown that individuals used both a care orientation and a justice orientation.

B. Gender and moral voice

1. Studies of adult moral development have found the use of feminine and masculine themes in both males and females.

2. Most adults use more than one moral orientation, and many studies show that there appear to be no gender differences in moral orientation.

• A multicultural view: Moral orientation in the United States and China

XII. College

College cultivates intellectual development and fosters a progression in ways of thinking. The United States has the most educated population, although there are ethnic differences in completion rates. Most studies have shown that the benefits of college can be realized at any type of school. Faculty-student contact is an important variable in cognitive growth.

A. Who attends college?

1. The rate of college enrollment for younger students has grown substantially, but the number of older students has been growing even more rapidly.

2. Students attend college for many reasons, including to obtain an education and to satisfy parental expectations.

B. Women and racial/ethnic minorities

1. Women are more likely than men to attend college and to complete it within four years of starting.

2. Although no differences between men and women were found in the cognitive structures or learning styles, there is a difference in how they view acquisition of knowledge.

3. The college student body has become more racially and ethnically diverse in the last two decades.

4. There are differences between African Americans and white students in terms of attrition rates, overall progression rates, and other variables, although these differences disappear when other variables are controlled.

5. Higher dropout rates among ethnic minorities may be due to inhospitable climate on most predominantly White college campuses.

XIII. Work

Work is a major social role of adult life and forms a critical part of one's identity. Occupation refers to all forms of work, whereas career usually refers to professional occupations.

A. Career stages

1. Greenhaus proposed a five-stage ladder of career development, with each stage consisting of an approximate age range and a set of major tasks.

   a. Preparation for work includes self-exploration to discover interests, talents, and preferences.

   b. Organizational entry involves finding a job.

   c. The early career stage involves gaining competence on the job as well as developing balance between fitting into the organization and learning about other options and directions for one's career.

2. It is important to develop a balance between work and nonwork commitments.

B. Gender, race, and socioeconomic status

1. Gender, race, and socioeconomic status affect which jobs people attain. **Discrimination** is the valuation by the labor market of personal characteristics of a worker that are not related to productivity.

2. Most jobs are held almost exclusively by men or women; this is called **occupational segregation**. Few jobs are truly integrated.

3. Occupations that depend on education have been more receptive to women than occupations that require physical strength and skill.

4. Females' aspirations toward gender-appropriate occupations are influenced by many variables.

5. The primary sector includes high-wage jobs that provide good benefits, job security, and advancement opportunities. The secondary sector includes low-wage jobs with few fringe benefits.

   a. Many ethnic and racial minorities are employed in the secondary sector.

   b. There are more gender similarities than differences between male and female African American youth in the school-to-work transition.

XIV. Growth and change

Key Concepts

Directions: Identify each of the following key concepts discussed in this chapter.

1. Early adulthood is generally the years between _____ and _____.

2. _____ is the extra capacity each body organ has for responding to particularly intense or prolonged effort or unusually stressful events.

3. Young adults have sex with more different partners than do older people, which puts them at higher risk for contracting _____.

4. Loss in functioning caused by exposure to unhealthy environments and health-compromising behaviors results from _____. Smoking, drug abuse, and unsafe sex are examples of _____.

5. Three health behaviors that people engage in to maintain or improve their health are _____, _____, and _____.

6. The primary benefit of exercise is to the _____ system. The excessive accumulation of body fat is called _____.

7. _____ is responsible for more preventable illnesses and deaths than any other single health-compromising behavior.

8. The breathing in of secondhand smoke from other people's cigarettes is called _____.

9. Heavy drinking greatly increases the risk of _____ in infants.

10. _____ is described by the inability to control one's drinking, a high tolerance for alcohol, and withdrawal symptoms.

11. Risk for AIDS is greatest for _____, _____, and _____. For sexually active people, _____ provide the best protection from HIV.

12. According to the _____, the pattern of physical response to stress takes place in three stages: _____, _____, and _____.

13. During _____, the individual determines if a stressor is positive, neutral, or negative. _____ refers to a person's assessment of whether he or she can cope with the negative stressor.

14. The physical and psychological symptoms of a person who has been the victim of a highly stressful event are called _____.

15. The five stages of the sexual response cycle are _____, _____, _____, _____, and _____.

16. An inability to function adequately sexually or to enjoy sexual activities is called _____.

17. The most common male sexual dysfunction is _____. If a woman has never experienced an orgasm, she is considered to have _____.

18. When a couple has been having sexual relations without contraception and cannot conceive a pregnancy, the problem of _____ is present.

19. The two major causes of female infertility are _____ and _____. Male infertility may be due to _____.

20. The final stage of cognitive development according to Piaget is _____. Some theorists have proposed other formulations, given the limitations of Piaget's conception of mature thought; these models are called _____.

21. _____ consists of generating new questions about oneself, one's work, or one's surroundings. Understanding and seeking out contradictions, dialectical thinking, and metasystematic operations are examples of the _____.

22. According to Schaie, the _____ is the stage when the person is building basic skills and abilities. Young adults, while in the _____, attempt to direct their intelligence toward goals. When in the _____, people strive to meet personal goals. In the _____, people apply postformal thought to practical problems. In late adulthood, people have fewer goals and fewer responsibilities; this is the _____.

23. When individuals see things in terms of right or wrong, good or bad, they are in what Perry called _____. In _____, people see truth as relative and the context meaningful.

24. When women integrate subjective and objective knowing, they are in _____.

25. Kohlberg, in describing moral orientation, emphasized the _____, while Gilligan stressed a(n) _____ perspective. According to research, people tend to use _____ in their moral orientation.

26. The largest differences in cognitive growth are among those who _____ and those who _____. Informal interactions between _____ and students are important in cognitive growth.

27. Higher dropout rates among minority populations might be due to _____.

28. _____ refers to all types of work, whereas career refers to _____.

29. The five-stage ladder of career development proposed by Greenhaus consists of _____, _____, _____, _____, and _____.

30. The _____ includes high-wage jobs with good fringe benefits and opportunities for advancement. _____ is the valuation of personal characteristics that are not related to work productivity. When most jobs are held almost exclusively by either men or women, the situation called _____ is present.

Multiple-Choice Self-Test

Factual / Conceptual Questions

1. Peak strength is reached during the
   a. late teens.
   b. early twenties.
   c. late twenties.
   d. early thirties.

2. Organ reserve refers to the
   a. extra capacity each body organ has for responding to stressful events.
   b. amount of development that an organ undergoes after maturity is reached.
   c. amount of extra fat that can be used by the organ system before damage occurs.
   d. estimated amount of time before organ deterioration results in breakdown.

3. Which of the following senses tends to show increases in sensitivity the longest?
   a. Hearing
   b. Taste
   c. Touch
   d. Vision

4. Which stage follows the plateau stage of the sexual response cycle?
   a. Desire
   b. Orgasm
   c. Excitement
   d. Resolution

5. The most common male sexual problem during young adulthood is
   a. erectile dysfunction.
   b. low sexual desire.
   c. premature ejaculation.
   d. primary orgasmic dysfunction.

6. According to Schaie, all of Piaget's stages are encompassed in the
   a. achieving stage.
   b. acquisitive stage.
   c. executive stage.
   d. responsible stage.

7. In order to achieve contextual relativism, individuals must be able to
   a. accept basic dualism.
   b. achieve formal operations.
   c. experience silent knowing.
   d. understand multiple perspectives.

8. According to Gilligan, the primary motivation for moral judgment is
   a. empathy.
   b. justice.
   c. rewards.
   d. survival.

9. Problem-solving performance is positively associated with
   a. age.
   b. gender.
   c. level of education.
   d. personality.

10. As compared to individuals who directly go to a four-year college, students who transfer from community colleges are
    a. more likely to obtain a master's degree.
    b. more likely to obtain a bachelor's degree.
    c. just as likely to obtain a bachelor's degree.
    d. less likely to obtain a bachelor's degree.

Application Questions

1. Jim and Tina, who are typical young adults, are both the same age. Which of the following statements about their physical growth is true?
    a. Tina and Jim will both reach their maximum height at about the same time.
    b. Tina and Jim will both reach their maximum bone mass at about the same time.
    c. Jim will go through the process of bone ossification before Tina.
    d. Tina and Jim should have the same amount of average body fat.

2. Charlie, a typical adult, is likely to experience noticeable decreases in respiratory efficiency at about _____ years of age.
    a. twenty
    b. thirty
    c. forty
    d. fifty

3. Danielle often has a glass of red wine with her dinner. The effect of this is likely to
    a. increase her risk of coronary heart disease.
    b. decrease her risk of cirrhosis of the liver.
    c. decrease her risk of obesity.
    d. actually increase her longevity.

4. Which of the following is the best example of eustress?
    a. Dorian was just fired from his job.
    b. Helena has just given birth to her first child.
    c. Ming feels ill-prepared for a physics exam he's about to take.
    d. Kim has just been pulled over by the police for going through a stoplight.

5. Frank views sex as an enjoyable physical activity, not an emotional activity. His view of sex would most likely be classified as
    a. chauvinistic.
    b. recreational.
    c. relational.
    d. traditional.

6. Bruce and Robin are having difficulty conceiving a child. Who is more likely to seek medical help first?
    a. Bruce
    b. Robin
    c. Both equally
    d. Neither is likely to seek help.

7. Kayla is a formal operational thinker. She is likely to have difficulty
    a. dealing with contradictions.
    b. solving concrete problems.
    c. understanding abstract concepts.
    d. using scientific reasoning.

8. Max, who has a wife and two children, has decided to go back to college in order to get a better-paying job. His decision came after discussing the issue with the family and weighing all the options. According to Schaie, Max is most likely functioning at the _____ stage.
    a. achieving
    b. executive
    c. reintegrative
    d. responsible

9. Rebecca is from a low-income family whose parents are not well educated. If she goes to college, she will most likely attend a
    a. large public university that grants Ph.D.'s.
    b. two-year community college.
    c. small, private, liberal arts college.
    d. four-year university that does not have a Ph.D. program.

10. Forty-two-year-old Marty is in the process of reassessing his job as a salesman and is thinking of going into business for himself. According to Greenhaus, Marty is in the _____ stage of career development.
    a. early career
    b. late career
    c. mid-career
    d. organizational entry

Answer Key

Key Concepts

1. twenty, forty
2. Organ reserve
3. sexually transmitted diseases (HIV)
4. pathological aging, health-compromising behaviors
5. consuming a healthy diet, exercise, weight control
6. cardiovascular, obesity
7. Smoking
8. passive smoking
9. fetal alcohol syndrome
10. Alcoholism
11. homosexual men, intravenous drug users, minority populations, condoms
12. general adaptation syndrome, alarm, resistance, exhaustion
13. primary appraisal, Secondary appraisal
14. posttraumatic stress disorder
15. desire, excitement, plateau, orgasm, resolution
16. sexual dysfunction
17. premature ejaculation, primary orgasmic dysfunction
18. infertility
19. failure to ovulate, blockage of the fallopian tubes, low sperm count (low sperm mobility, poor semen quality, blockage of the ducts of the reproductive tract)
20. formal operations, postformal thought
21. Problem finding, fifth stage of cognitive development
22. period of acquisition, achieving stage, responsible stage, executive stage, reintegrative stage
23. basic dualism, contextual relativism
24. constructed knowing
25. ethic of justice, empathy, both
26. attend college, do not attend college, faculty
27. inhospitable climates on most predominantly White college campuses
28. Occupation, professional occupations
29. preparation for work, organizational entry, early career, mid-career, late career
30. primary sector, Discrimination, occupational segregation

Multiple-Choice Self-Test: Factual / Conceptual Questions

1. Choice (d) is correct. Not until the very late twenties and early thirties do both males and females reach their peak strength. Choices (a), (b), and (c) are all too early.

2. Choice (a) is correct. Organ reserve, which decreases with age, is the extra amount of potential that the organ systems have to respond to stressful situations. The other choices do not have any particular term associated with them.

3. Choice (c) is correct. The sense of touch shows the longest period of increase. It peaks around forty-five years of age. Choice (a), hearing, peaks at about twenty; choice (b), taste, peaks at about twenty and then remains fairly constant until age forty; choice (d), vision, peaks between the ages of twenty and thirty.

4. Choice (b) is correct. Plateau is the third stage of the sexual response cycle. It is followed by orgasm, the fourth stage. Choice (a), desire, is the first stage; choice (c), excitement, is the second stage; and choice (d), resolution, is the fifth stage.

5. Choice (c) is correct. Premature ejaculation, which occurs either immediately before, during , or after insertion, is the most common sexual problem in men. Choice (a), erectile dysfunction, occurs in only about 10 percent of men; choice (b), low sexual desire, is found in both men and women but is not very common in young adults. Choice (d), primary orgasmic dysfunction, is found only in women.

6. Choice (b) is correct. The acquisitive stage is Schaie's first stage, which involves developing efficient ways to acquire information. Schaie believed that Piaget's four stages represented increasingly efficient ways of dealing with information and problems. Schaie's other stages, choices (a), (c), and (d)—achieving, executive, and responsible, respectively—involve the utilization of information.

7. Choice (d) is correct. Contextual relativism involves the understanding that truth is relative, meaning it depends on the context and the framework of the person who is trying to understand the event. In order to do this, one needs to be able to understand multiple perspectives, not just one. Choice (a), accept basic dualism, involves single perspective-taking; choice (b), achieve formal operations, may be helpful for achieving contextual relativism but is not sufficient; while choice (c), experience silent knowing, involves a passive approach to knowledge and the unconditional acceptance of other authorities without question.

8. Choice (a) is correct. Gilligan emphasizes a morality rooted in care as opposed to justice. For that reason, empathy, the ability to relate to another's feelings, is vital in making moral judgments. Choice (b), justice, is Kohlberg's emphasis; choices (c) and (d), rewards and survival, respectively, refer to the lower levels of judgment for both Gilligan and Kohlberg.

9. Choice (c) is correct. Studies have found correlations between problem solving and education level; individuals with more education (especially college) are better problem solvers. The other choices (a), (b), and (d)—age, gender, and personality, respectively—are not correlated with problem solving.

10. Choice (c) is correct. Contrary to popular belief, individuals who attend a community college and then enter a four-year institution seem to be just as likely to obtain a bachelor's degree as those who start out in a four-year college. Choices (a), (b), and (d) do not reflect the actual data.

Multiple-Choice Self-Test: Application Questions

1. Choice (b) is correct. Men and women reach their maximum bone mass at about age thirty. Females tend to reach maximum height before males, so choice (a) is incorrect, and they also go through bone ossification before males, making, choice (c) incorrect. Females have a greater percent body fat throughout adulthood, so choice (d) is also incorrect.

2. Choice (c) is correct. Although respiratory efficiency decreases starting at about age twenty-five, it is typically first noticed at about age forty. Thus the other answers are incorrect.

3. Choice (d) is correct. Light to moderate alcohol consumption (particularly red wine) actually has some positive effects in that it decreases the risk of coronary heart disease (choice [a]) and thus increases longevity. However, alcohol abuse has just the opposite effect and can greatly decrease longevity. Choices (b) and (c), cirrhosis of the liver and obesity, respectively, actually show increases, not decreases, as the amount of drinking increases.

4. Choice (b) is correct. Eustress refers to positive stress, which involves events that are viewed as positive by the individual but nevertheless are stressful. Choice (b), birth of a child, fits this definition best, while choices (a), (c), and (d) are forms of distress, or negative stress.

5. Choice (b) is correct. Recreationally oriented sex does not involve love or intense emotions but rather simply focuses on the pleasure. Choice (a), chauvinistic, might be a subjective interpretation of Frank's attitude, but it is not one of the sexual behavior categories. Choice (c), relational, involves a loving relationship but not necessarily marriage or firm commitment. Choice (d), traditional, involves the attachment of particular religious or moral beliefs concerning sex, generally indicating that it should occur only as part of a marriage.

6. Choice (b) is correct. Females are more likely to seek help first if a couple is having difficulty conceiving, even though 40 percent of the time the difficulty stems from the male, 40 percent of the time from the female, and the remainder is a combination of both. Thus the other choices are not correct.

7. Choice (a) is correct. Although they may be good at solving problems, choice (b); dealing with abstract concepts, choice (c); and using scientific reasoning, choice (d); formal operational individuals still have difficulties dealing with contradictory information. Not until they reach the postformal stage, choice (a), can they begin to deal with contradictions effectively.

8. Choice (d) is correct. Schaie's responsible stage involves taking into consideration the effect of one's decisions on others, particularly family members. Decisions are not made in isolation since their consequences affect more than just the person making the decision. This decision will clearly affect not just Max but also his wife and his children, and Max is taking their views into consideration. Choice (a), achieving, is where an individual might make a decision, but that decision typically affects only that individual. Choice (b), executive, reflects an even broader viewpoint, similar to that of middle manager; choice (c), reintegrative, reflects an older individual looking at "the big picture."

9. Choice (b) is correct. Children from low-income families, especially if the parents are not well educated, tend to go to community colleges. Children from higher-income families, especially if the mother is well educated, tend to go to large public universities that grant Ph.D.'s, choice (a). Choices (c) and (d), small, private, liberal arts college and four-year university that does not have a Ph.D. program, respectively, are not strongly associated with income or education level.

10. Choice (c) is correct. Marty's reassessment, coupled with his age, points to Greenhaus's mid-career stage of career development, in which a person reappraises past career decisions and either reaffirms or modifies them. Choices (a) and (d), early career and organizational entry, respectively, involve initial entry into a career, while choice (b), late career, involves preparation for retirement.

CHAPTER 13
Early Adulthood: Psychosocial Development

Learning Objectives

1. Describe the major characteristics of psychosocial development during the early adulthood period. Distinguish between timing of events and normative crisis theories.

2. Describe Vaillant's crisis theory.

3. Describe Levinson's seasons of life approach to adulthood.

4. Describe Erikson's theory of psychosocial development during adulthood.

5. Discuss the development of intimacy during adulthood. Indicate the characteristics of friendships.

6. Describe Sternberg's triangular theory of love. Identify the various types of love.

7. Discuss the process of mate selection and the relevant variables.

8. Identify and describe the different types of marriage and explain how they affect marital equality and satisfaction.

9. Discuss alternatives to marriage, including singlehood, heterosexual cohabitation, and lesbian/gay relationships.

10. Describe how marriage has changed over the years. Discuss the effects of divorce and remarriage on the family.

11. Identify the challenges that come with parenthood and indicate how children might alter marital relationships.

12. Discuss the effects of single parenthood.

13. Discuss the effects of stepparents and blended families.

14. Discuss the consequences of not having children on long-term marital relationships.

Chapter Overview

Significant changes continue to take place in early adulthood. As individuals enter adulthood, development has less to do with biology and more to do with cultural, social, and personal factors. Social clocks are internalized age expectations that govern when people experience major life transitions; their influence has declined as age grading has become less rigid. The Grant Study indicates that development is a lifelong process, that sustained relationships have more of an effect on the shape life takes than isolated events do, and that the maturity of adaptive mechanisms determines the level of mental health.

Levinson identified three eras in adult male life. During the novice phase, men have a Dream, form mentor relationships, develop an occupation, and establish intimate relationships. Some researchers have found that women's experiences are not adequately described in the Grant Study or Levinson's research. From Erikson's perspective, a young adult is faced with the need to establish his or her identity and then form close, intimate relationships. Friendships provide young adults with support and can contribute to an individual's well-being. Love is another form of intimacy. Young adults are delaying marriage and typically experience serial monogamy as they go from one love relationship to another. Sternberg's triangular theory of love highlights intimacy, passion, and decision/commitment as love's essential components. Most people meet their mates in familiar places or are introduced by friends or family. This preselection is likely to result in similarity in race/ethnicity, age, and educational level. Although most people say the ideal marriage is an equal partnership, most contemporary marriages are junior-partner relationships or conventional relationships. Marital equality leads to greater marital happiness and lower marital conflict. Marriage is associated with psychological well-being, with men benefiting more than women. Alternative lifestyles have become more commonplace, including singlehood and heterosexual cohabitation, which is sometimes seen as part of the courtship process and a way to test for compatibility prior to marriage. Most gay men and lesbians are involved in close, steady same-sex relationships. High divorce rates are due to increased expectations from marriage and to decreased expectations for marital permanence. Divorce often leads to remarriage.

Reasons for having children vary. Enormous changes in the lives of new parents occur with the birth of the first child. Mothers feel the strain of change more fully than fathers because the primary responsibility for infant care usually falls on them. Single parenthood is often associated with poverty, which can create problems. Many single-parent families successfully raise happy families. Remarriage often leads to the creation of stepparent or blended families, and these families experience more within-family conflict because of the complexity of the relationships. Couples who choose to be child-free are likely to be college educated and career oriented. Their life satisfaction differs minimally from those who choose to be parents.

Chapter Outline

I. Theories of adult development

Reaching early adulthood is not the end of development; it, too, is marked by significant change. As individuals enter adulthood, their development has less to do with biology and more to do with cultural, social, and personal factors. As a result there is more diversity in adult development than in child or adolescent development.

A. Timing of events: Social clocks

1. This approach focuses on the importance of the developmental context.

2. The developmental context is described by a **social clock** that tells us whether we are "on time" in following an age-appropriate social timetable.

a. These social norms dictate when certain life transitions should occur.

b. People who follow this expected pattern experience fewer difficulties than people who deviate from it.

3. Society has become less rigid in its expectations of when significant life events should occur. But these age-graded roles have not disappeared.

4. Timing of events theories are better than normative-crisis theories to explain dissimilarities among groups.

B. Crisis theory: Vaillant and the Grant Study

1. Vaillant studied 204 white men in a longitudinal study and came to several conclusions.

a. Growth and development are a lifelong process.

b. Isolated events rarely mold individual lives. What is more important are the relationships with others.

c. **Adaptive mechanisms**, or coping styles, determine individuals' level of mental health. Vaillant found four types of adaptive mechanisms—mature, immature, psychotic, and neurotic.

2. Vaillant found that individuals were more likely to use one adaptive mechanism over another at certain ages. Some subjects made maturational shifts in adaptive styles. Several variables were associated with this shift.

a. A healthy brain leads to mature adaptive mechanisms. Injuries and alcoholism lead to less mature mechanisms.

b. Sustained loving relationships lead to mature adaptive mechanisms. Close, loving relationships provide models for coping with life events.

3. During **career consolidation**, between the twenties and forties, men tended to work hard, devote themselves to career achievement, and sacrifice play.

C. Crisis theory: Levinson's seasons of adult lives

1. Levinson used the **biographical method** to learn about his subjects' lives. The method involves reconstructing the life course through interviewing and using other sources.

2. Levinson identified three eras, or seasons, in the adult male life, two of which occur in early adulthood; during each era, a man builds a life structure. It is then followed by a transition, and then he builds a new life structure.

a. The novice phase is characterized by exploration of the possibilities of adult life, testing of some initial choices, and creating a provisional entry life structure. The age thirty transition allows reassessment and improvement to this first adult life structure. The phase has four major tasks: forming a Dream, forming mentoring relationships, developing an occupation, and establishing intimate relationships and finding the special woman.

    b.   In the second phase, the culminating phase, the young man establishes occupational goals and makes plans for advancing them. He is settling down and is more independent and self-sufficient. Around forty, the man enters midlife transition.

   3.   Because Levinson excluded women from the study, there is some question about their course of development. Levinson later reported that his formulations fit women too.

    a.   The Dreams of women may differ from those of men.

    b.   Women were also unlikely to have had mentors.

    c.   Integrating career and family was difficult for women for several reasons, including their husbands' expectations that their wives would support their own Dreams.

  D. Crisis theory: Erikson's intimacy versus isolation

   1.   In **intimacy versus isolation**, the crisis of early adulthood builds on Erikson's earlier stages of ego development.

    a.   During this stage, the individual must develop the ability to establish close, committed relationships and to tolerate the threat of fusion and loss of identity that intense intimacy raises.

    b.   The avoidance of intimacy leads to isolation and self-absorption.

   2.   Critics have suggested that identity and intimacy develop simultaneously.

II. Intimate relationships

During early adulthood, attachment to friends and lovers increases while attachment to family decreases. Although family members continue to be important in young adults' lives, they are not as important as they were during earlier life stages.

  A. Friendship

   1.   Friendships are particularly important during early adulthood, since young adults rely increasingly on friends for intimacy and support.

   2.   The essential elements of friendship include its voluntary nature and its ability to provide many important forms of support, such as validation and acceptance.

   3.   In other cultures, friendships are often based on more basic survival needs.

   4.   Friendships provide many mental and physical health benefits.

   5.   Men and women tend to have different styles of friendships.

    a.   Women tend to talk with their friends in more deep and more self-revealing ways and to define friendships in terms of emotional sharing of confidences.

    b.   Men tend to define friendships in terms of proximity and shared activities and interests.

c.   Gender differences may be related to issues of power and control.

6.   Single adults have more cross-gender friendships than any other group.

- Working with Marilyn Kline, suicide hotline worker: Helping individuals through crises

B.   Love

1.   Since young adults are waiting longer to marry, they experience more love relationships. Each of these relationships is likely to reflect **serial monogamy**.

2.   Sternberg developed a triangular theory of love and argued that love has three essential components: intimacy, passion, and decision/commitment.

   a.   The three components have different properties and vary in different kinds of love relationships.

   b.   According to Sternberg, there are seven combinations of these three components.

3.   Men and women place different values on the instrumental and expressive aspects of love.

   a.   Women report significantly higher confidence in expressing liking, love, and affection to men than men do for women. Women also place more emphasis on expressive qualities like emotional involvement and verbal self-disclosure.

   b.   Men consider practical help, sharing physical activities, spending time together, and sex more important.

C.   Mate selection

1.   Most people's partners are like them in race/ethnicity, age, and educational level.

2.   Most people meet their partners in conventional ways in familiar places like school, work, a private party, or a religious institution.

3.   People are more vulnerable to falling in love when their life is in turbulence.

4.   Getting to know someone as a friend is more likely to lead to a long-term relationship than responding to passion first and then trying to build emotional intimacy.

III. Marriage

During early adulthood, almost everybody finds a marriage partner. Marriage is the socially sanctioned union of a man and a woman that, to some extent, symbolizes being an adult.

A.   Marriage types

1.   The **equal-partner relationship** is characterized by negotiating about shared concerns and responsibilities. Everything is open for renegotiation.

2.   **Conventional relationship** describes a marriage in which the man is the head of the household and sole economic provider, and the woman is the mother and the homemaker.

3. The **junior-partner relationship** has elements of both equal-partnership and conventional relationships.

B. Marital equality

1. Many women work the second shift, meaning that they work the first shift at work and the second shift in the family.

2. Family size, social class, ethnicity, husband's income, and wife's employment are associated with the degree of the husband's dominance in the marriage.

C. Marital satisfaction

1. Different types of marriages are related to different levels of satisfaction with marriage.

   a. Both spouses in equal partnerships express the highest levels of marital satisfaction and psychological well-being.

   b. Equality is a desirable basis for marriage and is related to greater marital happiness and lower marital conflict and aggression.

2. Married people fare better than unmarried people with regard to mortality, morbidity, mental health, and more general measures of psychological well-being.

   a. Formerly married people have the lowest levels of well-being of all types, and never-married people have intermediate levels.

   b. Men seem to benefit more from marriage than women.

   c. Differences in personal happiness between married and never-married individuals have decreased in recent years.

- A multicultural view: Cross-cultural similarities in wife abuse

IV. Alternative lifestyles

Some adults spend significant portions of their lives as singles, and some never marry.

A. Singlehood

1. Singles are not a homogeneous group.

2. One-third of the men and one-fifth of the women are single by choice.

B. Heterosexual cohabitation

1. The trend toward **cohabitation** is replacing early marriage.

2. Cohabitation can serve many purposes.

   a. It can be perceived as part of the courtship process.

   b. Living together can be seen as a temporary arrangement prior to marriage.

       c.   It may be a good way to test for compatibility before marriage.

    3.   Heterosexual cohabitation typically does not last long. Within a few years, most relationships have either broken up or ended in marriage.

    4.   The research on the influence of cohabitation on the quality of marriage is inconclusive. Some studies suggest that cohabitation makes no difference in level of satisfaction with marriage; others suggest that it can have a negative effect.

        a.   Female cohabitors tend to be White, less educated, and less likely to be employed. They are likely to live in large metropolitan areas and more likely to have grown up in a single-parent family.

C. Lesbian/gay sexual preference

    1.   **Homophobia** discourages many gay men and lesbians from making their sexual identity public.

    2.   The percentages of gay men and lesbians are small, but they still represent a great many individuals.

    3.   Most gay men and lesbians live in larger cities and the surrounding suburbs.

D. Lesbian/gay cohabitation

    1.   It is estimated that one-half of gay male couples and three-quarters of lesbian couples live together.

    2.   Most couples form equal partnerships and share household tasks and decision making.

    3.   Gay male couples do not differ from heterosexual men in their levels of relationship satisfaction, and lesbians do not differ from wives in their levels of relationship satisfaction.

V. Changing families

The image of a breadwinner husband and a homemaker wife with two children no longer reflects the typical marriage.

A. Divorce

    1.   About 50 percent of first marriages and 40 percent of all marriages end in divorce.

        a.   Most divorces occur during early adulthood.

        b.   The age at which people divorce has been rising since the mid-1970s.

        c.   The probability of marital success dropped between 1970 and 1990.

    2.   Two social changes have contributed to the rising divorce rates.

a. There are increased expectations of marriage, coupled with a breakdown of consensus about marital and gender roles and the issue of equality within marriage.

b. There has been a decline in the belief that marriage really means "until death do us part." Many young adults witnessed their mothers becoming **displaced homemakers** and thus fear becoming fully committed to marriage.

B. Remarriage

1. People remarry at about the same rate at which they marry; 72 percent of divorced people remarry, with divorced young adults remarrying at the highest rates.

2. About half of these remarriages will end in divorce.

3. People who have divorced and remarried several times report less happiness.

4. There is a relationship between the types of relationships marriage partners have with ex-spouses and the quality of their current marriages.

5. Relationships with ex-spouses that are low in conflict and low in emotional attachment have the best outcome for the new marriage.

6. Some individuals choose not to remarry because of a redefinition of their sexuality from heterosexual to lesbian.

VI. Parenthood

People have children for different reasons. Whatever the reason, pregnancy and childbirth are major life experiences.

A. Transition to parenthood

1. There is less preparation for the parenting role than for any other role in early adulthood.

2. Both fathers and mothers feel the strain of new parenthood, but mothers feel it more fully.

3. The gap between the mother's expectations of fulfillment and the realities of exhaustion and distraction is often enormous.

4. Expecting a baby arouses anxieties in men about their capacity to provide.

5. Employment outside the home may cause problems since women still carry 90 percent of the responsibility for the children, leaving mothers with the heavy demands of two jobs.

6. Marital satisfaction declines before and after the birth of the first child.

a. Having a baby does not bring couples with distressed marriages closer together.

b. Couples may regain satisfaction by successfully negotiating how they will divide the new family responsibilities.

- Perspectives: How does the timing of parenthood influence the parenting experience?

B. Single parenthood

   1.   There is a rise in the number of single parents due to increasing numbers of divorce and delayed marriages.

   2.   Many children of single parents live in poverty, making it difficult to separate the effects of single parenting from the effects of poverty.

   3.   The problems of single parenting are particularly acute for African American families.

   4.   Extended families provide many single parents with support systems.

   5.   Many single parents successfully raise happy and healthy children despite the particular difficulties they face.

C. Stepparent/blended families

   1.   A blended family results when remarriage reconstitutes a single-parent family into a family with a stepparent.

   2.   Blended families show the highest number of within-family problems.

   3.   The complexity of the relationships in these families is significant.

   4.   Adults in stepfamilies have more difficulty than children do in coping with stepsibling relationships.

      a.   Being a stepparent is an ambiguous role.

      b.   Men generally have an easier time being stepfathers than women do being stepmothers.

      c.   Stepmothers tend to be more involved with their stepchildren than are stepfathers, but neither is as involved as the biological parent.

   5.   In comparing self-esteem and behavior problems of stepchildren and children in nuclear and single-parent families, it was concluded that stepchildren do not differ greatly from children in these other families.

D. Child free

   1.   Only about 5 percent of married couples choose not to have children.

   2.   People who choose not to have children pay a social price.

   3.   In couples who choose to forgo parenthood, the woman almost always makes the initial decision and remains more committed to the decision than the man.

      a.   An **early articulator** is someone who knew from childhood that she or he did not want children.

b. A **postponer** is likely to be less definite about whether he or she wants children.

4. Women who complete their education, postpone marriage, and hold jobs outside their home tend to have higher childlessness rates.

5. Many women on the career path feel ambivalence about childbearing.

6. Couples with no children tend to have a slightly higher degree of overall satisfaction and closeness than couples with children.

VII. Looking back/looking forward

Key Concepts

Directions: Identify each of the following key concepts discussed in this chapter.

1. _____ are internalized expectations that tell us when certain life events should happen.

2. Vaillant found that coping styles, or _____, determine people's level of mental health.

3. The development of mature adaptive mechanisms is related to sustained and loving relationships and _____.

4. According to Vaillant, during _____, men tend to work harder, devote themselves to career advancement, and sacrifice play.

5. The method of research used by Levinson is known as the _____.

6. Based on Levinson's work, the _____ phase of early adulthood includes forming a(n) _____, forming _____, developing an occupation, and establishing _____.

7. The final two periods of early adulthood, according to Levinson, form the _____.

8. In early adulthood, individuals must resolve the crisis of _____, according to Erikson.

9. Avoiding intimacy may lead to _____.

10. With regard to friendships, men stress _____ and women stress _____.

11. As individuals move from one monogamous relationship to the next monogamous relationship, the pattern of _____ occurs.

12. The three elements of Sternberg's triangular theory of love are _____, _____, and _____.

13. _____ are what bring people together into romantic or sexual relationships. We tend to meet partners in _____ ways.

14. The _____ is characterized by negotiations about shared concerns and responsibilities in a marriage. In the _____, the man is the breadwinner and head of household, and the woman is the mother and responsible for the domestic tasks. _____ are relationships where the wife brings in some of the income and takes on some decisions with the husband helping the wife at home.

15. Spouses in _____ relationships express the highest levels of marital satisfaction and psychological well-being.

16. Married people are _____ than never-married people. _____ have the lowest levels of well-being.

17. The advantage of being single is _____, and the disadvantage is _____.

18. Living together is known as _____.

19. People who live together are likely to possess personal and demographic characteristics that _____ the risk for divorce.

20. The fear, dread, hostility or prejudice directed toward gay people is called _____.

21. Most divorces occur during _____. Besides a decline in marriage's permanency, _____ are believed to play a role in divorce.

22. Women who committed themselves to the conventional roles of wife and mother but then lost these roles because of separation, divorce, or widowhood and were unprepared for employment and single parenthood are known as _____.

23. Women who expressed high need for _____ experienced less postpartum depression two months after their baby's birth.

24. Marital satisfaction _____ after the birth of the first child.

25. About _____ percent of married couples choose not to have children.

26. A person who knew from childhood that she or he did not want children is a(n) _____. Someone who is less definite about whether he or she would have children is called a(n) _____.

Multiple-Choice Self-Test

Factual / Conceptual Questions

1. The period of adulthood represents a time of _____ than childhood and adolescence.
   a. greater physical maturation
   b. greater diversity
   c. greater growth
   d. fewer choices

2. As compared to normative-crisis theories, timing of events theories are better able to explain
   a. age changes.
   b. dissimilarities among groups.
   c. individual motivations.
   d. situational variables.

3. Which of the following adaptive mechanisms leads to more mature levels of mental health?
   a. Fantasy
   b. Hypochondria
   c. Repression
   d. Sublimation

4. All of the following are functions of mentors *except*
   a. teaching.
   b. guiding.
   c. being intimate.
   d. serving as a model.

5. For Erikson, the crisis in early adulthood involves
   a. identity.
   b. intimacy.
   c. autonomy.
   d. generativity.

6. Which of the following is *not* an essential component of the triangular theory of love?
   a. Passion
   b. Affiliation
   c. Intimacy
   d. Commitment

7. The highest levels of marital satisfaction are associated with _____ marriages.
   a. conventional
   b. equal-partnership
   c. junior-partnership
   d. liberal

8. As compared to never-married individuals in the 1970s, never-married individuals today are
   a. less likely to be employed.
   b. less healthy.
   c. happier.
   d. more depressed.

9. One of the major reasons for the increase in the divorce rate is that
   a. gender roles are becoming more stereotyped.
   b. more individuals are cohabiting and have trouble with the marital transition.
   c. people are getting married at a much younger age and fail to make a mature decision.
   d. there is a decline in the belief that marriage should be permanent.

10. The choice of whether or not to have children seems to
    a. rely more heavily on the husband.
    b. rely more heavily on the wife.
    c. be most often a completely mutual decision.
    d. be made by the dominant member of the couple regardless of their gender.

Application Questions

1. Suzanne and Franklin plan to have a child about a year after they're married because that's what many of their friends have done. Their decision is most consistent with
   a. lifespan role theory.
   b. normative-crisis theory.
   c. psychosocial theory.
   d. timing of events theory.

2. Forty-five-year-old Sid throws tantrums when he doesn't get what he wants. Vaillant would label him a
   a. generative man.
   b. perpetual boy.
   c. neurotic.
   d. psychotic.

3. Bill is moving out of the early adulthood era and into the transition to middle adulthood. According to Levinson, Bill will spend this transition
   a. building new life structures.
   b. in quiet solitude.
   c. trying to recapture his youth.
   d. repressing previous life experiences.

4. Twenty-two-year-old Lee seems incapable of establishing a close relationship with anyone. Erikson would say that Lee is having difficulty with the psychosocial conflict involving
   a. identity.
   b. intimacy.
   c. the superego.
   d. sexuality.

5. Tim, Al, and Sam are friends in their early twenties. They will probably spend much of their time together
   a. discussing their problems concerning relationships.
   b. planning for the future.
   c. providing emotional support for one another.
   d. watching or playing sports.

6. Nina and Marv have been married for thirty-two years, and although they are very much committed to their marriage, they feel no passion and fail to share their feelings. Their love would be classified as
   a. liking.
   b. empty.
   c. companionate.
   d. fatuous.

7. Barb and Rick share responsibilities for maintaining their household and actively discuss the various tasks. Their marriage type is
   a. conventional.
   b. equal partnership.
   c. junior partnership.
   d. new wave.

8. Brent and Jeff are a cohabiting gay couple. As compared to heterosexual married couples, Brent and Jeff will
   a. have lower levels of satisfaction in their relationship.
   b. have lower levels of sexual satisfaction with their partner.
   c. share more information about their sexuality with each other.
   d. show equivalent levels of interpersonal communication.

9. Justine got married right out of high school, had three children, and spent the next ten years raising them. After fourteen years of marriage, her husband suddenly divorced her, leaving her with the children, no job, and no skills. The term that best fits Justine's predicament is
   a. displaced homemaker.
   b. emancipated mom.
   c. traditional housewife.
   d. unconventional parent.

10. Ken and Mary Jo have just had their first child. Most likely, their level of marital satisfaction will
   a. increase dramatically.
   b. increase some.
   c. stay about the same.
   d. decline.

Answer Key

Key Concepts

1. Social clocks
2. adaptive mechanisms
3. a healthy brain
4. career consolidation
5. biographical method
6. novice, Dream, mentoring relationships, intimate relationships
7. culminating phase
8. intimacy versus isolation
9. isolation and self-absorption
10. shared activities/interest, emotional sharing
11. serial monogamy
12. intimacy, passion, decision/commitment
13. Similarities, conventional
14. equal-partner relationship, conventional relationship, Junior-partner relationship
15. equal partnerships
16. happier, Formerly married people
17. freedom, loneliness
18. cohabitation
19. increase
20. homophobia
21. early adulthood, increased expectations of marriage
22. displaced homemakers
23. affiliation
24. declines
25. 5
26. early articulator, postponer

Multiple-Choice Self-Test: Factual / Conceptual Questions

1. Choice (b) is correct. As age increases individual differences also increase, which means there is greater diversity among people. There is greater physical maturation earlier in life rather than later, so choice (a) is incorrect; growth begins to slow as most physical and mental aspects reach their peak, so choice (c) is incorrect; and adults actually have more choices, making choice (d) also incorrect.

2. Choice (b) is correct. The normative-crisis theories often hypothesize stages of development that everyone goes through and thus promote similarity, while timing of events theories indicate that the same event may have different results depending on its timing, which can lead to dissimilarities. Choices (a), (c), and (d)—age changes, individual motivations, and situational variables, respectively—are accounted for equally well (or poorly) by each theory.

3. Choice (d) is correct. Sublimation is the redirecting of typically negative responses into more positive actions. This can be viewed as positive, whereas choices (a), (b), and (c)—fantasy, hypochondria, and regression, respectively—produce negative or neutral consequences.

4. Choice (c) is correct. Mentors are teachers, choice (a); guides, choice (b); and serve as models, choice (d). Although a mentor may also be a friend, that is not one of the primary purposes (since often the mentor's role may necessitate being objective and critical), thus intimacy is not a typical function.

5. Choice (b) is correct. Erikson believed that the crisis of the young adulthood period is intimacy versus isolation. Choice (a), identity, is the crisis during adolescence; choice (c), autonomy, is one of the childhood crises; and choice (d), generativity, is the middle-age crisis.

6. Choice (b) is correct. Passion, choice (a); intimacy, choice (c); and commitment, choice (d), make up the three major components of Sternberg's theory. Affiliation is not one of them.

7. Choice (b) is correct. Marriages in which both partners have true equality seem to show the highest level of satisfaction. Choice (c), junior partnership, has somewhat higher satisfaction than choice (a), conventional, while choice (d), liberal, is not a type of marriage.

8. Choice (c) is correct. Since being single is viewed more positively than it was twenty-five years ago, there is less social pressure to marry. Thus, never-married individuals seem to be happier now than they were in the past. Choices (a), (b), and (d)—less likely to be employed, less healthy, and more depressed, respectively—have no support in the current literature.

9. Choice (d) is correct. Studies suggest that despite the vow "till death do us part," marriage is not viewed as permanent. In a sense the lack of permanence increases the divorce rate, which serves to further reinforce the perception. Choice (a) is inaccurate—actually, stereotypes seem to be decreasing—and although choice (b) is true, it does not seem to contribute to the divorce rate. Contrary to choice (c), people actually marry later now, even though younger marriages are at greater risk for divorce.

10. Choice (b) is correct. Studies suggest that the wife has a greater say in whether or not a couple will have children.

Multiple-Choice Self-Test: Application Questions

1. Choice (d) is correct. The timing of events model implies that there are certain on-times and off-times for events, and this timing is determined by social pressures to conform. The example

clearly illustrates that. The other theories cited—lifespan role, choice (a); normative crisis, choice (b); and psychosocial, choice (c)—do not really comment about specific timing.

2. Choice (b) is correct. Vaillant would characterize this immature behavior on the part of an adult as being a perpetual boy. The opposite of that, mature responding, is captured in choice (a), generative man. Choices (c) and (d), neurotic and psychotic, respectively, are not part of Vaillant's work.

3. Choice (a) is correct. For Levinson, the transitions between different eras of adulthood involve the building of new life structures and are often turbulent times. Thus choice (b), quiet solitude, is incorrect, since upheaval typically occurs, nor is choice (c), trying to recapture his youth, necessarily true (although some may attempt to do that); and choice (d), repressing previous life experiences, is not part of Levinson's theory.

4. Choice (b) is correct. The issue of the young adulthood period is the establishment of intimate relationships with others. Choice (a), identity, is the issue of adolescence, while choice (c), the superego, is not part of Erikson's theory. Although sexuality, choice (d), may be related to intimacy, Erikson looks at both sexual and nonsexual relationships as being part of the young adulthood crisis.

5. Choice (d) is correct. Males tend to spend their time in activities that often center around common interests such as sports. Females, on the other hand, are more intimately involved with one another and tend to focus on those things mentioned in choices (a), (b), and (c).

6. Choice (b) is correct. Sternberg's triangular theory of love has three components: passion, intimacy, and commitment. This example describes a couple that possesses only commitment, which Sternberg classifies as empty. Choice (a), liking, involves only intimacy; choice (c), companionate, involves intimacy with commitment but no passion; and choice (d), fatuous, involves passion and commitment with no intimacy.

7. Choice (b) is correct. Equal partnerships occur when tasks are equally shared and discussed. Choice (a), conventional, is where the husband is the breadwinner and the wife the homemaker; choice (c), junior partnership, is where the husband is the primary breadwinner but the wife contributes; however, housework is still the wife's primary responsibility. Choice (d), new wave, is a nonexistent type.

8. Choice (c) is correct. Gay couples actually communicate more than heterosexual couples, especially with regard to issues about their sexuality. Their levels of satisfaction with their relationship tend to be at least equal to if not greater than that of heterosexual couples, so choices (a) and (b) are incorrect. Their levels of interpersonal communication are also higher, so choice (d) is also incorrect.

9. Choice (a) is correct. The scenario describes what has been termed a "displaced homemaker": the wife gives up her career aspirations early in order to raise a family and then suddenly finds herself without any marketable skills when a divorce occurs and she needs to enter the job market. The other choices are not terms that describe this scenario.

10. Choice (d) is correct. Marital satisfaction shows a U-shaped curve across the family life cycle, with the highest levels being immediately after marriage and after retirement. As children enter the picture, marital satisfaction begins to decline; it reaches its lowest point right before the children leave home.

CHAPTER 14

Middle Adulthood: Physical and Cognitive Development

Learning Objectives

1. Discuss the changes in life expectancy and differentiate between primary and secondary aging.

2. Describe the major physical changes associated with middle age, including strength and appearance.

3. Describe the major changes in the various body systems (cardiovascular, respiratory, and sensory) associated with middle age.

4. Characterize the health concerns of middle adulthood.

5. Identify and describe the major forms of cancer associated with middle age.

6. Discuss the changes in female reproduction during middle age. Identify the signs of and treatment for menopause.

7. Discuss the changes in male reproduction during middle age. Identify the characteristics of the male climacteric.

8. Describe the changes in sexuality and sexual functioning during middle age.

9. Discuss the issues surrounding the question "Does intelligence decline with age?" Describe the findings from early cross-sectional and longitudinal studies and later findings from sequential studies.

10. Distinguish between fluid and crystallized intelligence and describe the changes in each across adulthood.

11. Define what is meant by competence and distinguish between practical intelligence and expertise.

12. Describe the adult learner and differentiate between the skills needed for independent learning and those needed for organized instruction.

13. Discuss why certain individuals return to college during adulthood.

14. Discuss the changes in work and job satisfaction during the middle adulthood years. Describe the influences of race and gender on these changes.

15. Describe the effects of unemployment on middle-aged individuals.

Chapter Overview

Changes in appearance and physical functioning occur in middle adulthood, roughly the period from ages forty to sixty. Primary aging refers to the normal, age-related changes that everyone experiences, while secondary aging refers to pathological aging. During middle adulthood the loss in strength is so minimal that increased skill and experience often compensate. In middle adulthood, the physical signs of aging appear in the hair and skin, and weight tends to increase. The cardiovascular, respiratory, and sensory systems experience declines in function. Health behaviors in early adulthood can lead to healthy middle and later years. Rates of breast and prostate cancer increase during the middle years. The climacteric occurs in both men and women, and these changes affect sexual functioning. All phases of the sexual response cycle continue, but with diminished speed and intensity.

Cross-sectional studies of intelligence suggested that competence declines with age starting around age forty, whereas longitudinal studies show gain until around age sixty. Schaie's sequential studies reveal at least modest gain for all abilities from early adulthood to early middle age. Abilities peak at different ages, change at different rates, and differ systematically for women and men. Schaie's studies also show large differences in how long individuals maintain their mental abilities. Another perspective of examining intelligence in adulthood involves fluid and crystallized intelligence. Crystallized intelligence improves with age, whereas fluid intelligence declines.

Middle-aged individuals tend to do well on measures of practical intelligence and more poorly on conventional laboratory measures. Adults who are experts in their domain rely on frequently used skills and experience to compensate for any declines. Most adults conduct at least one major learning effort each year for a variety of reasons. Some even return to college for self-improvement and career development. Work in middle adulthood calls for reappraisal of early career decisions and new choices that provide continuing challenge. Workers may experience plateauing. Women and racial and ethnic minorities are more likely to plateau before reaching the top because of stereotyping and unequal treatment. Women who work and provide caregiving to their family experience added pressures. Unemployment during middle adulthood has particularly severe effects, especially for men, because they have less social support than women.

Chapter Outline

I. Physical development

II. The biology of aging

    A. Changes in appearance and functioning of the body characterize middle adulthood, which spans roughly ages forty to sixty.

    B. The timing of middle adulthood depends on **life expectancy**.

    C. The changes in middle adulthood are due to **primary aging** and **secondary aging**.

        1. Primary aging refers to the normal, age-related changes that everyone experiences.

        2. Secondary aging refers to pathological aging, and it shows more variability.

III.   Physical functioning in middle adulthood

Most adults do not feel the impact of the decline before age fifty, and some do so much later than that.

A.   Strength

1.   Strength slowly but steadily declines after peaking in early adulthood, but people differ in the amount of strength lost.

2.   Expending maximum effort only at the exact moment it is required helps to conserve energy and makes the decline barely noticeable to most people.

3.   Atrophy of the muscle fibers leads to loss of muscular strength and is part of the aging process, but it can be reduced through exercise.

4.   Bone mass also begins to decrease, although the process can be slowed by ingesting sufficient levels of calcium, doing weight training, and taking replacement estrogen after menopause.

5.   Starting good nutrition and exercise habits in early adulthood can reduce potential problems later in life.

B.   Age-related changes in appearance

1.   The signs of aging become apparent. The skin becomes less elastic and begins to sag and wrinkle.

2.   Graying begins due to loss of pigment, and hair becomes thinner.

3.   People tend to gain weight through the mid- to late fifties as fatty tissue and muscle are redistributed throughout the body.

a.   Middle-aged adults tend to store fat in the thighs, abdomen, waist, back, and upper arms.

b.   The "middle-age spread" is not inevitable with regular exercise and proper diet.

C.   Cardiovascular system changes

1.   The cardiovascular system loses efficiency during middle adulthood.

2.   Maximum oxygen consumption and the heart rate attained during maximum levels of exertion decline.

3.   Continuous and regular exercise helps to counteract these changes.

D.   Respiratory system changes

1.   The breathing apparatus and tissues of the lungs change due to primary aging.

2.   The amount of oxygen in the blood after passing through the lungs decreases with age.

3. Lifelong endurance training increases **vital capacity**, which is the total volume of air that moves in and out of the lungs during maximal exertion.

E. Sensory system changes

1. By age fifty, most people require reading glasses or bifocals if they already wear glasses as the lens of the eye continually grows fibers without shedding the old ones. This results in the lens thickening and gradually losing its capacity to accommodate.

2. Hearing loss begins gradually in early adulthood and progresses until the eighties.

3. Most adults are able to function normally despite these losses.

IV. Health in middle adulthood

Adults become more aware of health issues than when they were younger. They pay more attention to body monitoring, reflecting the realities of chronic disease and the effects of lifelong behaviors taking their toll. **Morbidity** refers to the number of cases of disease, while **mortality** refers to the number of deaths. Most middle-aged adults are not much different in physical health than young adults.

A. Health and health-compromising behaviors

1. Behaviors at younger ages lay the groundwork for health and well-being in later life.

2. Health-promoting behaviors positively affect health in several ways.

   a. The cardiovascular and respiratory systems benefit.

   b. Weight is controlled.

   c. Exercise enhances the ability to cope with psychosocial stressors.

3. Health-compromising behaviors are often linked; for example, individuals who smoke heavily are also likely to drink heavily.

4. Research has shown that drinking to "drown sorrows" is more of a risk factor for cancer and coronary heart disease than "pleasure" drinking.

• Perspectives: The gender gap in life expectancy

B. Breast cancer

1. Lifestyle factors play a role in breast cancer.

2. More new cases of breast cancer than lung cancer are diagnosed each year.

3. The overall incidence of breast cancer is higher for White women than for African American women, but the death rate is greater for African Americans and may be related to socioeconomic factors.

4. Cultural factors may also be important in breast cancer screening and seeking and following medical care.

C. Prostate cancer

1. Prostate cancer is the most common cancer in men, and its incidence has increased since 1968.

2. Causes of prostate cancer are unknown but may be related to family history, ethnicity, socioeconomic status, diet, and environmental factors.

3. Prostate cancer is slow-growing and unlikely to produce symptoms.

a. It is typically discovered during surgery, digital exam, or a blood test called PSA.

b. The blood test may fail to detect cancer and sometimes can falsely indicate cancer.

4. There is no standard recommended treatment for prostate cancer. Some treatments may include removal of the prostate and/or radiation.

V. Reproductive changes

The gradual reduction in sex hormone production is called the **climacteric**; it is more noticeable in women than in men.

A. Menopause

1. When a previously menstruating woman has an entire year without a menstrual period, she has reached **menopause**.

2. Attitudes regarding menopause are generally negative, but not all cultures share this view of menopause.

3. Decreased ovarian functioning causes menopause, which ultimately leads to reduced levels of estrogen and progesterone.

4. Menopause occurs in three stages.

a. Premenopause is characterized by the ovaries gradually reducing hormone production.

b. Menopause is the second stage of the female climacteric.

c. Postmenopause, the third stage, occurs when hormonal levels stabilize and menopausal signs subside.

5. The most common physical sign of menopause is the hot flash. Vaginal changes are another common sign of menopause. Only about 10 percent of women experience severe symptoms.

6. The surgical removal of the uterus, called **hysterectomy**, is performed as a treatment for cancer and can cause sudden onset of menopause. **Oophorectomy**, which is the surgical removal of the ovaries, always triggers menopause.

7. **Estrogen replacement therapy (ERT)** and **hormone replacement therapy (HRT)** are options to alleviate menopausal symptoms by replacing the natural decrease in hormones.

    a. These replacement therapies can increase the risk for cancer.

    b. In combination with exercise and diet, they can help prevent **osteoporosis**.

    c. Women who take hormones are generally more affluent and healthier than those who do not and would have lower rates of disease anyway.

- A multicultural view: Japanese and North American attitudes toward menopause

B. The male climacteric

    1. Unlike menopause, the male climacteric does not lead to sterility.

    2. Decreased testicular functioning characterizes the male climacteric, causing a reduction in the number and vitality of sperm and a gradual reduction in testosterone production.

    3. The most notable changes affect the prostate gland, with **hypertrophy** occurring, causing pressure on the urethra and restricting and eventually blocking urine flow.

    4. Many signs of the male climacteric are similar to those attributed to menopause.

VI. Sexuality in middle adulthood

The changes in the reproductive systems of men and women have implications for sexual functioning.

A. Female sexuality

    1. Most women find that the hormonal changes of menopause affect their sexual responsiveness.

    2. The cycles of sexual response continue, but with diminished speed and intensity.

    3. A reduction of vaginal lubrication can cause irritation or pain during intercourse.

    4. There is no evidence of decline in postmenopausal women's physical capacity for sex.

B. Male sexuality

    1. Erections take longer to obtain and are not as hard as they were earlier in life.

    2. Changes in orgasm are also experienced by aging men, with a reduction in intensity and an increase in the refractory period.

VII. Gradual decline

Most of the decline of primary aging is so slight that it has only a minor impact on daily life. The speed of decline and the risks of morbidity and mortality associated with secondary aging are linked to genetic make-up, health behaviors, and health-compromising behaviors.

VIII. Cognitive development

Middle adulthood is often referred to as the time of life when adults are responsible for maintaining and enhancing the culture, but in contemporary America, youthfulness is more admired, and middle adulthood is thought to be "over the hill."

IX. Does intelligence decline with age?

It is difficult to determine the course of cognitive competence or intelligence over the adult years due to several factors.

A. Early negative studies

1. Early studies suggested that intellectual decline begins in the teenage years.

2. Later studies suggest that the decline occurs in early adulthood.

3. More recent research has studied whether the differences in performance are due to age-related declines or to other variables.

B. Cross-sectional versus longitudinal studies

1. Cross-sectional studies assume that the older subjects perform at the same level as the younger subjects did when they were young. However, cohort differences may challenge this assumption.

2. Cross-sectional studies may "create" age decline because they confound cohort differences with age.

3. Longitudinal studies measure intelligence across adulthood and minimize negative age patterns.

4. Longitudinal studies may be biased in a positive direction since people who perform poorly are less likely to be available for retesting.

5. In contrast to cross-sectional studies, longitudinal studies suggest a more positive view of intellectual competence in middle adulthood.

C. Schaie's sequential studies

1. Schaie began a longitudinal study of a cross-sectional sample that resulted in a sequential study. The study assessed the mental abilities of more than five thousand adults.

2. The SLS used the Primary Mental Abilities battery and assessed a number of abilities.

3. The results indicate no uniform pattern of age-related changes in adulthood across all intellectual abilities. Abilities tend to peak at different ages, change at different rates, and differ systematically for women and men.

4. Age-related changes in word fluency were found. All abilities showed some decline by age sixty-seven, but the declines were modest until the eighties.

5. Research also revealed that age-related declines depend on the ability being measured.

6. Individual performance varied widely, with some showing stability and some showing decline. Schaie identified seven factors that reduce the risk of cognitive decline in old age.

7. Age-related decline in intellectual abilities is multifaceted and multidimensional.

   a. The onset and rate of decline differ for the various abilities and with gender.

   b. Number skills show the sharpest decline overall, and word fluency begins to decline the soonest.

   c. Environmental and personality factors account for the large differences in how long individuals maintain their mental abilities.

X. Fluid and crystallized intelligence

Horn studied fluid and crystallized intelligence, two general types of abilities, both of which are influenced by hereditary and environmental factors.

A. Two types of intelligence

   1. **Crystallized intelligence** refers to learned cognitive processes and primary abilities.

   2. **Fluid intelligence** is the ability to process new information in novel situations. It depends more on neurological development and less on education.

   3. Each type changes differently with age.

      a. Crystallized intelligence improves or stabilizes with age.

      b. Fluid intelligence peaks in late adolescence and declines rapidly from early adulthood to old age.

B. Negative assessment

   1. Fluid intelligence is seen as the most salient indicator of intellectual capacities since it allows a person to understand relations, comprehend implications, and draw inferences, and it is independent of cultural and experiential influences.

   2. Age-related declines in fluid intelligence result from accumulations of small losses of brain function.

C. Conflicting views

   1. Horn's theory has been criticized on several grounds, primarily because it is based on cross-sectional research and confounds cohort differences with age differences.

   2. Longitudinal research is criticized for painting a falsely positive picture.

   3. Different patterns of age-related declines may be due to speed rather than to fluid-crystallized differences.

XI. Competence

Performance on traditional laboratory problem-solving tasks decreases during the adult years, while performance in the real world increases at least through middle age. Traditional laboratory problem-solving tasks have limited value testing intellectual development in middle adulthood. **Practical intelligence** involves the application of intellectual skills to everyday activities, whereas **expertise** and wisdom refer to behaviors that require intelligence as well as specialized experience in specific domains.

A. Practical intelligence

   1. Performance on more practical problem-solving tasks increases from age twenty to age fifty and then declines after that.

   2. These findings are consistent with real-life experience, in which middle-aged adults typically are more knowledgeable than young adults.

B. Expertise

   1. Experience is highly relevant to competence and much less relevant to abstract assessment of cognitive abilities.

   2. This explains why older adults hold many of the most responsible and challenging leadership positions in society but perform at lower levels on conventional psychometric and abstract problem-solving tasks than younger adults do.

   3. Despite declining fluid abilities, older adults continue to function efficiently when given tasks that allow them to use their expert knowledge.

      a. Experience may maintain or preserve abilities that would decline in the absence of experience.

      b. Development of competence may depend on a certain level of fluid intelligence, whereas maintenance of competence no longer requires the same level.

      c. Increased experience may somehow lead to compensation for declining abilities.

   4. Skill appears to matter more than age in domain-specific tasks, whereas age is important in general, abstract tasks.

   5. Aging appears to lead to poorer performance in nonpracticed tasks and slower acquisition of new skills, particularly those that depend on new types of knowledge.

XII. The adult learner

Adults have a variety of motivations for adult learning, including job or occupation, managing home and family, hobby or leisure time activity, and puzzlement.

A. Adult education

   1. Adult education refers to all non-full-time educational activities.

   2. Most of the learning done by adults is self-planned, and these activities are very important to them.

3. Life changes, or transitions, are often the impetus for adult learning.

4. Triggers, or a specific life event that generates the decision to learn at that time, often precipitate a transition.

5. Career transitions are the most common trigger for men and women. Family is more often the trigger for women than for men.

6. Family may also serve as a barrier to women pursuing adult education.

B. Returning to college

1. Adults have been returning to college in record numbers.

2. Typically adults return to college because they are dissatisfied with their lives and regard finishing their education as a way to improve themselves.

3. Older students experience cognitive gains in critical thinking.

4. Career development is the most frequent reason for returning to college in the middle years.

- Working with Carol Singer, associate dean of continuing education: Counseling students returning to college

XIII. Work in middle adulthood

Midlife workers are confronted with fear of job loss and **plateauing**, which is reaching a point of constricted occupational opportunity. Mid-to-late-career stages are often accompanied by negative emotions and feelings of personal failure. Some workers experience **burnout**, or disillusionment and exhaustion on the job.

A. Age and job satisfaction

1. Older people are more satisfied with their jobs than younger people are.

2. There appear to be distinctly different age satisfaction curves among nonprofessionals, elite professionals, and ordinary professionals.

B. Racial and ethnic minorities

1. Racial and ethnic minorities are more likely to plateau long before they reach their corporate dream.

2. As minorities climb the corporate ladder, they become more isolated from same-sex or same-race superiors or peers. Their status becomes more obviously "token," and they are more likely to feel alienated.

3. Minorities and women face problems that do not affect White males. As a result they must meet higher performance standards than White men, with fewer resources and more barriers.

C. Gender

1. Men constitute the majority of full-time workers age fifty and older, and women comprise the majority of part-time workers.

2. New family issues, like providing care for aging parents, may put pressure on midlife women's employment.

3. Caregivers are more likely than other employees to report conflicts between work and family responsibilities and are more likely to miss work.

D. Unemployment

1. Unemployed workers feel as if they are without part of themselves, since work is an important aspect of one's identity.

2. Responses to job loss follow the stages of initial shock, relief/relaxation, efforts to become reemployed, frustration, and resignation to being out of work.

3. Unemployment has a negative impact on physical, mental, and social well-being.

4. The psychological impact of unemployment may be greater for male workers than for female workers.

XIV. Change and growth

Key Concepts

Directions: Identify each of the following key concepts discussed in this chapter.

1. The statistical estimate of the probable number of years remaining in the life of an individual based on the likelihood that members of a particular birth cohort will die at various ages is called _____.

2. _____ refers to the normal, age-related changes that everyone experiences.

3. Pathological aging is sometimes called _____.

4. Changes in strength for most people are _____.

5. _____ can help to counteract age-related changes in the cardiovascular system.

6. The total volume of air that moves in and out of the lungs during maximal exertion is called _____.

7. The process of changing the shape of the lens to focus is _____.

8. The number of cases of a disease is _____; _____ refers to the number of deaths.

9. The death rates from breast cancer among African American women is _____ than for White women.

10. The most common cancer in men is _____. A blood test used to detect this cancer is called _____.

11. The process of a reduction of sex hormone production is called the _____; in women it is known as _____.

12. The most common sign of menopause is the _____ and _____.

13. The surgical removal of the uterus is _____, and the surgical removal of the ovaries is _____.

14. Two replacement treatments for menopause are _____ and _____.

15. The degeneration of the bone is called _____.

16. In the male climacteric, the overgrowth of glandular cells is called _____.

17. The early studies of age-related changes in intelligence suggest that it starts to decline in the _____. Cross-sectional studies confound _____ differences with age. Longitudinal research suggests that mental abilities are _____ in middle adulthood.

18. Schaie's research combined cross-sectional samples with longitudinal study to form a(n) _____ study. _____ was the only primary ability that clearly decreased in middle adulthood.

19. _____ is learned cognitive processes and primary abilities. The ability to process new information in novel situations is _____, and it _____ with age.

20. The application of intellectual skills to everyday activities is termed _____. _____ and wisdom refer to behaviors that require intelligence as well as specialized experience in ____ domains.

21. Many adults pursue education because they've experienced some _____.

22. Reaching a point of constricted occupational opportunity is called _____. If a worker experiences disillusionment and exhaustion on the job, _____ occurs.

23. Most full-time workers are _____, while most part-time workers are _____.

24. The psychological impact of unemployment may be greater for _____ workers.

Multiple-Choice Self-Test

Factual / Conceptual Questions

1. Since 1900, life expectancy for White males has increased by about _____ years.
   a. eleven
   b. eighteen
   c. twenty-six
   d. thirty-three

2. Middle-aged individuals tend to store fat in all of the following locations *except*
   a. lower legs.
   b. thighs.
   c. upper arms.
   d. waist.

3. Which of the following is true concerning death rates during adulthood?
   a. Death rates for heart disease and cancer are greater for males.
   b. Death rates for heart disease and cancer are greater for females.
   c. Death rates for heart disease are greater for males, while death rates for cancer are greater for females.
   d. Death rates for heart disease are greater for females, while death rates for cancer are greater for males.

4. Which of the following is the most common form of cancer in men?
   a. Colon
   b. Liver
   c. Lung
   d. Prostate

5. All of the following are typical changes in male sexuality associated with middle age *except*
   a. increased refractory period.
   b. premature ejaculation.
   c. reduced semen production.
   d. slower erections.

6. Early studies of adult intelligence led researchers to conclude that
   a. as age increases, intelligence tends to decrease.
   b. intelligence peaks at age forty and then remains constant throughout the remaining adult years.
   c. most individuals continue to increase in intelligence across adulthood.
   d. the only declines in intelligence found during adulthood are directly attributed to disease.

7. The major advantage of using the sequential design to study intelligence is that it
   a. allows for comparisons among cohorts at one time and traces actual development over time.
   b. allows researchers to examine changes through direct experimental manipulation.
   c. provides a more reliable measure of intelligence.
   d. uses more subjects than either longitudinal or cross-sectional studies.

8. As age increases, fluid intelligence _____ and crystallized intelligence _____.
   a. increases, increases
   b. decreases, decreases
   c. increases, decreases
   d. decreases, increases

9. Adults who participate in adult education tend to
   a. be blue-collar workers.
   b. be unemployed.
   c. be well educated.
   d. live in larger cities.

10. In general, older people are
    a. more satisfied with their jobs than younger workers.
    b. more satisfied with their jobs than middle-aged workers but less satisfied than younger workers.
    c. just as satisfied with their jobs as middle-aged workers but less satisfied than younger workers.
    d. just as satisfied with their jobs as all other workers.

Application Questions

1. Lydia has just celebrated her sixty-fifth birthday and is in good health. She can probably expect to live another _____ years.
   a. six
   b. eleven
   c. nineteen
   d. twenty-five

2. As a teenager, Val enjoyed lying out at the beach in the sun and wind, while her identical twin sister, Sal, preferred the indoors. Now that they have both reached their mid-forties, we can expect that Val will
   a. have more wrinkles than Sal.
   b. have darker skin than Sal.
   c. have a more youthful look than Sal.
   d. continue to look the same as Sal.

3. Thirty-year-old Bernie wears glasses because he is nearsighted. Chances are that by the time he reaches fifty
   a. he'll need a much stronger prescription for his nearsightedness.
   b. he'll need bifocals.
   c. his need for glasses will decrease.
   d. he'll develop glaucoma.

4. Who is most likely to smoke cigarettes?
   a. Dawn, a White woman who has five or six drinks per day and prefers hard liquor
   b. Karen, a Black woman who has two or three glasses of wine per day
   c. Bradley, a Black man who drinks three or four beers per day
   d. Dominick, a White man who drinks four or five glasses of wine or beer per day

5. Fifty-six-year-old Maya is experiencing night sweats, some insomnia, and occasional warm sensations that travel from her chest to her face. Maya seems to be having symptoms most often associated with
   a. breast cancer.
   b. cardiovascular disease.
   c. menopause.
   d. stroke.

6. Which of the following tasks would a psychologist most likely use to test crystallized intelligence?
   a. A vocabulary test
   b. Putting together a complex puzzle
   c. Stacking blocks
   d. A concept formation test

7. Of the following, who is using practical intelligence?
   a. Consuela, who is learning to drive a car
   b. Hiroshi, who is planning what to plant in his vegetable garden
   c. Mary Lou, who is studying for her nutrition exam
   d. Mitch, who is assisting a TV repairman

8. Kurt has been working as a mason for over fifteen years. When he prepares his mortar, he doesn't measure anything but just looks and feels it for proper consistency. Kurt's approach to his work demonstrates
   a. expertise.
   b. fluid intelligence.
   c. practical knowledge.
   d. recklessness.

9. Fifty-year-old Ed does not see any more advancement in his job as an accountant for a major corporation. He feels his job has become quite routine and predictable. Ed is most likely experiencing
   a. burnout.
   b. plateauing.
   c. retrenchment.
   d. surfing.

10. Forty-seven-year-old Natalie, who has been with the same company for seventeen years, has just been let go as the company downsizes after a merger. Natalie's initial reaction to her job loss is likely to be
   a. depression.
   b. frustration.
   c. relief.
   d. shock.

Answer Key

Key Concepts

1. life expectancy
2. Primary aging
3. secondary aging
4. barely noticeable
5. Exercise
6. vital capacity
7. accommodation
8. morbidity, mortality
9. higher
10. prostate cancer, PSA
11. climacteric, menopause
12. hot flash, atrophy of the vagina
13. hysterectomy, oophorectomy
14. estrogen replacement therapy, hormone replacement therapy
15. osteoporosis
16. hypertrophy
17. teenage years, cohort, stable
18. sequential, Word fluency
19. Crystallized intelligence, fluid intelligence, declines
20. practical intelligence, Expertise, specific
21. transition (trigger)
22. plateauing, burnout
23. male, female
24. male

Multiple-Choice Self-Test: Factual / Conceptual Questions

1. Choice (c) is correct. In 1900 the life expectancy was 46.6 years for a White male; in 1990 it was 72.7 years, and continues to increase. The difference is 26.1 years.

2. Choice (a) is correct. Middle-aged adults store fat in the thighs, abdomen, waist, back, and upper arms, not in the lower legs.

3. Choice (a) is correct. Statistics show that death rates for cancer and cardiovascular disease are higher for males across the entire lifespan.

4. Choice (d) is correct. For men, prostate cancer is the most common form of cancer. The other forms—colon, liver, and lung—are less common for men.

5. Choice (b) is correct. As men age, it takes them longer to obtain an erection, choice (d); there is lower semen as well as sperm production, choice (c); and it takes a longer time to be sexually responsive after intercourse, choice (a). Premature ejaculation is a problem typically found in younger individuals.

6. Choice (a) is correct. Early studies, which were primarily cross-sectional studies, showed decreases in intelligence associated with age. The differences were most likely due to cohort rather than to age differences. Choices (b), (c), and (d) are not correct.

7. Choice (a) is correct. A sequential study combines aspects of longitudinal and cross-sectional studies and thus allows for a better examination of age effects and cohort effects separately. It does not involve experimental manipulation, so choice (b) is incorrect; nor is it necessarily any more reliable, making choice (c) incorrect. It also does not require more subjects, so choice (d) is incorrect as well.

8. Choice (d) is correct. Fluid intelligence, the ability to process new information, decreases, while our storehouse of knowledge, crystallized intelligence, increases.

9. Choice (c) is correct. Adult education involves a wide range of courses and programs. In general, individuals who are already well educated tend to get more education. White-collar workers are more likely to take adult education courses than blue-collar workers, so choice (a) is incorrect. Adults who live in suburbs and those who are currently employed also tend to take adult education courses, making choices (b) and (d) incorrect as well.

10. Choice (a) is correct. Studies of job satisfaction indicate that as age increases, job satisfaction increases. Thus, older workers seem more satisfied than any other group.

Multiple-Choice Self-Test: Application Questions

1. Choice (c) is correct. A female who reaches sixty-five years of age can expect to live to be eighty-four years of age, an additional nineteen years.

2. Choice (a) is correct. Exposure to sun and wind early in life decreases the elasticity of the skin, causing wrinkles. Sal, who did not have that exposure, should have fewer wrinkles. Skin also becomes paler as age increases, which eliminates choice (b).

3. Choice (b) is correct. Individuals who are nearsighted generally need bifocals as they age because of loss of close vision due to the inflexibility of the lens. Bernie's nearsightedness will probably stay about the same, making choices (a) and (c) incorrect, and although glaucoma

becomes a greater risk as people age, it is not related to Bernie's nearsightedness, so choice (d) is also incorrect.

4. Choice (a) is correct. The relevant variables in this question are sex (females being more likely to smoke than males), amount of drinking (heavier drinkers smoke more), and choice of liquor (hard liquor drinkers smoke more than beer or wine drinkers). Dawn fits all these variables, while the others do not.

5. Choice (c) is correct. The list of symptoms is consistent with menopause, not breast cancer, cardiovascular disease, or stroke. The warm sensations are hot flashes.

6. Choice (a) is correct. Crystallized intelligence involves our repository of accumulated knowledge, which would include such things as general knowledge and, in this case, vocabulary. The other choices—putting together a puzzle, stacking blocks, and a concept formation test—rely more on fluid intelligence.

7. Choice (b) is correct. Practical intelligence involves the application of intelligence to everyday activities. The best example of this is planning a vegetable garden, since it requires not only the knowledge of what will grow well, but also what the gardener's family will eat and how much. The other choices—learning to drive a car, studying for a nutrition exam, and assisting a TV repairman—tend to require more expert knowledge than practical intelligence.

8. Choice (a) is correct. Kurt is able to skip steps because he has learned his work very well and uses different cues to make his decision. This is characteristic of what an expert does.

9. Choice (b) is correct. Apparently Ed has reached his peak in his job and should not expect any further advancement (except, perhaps, cost-of-living adjustments). This is known as reaching the plateau of his career. Choice (a), burnout, occurs when there is too much stress for a prolonged period of time; choices (c) and (d), retrenchment and surfing, respectively, are not terms associated with career development.

10. Choice (d) is correct. Although the other choices—depression, frustration, and relief—are all emotions that may occur when loss of a job occurs, the immediate reaction is typically shock.

CHAPTER 15

Middle Adulthood: Psychosocial Development

Learning Objectives

1. Describe the overall variations in personality and other characteristics during middle adulthood.

2. Discuss the views that support the notion of a midlife crisis. Describe the data that support this view.

3. Discuss the views that support the notion that there is no midlife crisis. Describe the data that support this view.

4. Discuss the alternative view that argues for a midlife transition.

5. Describe the characteristics of long-term marriages. In particular, discuss marital satisfaction during the family life cycle.

6. Discuss the impact of divorce during middle adulthood.

7. Describe the kinds of issues members of the "sandwich generation" confront.

8. Describe how parents respond when their children leave the family to go off on their own.

9. Discuss the role of grandparents in middle-age adulthood, including off-time grandparenthood and grandparents as surrogate parents.

10. Discuss the changing relationship between middle-aged adults and their aging parents.

11. Describe middle-aged sibling relationships, including how siblings might deal with a family crisis.

12. Discuss the middle-aged adult's response to the death of a parent.

13. Describe how middle-aged individuals tend to use leisure time. Discuss leisure activities across the lifespan and identify the variables that influence leisure-time activities.

14. Distinguish between wills and advance directives. Explain why middle age is a good time to make these kinds of plans.

Chapter Overview

A number of contrasting images regarding middle age exist, including midlife as a boring plateau and as a time of inevitable crisis. Development theorists like Gould, Vaillant, and Levinson built on Erikson's model of midlife crisis. Erikson believed that middle-aged individuals experience a normative crisis in the task of generativity versus stagnation. Some researchers find little evidence of crisis, while others see it as the normative midlife experience. A number of variables, such as gender and socioeconomic status, determine whether the transition will result in a crisis. Men are more likely than women to experience a midlife crisis.

With regard to marriage, middle-aged and older marriages are happier than marriages in earlier stages of the family life cycle. Divorce has a significant impact on middle-aged women and often results in a lower standard of living. Family relationships are diverse during middle age. Marital satisfaction declines while parenting adolescent children. As these children grow into early adulthood, their relationships with their parents generally improve and are characterized by two-way emotional support. An "empty nest" generally results in improved marital satisfaction and opportunities for self-development and autonomy. Many young adults remain at home or return home, creating the potential for conflict.

Grandparents are called on to assist in many different ways, depending on socioeconomic status, race/ethnicity, and circumstances of the family. Support can be financial, emotional, and/or surrogate parenting. Most middle-aged individuals have warm and satisfying relationships with their aging parents. Aging parents often provide financial and emotional support to their middle-aged children. When their parents become frail, daughters tend to provide more care for their aging parents than do sons. Bereavement over parental death involves many emotions and can lead to growth and changes in levels of maturity and generativity.

There is evidence of both continuity and change in leisure activities during midlife, depending on whether the studies are cross-sectional or longitudinal. Leisure provides psychological benefits and can provide preparation for late adulthood. Wills and advance directives enable individuals to take control of after-death choices as well as choices about medical care and life-sustaining equipment. Midlife is a time to prepare for retirement. Highly committed professionals may avoid planning for retirement and have problems adjusting to retirement.

Chapter Outline

   I. A multiplicity of images of middle age

      A. Many images, often contradictory, exist of middle age. Like early adulthood, there is much variability to middle adulthood.

      B. People tend to believe that following an increase in desirable traits in early adulthood, there is a moderate decrease in middle age, paralleling an increase in undesirable traits in old age.

      C. Perceptions of life periods vary by social class, gender, and age.

  II. Crisis or no crisis?

Developmental theories reveal differing perspectives on the experience of midlife. Havighurst identified seven developmental tasks of middle age. The tasks are associated with **normative life events** and **nonnormative life events**. Erikson believed that middle-aged individuals experience a normative crisis in the task of **generativity versus stagnation**. Some researchers question whether Erikson's theory applies well to women. Stage theories of adult development focus on midlife crisis as a normal component of midlife. A **midlife crisis** refers to the radical changes within the personality associated with the adult's reexamination of goals, priorities, and life accomplishments in middle age.

A. Normative-crisis module: Midlife crisis

    1. Gould found the transformation of middle adulthood to be the most significant one in adulthood.

        a. Individuals begin to confront the long-held assumption of immortality resulting in a need to question and reassess priorities.

        b. How an individual negotiates the midlife crisis determines the individual's adaptation to old age.

    2. Vaillant argues that midlife brings forth a sense of life's limits and a need to use time wisely.

        a. Pain during the forties is seen as preparation for entering a new stage.

        b. A heightened self-awareness results and leads to further growth and opens the way for a sense of generativity.

    3. Using the biographical method, Levinson found that men come to terms with the Dream and how it didn't come to fruition; based on this, men revise the Dream and make changes in lifestyle.

        a. Drastic changes are made by some men; for others, the change is still important though less obvious.

        b. Men struggle within the self and the external world, and if this struggle is not experienced, a later developmental crisis is likely to occur.

    4. Women tend to experience nurturance and investment in relationships rather than a normative midlife crisis.

B. No crisis

    1. The evidence for midlife crisis comes from clinical impressions from people seeking help dealing with issues related to their stage of life or from nonrandomly selected samples.

    2. The frequency of midlife crisis is overestimated by clinicians.

    3. When middle-aged individuals are randomly selected, they rarely report a crisis.

    4. Costa and McCrea focus on the **trait** as a dimension of psychological functioning.

        a. Traits contribute to the person's basic tendencies.

        b. Specific behaviors may change, but basic tendencies do not.

    5. Cross-sectional studies show little consistency of traits.

        a. Longitudinal studies show that personality is quite stable after about age thirty.

      b.   Since personality is highly predictable over long periods of time, it enables individuals to prepare for successful aging.

C. Midlife transition

    1.   Another theory argues that men in their forties experience a transition to middle age in which their perspective on life changes, but they do not necessarily experience a crisis. Women (including women with careers) do not have the same experience, as they have organized their lives around the life cycle of the family, whereas men have organized their lives around work.

    2.   Not all men are willing to undergo self-examination, and this tendency can be categorized into four personality types based on degrees of life satisfaction and ability to confront stress.

        a.   Antiheroes and transcendent-generative men openly confront stress.

        b.   Pseudo-developed and punitive-disenchanted men deny stress.

    3.   Some men experience midlife crisis and others do not. Upper-class and well-educated middle-class men use the midlife transition to reexamine and change earlier choices and solutions.

III. Marriage and divorce

A. Long-term marriage

    1.   Research reveals that in discussing pleasant topics, elderly couples were more affectionate than middle-aged couples, while middle-aged couples displayed more interest, humor, anger, and disgust.

    2.   When discussing conflict in their relationship, older couples managed to express higher levels of affection and lower levels of negative feelings toward their partners.

    3.   Positive emotions are more likely to emerge in happy marriages than in unhappy marriages, even when discussing marital conflict.

    4.   Wives show more emotion and a greater range of emotions than husbands, while husbands show more defensiveness.

    5.   Husbands and wives mention very similar qualities to which they attribute long-term marriage.

B. The family life cycle

    1.   The **family life cycle** is a series of predictable stages through which families pass.

    2.   Families are placed into stages based on the ages of the children and the age of the wife.

    3.   The different stages of the family life cycle are associated with different levels of marital satisfaction.

4. Gender role attitudes correlated with household involvement of husbands and wives.

   a. More stage I and II families were characterized by equal partnerships.

   b. In stage III and IV families, the wives were likely to be modern and the husband traditional.

5. Gender role attitudes are correlated with employment of stage I and II wives; when husbands and wives were both traditional, the young wife was unlikely to be employed.

6. Wives reported distress when their husbands experienced competing demands, and the husbands reported distress when their wives spent large amounts of time at work.

7. Family life stage was highly correlated with strain for dual-earner families.

   a. Younger dual-earner husbands experienced more strain than older ones.

   b. Younger families experience higher role strain between occupational and family demands than middle-aged and older couples.

   c. The husband's role strain differentiates the harried families from the calmer ones.

8. Middle-aged families are happier than those in the earlier stages.

   a. Marital satisfaction follows a curvilinear path over the family life cycle.

   b. The presence of younger children creates demand, lowering marital interaction and happiness.

   c. In long-term marriages, marital satisfaction dips during the childrearing years.

   d. Children are rated as the largest source of marital conflict for middle-aged couples.

- Perspectives: The effects of middle-aged adult children's problems on older parents

C. Divorce

   1. Most divorces occur before middle age.

   2. Divorce during middle adulthood has a significant impact on women, men, and their children.

      a. Divorce can represent entry into a lifetime single status.

      b. For women, separation and divorce usually lower the standard of living significantly.

      c. For men, divorce or separation usually means that they see their children far less often, since custody of young children is frequently awarded to mothers. This has implications for the father-child relations and the well-being of men after age fifty.

3. Divorces that occur when the children are already out of the house can have significant effects.

   a. Recent parental divorce is associated with reduced intimacy and contact between fathers and their children.

   b. Lack of contact between fathers and children of recent divorce may be due to lack of interest on the part of the father, ongoing conflict with the ex-wife, forcing children to take sides, personal problems, and geographic distance.

4. Fathers may lack kinkeeping skills, which are skills that keep the individual in touch with other family members.

IV. Family relationships

Middle-aged adults have been called the **sandwich generation**; they are caught between the needs of adjacent generations.

A. Adolescent children

1. Adolescent children have the most detrimental impact on marital satisfaction.

2. An authoritative parenting style promotes adolescent development.

3. Having an adolescent may cause an adult to reassess his or her own self and goals, and this may cause crises.

4. For some families, adolescence is characterized by reduced interaction and closeness with families; this may not be true for all families, especially African American families, where the family represents a safe haven and where higher levels of parental control and family intimacy are reported.

5. Research reveals that there is conflict over control in every culture and in every historical period.

B. Young adult children

1. The parent-child relationship changes when the child becomes an adult.

2. Young adult children do not necessarily become fully independent and may rely on their parents for financial and emotional support, and they may return home for holidays, summer vacations, and whenever they feel the need.

3. When children are in their forties and their parents in their seventies, the support tends to shift from parent to child to child to parent, although ethnicity and family income may influence the flow of money between generations.

4. An "empty nest" generally results in improved marital satisfaction and opportunities for self-development and autonomy and even employment for wives.

5. Wives appear to benefit more than husbands from the empty nest.

6. Many young adults never leave home or return one or more times to the parental household.

    a. Children's marital status is the best predictor of coresiding.

    b. All racial and ethnic minorities are more likely than Whites to live in multigenerational households.

    c. Coresiding adults and their parents influence each other and monitor each other. This can lead to conflict.

- Working with Joan Stone, victim advocate: Helping victims of abusive family relationships

C. Grandparenting

    1. In general, couples become grandparents in their late forties and early fifties, and the role of grandparenting is likely to last three or four decades.

    2. Timing affects how people experience the transition to grandparenting.

        a. "Right time" grandparenting is in late middle age and can be a positive experience. Very early "off-time" grandparenting can be very distressing.

        b. Social class influences timing of grandparenthood.

    3. Grandparents are generally viewed as a valuable resource. The way that resource is used depends on the family's circumstances.

        a. Grandparents can provide a sense of family continuity and family history.

        b. Grandparents can provide substantial assistance to their adult children and grandchildren.

    4. Some gender differences exist in how grandparents view their relationships with their grandchildren.

        a. Grandmothers report greater satisfaction from relationships with their grandchildren than grandfathers.

        b. Grandfathers place greater stress on generational extension of the family and indulging grandchildren.

    5. Sometimes grandparents are called on to become surrogate parents.

        a. Some reasons for grandparents parenting their grandchildren are parental drug addiction, emotional problems, mental problems, incarceration, and AIDS.

        b. The role is associated with both challenges and rewards.

    6. Research suggests possible racial and ethnic differences in self-perceptions among grandparents and perceptions of grandchildren. Social class, unemployment, moving away from home, and marital status are confounding variables.

- A multicultural view: Diversity in intergenerational families

D. Aging parents

1. As middle-aged adults become grandparents, their own parents are likely to be reaching late adulthood; middle-aged adults and their aging parents report high levels of regard, closeness, warmth, and satisfaction.

2. Still-healthy aging parents tend to provide the most financial and emotional support to their children. Parents seem to give to their children in one way or another for as long as they are able.

3. Young-old parents tend to give more aid, while old-old parents tend to receive more aid.

4. Middle-aged adult children are second only to spouses in providing care to frail, aging parents. Daughters tend to be the principal caregivers, with sons tending to do more home repair and maintenance tasks; when acting as primary caregivers, sons tend to be managers rather than direct providers of care.

E. Siblings

1. Sibling relationships are among age peers and therefore last longer, are more egalitarian, more sociable, and more like friendships than other family relationships.

2. Sometimes siblings increase contact and get closer in middle adulthood as they face family crises and transitions.

3. Marriage separates siblings and reduces contact.

4. Helping aging parents is a new developmental task for middle-age siblings.

   a. Siblings go through a series of stages as they face this challenge.

   b. Parental caregiving arrangements can be a source of conflict for middle-aged siblings.

V. Bereavement

A parent's death involves many emotions because of the intensity and uniqueness of the parent-child relationship. **Bereavement** is the process of getting over another person's death.

A. Mourning for one's parents

1. Three tasks are evident as middle-aged children mourn the death of parents. Each task focuses on a different aspect of the child's relationship to the deceased parent.

   a. Stocktaking involves the exploration of changes.

   b. The reminiscence task involves recalling harsh and meaningful memories.

   c. Internalization and passage involve discussion about the present without denying the past.

B. Bereavement and growth

1. Bereavement for a parent during middle age may promote personal growth and maturity and help to resolve developmental tasks.

2. Research reveals that after the parent's death, there is a time of upheaval and a change in outlook on life.

C. Reactions to grief

1. Increased psychological distress and reduced sense of personal mastery are initial reactions to parental death.

2. Unresolved grief reactions include depression, thoughts of suicide, and other psychiatric symptoms.

3. Initial and residual grief is influenced by the expectedness of the parent's death, the extent of filial autonomy, age, and gender.

4. Many middle-aged adults deny the impact of the loss and express their feelings of pain through physical symptoms more than younger or older adults do.

    a. Younger adults may be protected by their greater physical capacities and sense of invulnerability, which act as buffers against the strain of readjustment.

    b. Older adults are better prepared for the death of another, as they are preparing for their own deaths.

    c. The deaths of spouses and siblings are most likely to affect middle-aged adults because they are members of the same generation.

VI. Leisure

A. Because of the many changes in midlife, adults often feel less constrained.

B. **Leisure** is choosing whatever activities one enjoys and participating in them at one's own pace.

C. The same activities can have different meanings for different individuals.

D. As people enter middle age, their view of leisure shifts.

1. Validation and gratification may come from leisure activities.

2. A shift occurs from activities requiring physical exertion and high-intensity involvement to more sedentary, moderate-intensity activities.

3. There is also some continuity in level and types of leisure activities over the life course.

E. Higher socioeconomic status is associated with greater leisure involvement.

F. Racial and ethnic minorities have had more limited leisure options.

G. Gender affects the leisure activities people choose.

    1.   Women tend to engage in social and home-based activities and in cultural activities.

    2.   Men are more likely to be involved in exercise and outdoor recreation, to attend spectator sports, and to travel.

H. Involvement in leisure activities seems to promote psychological well-being.

    1.   The degree of satisfaction is more important than the number and types of activities.

    2.   Pursuing satisfying leisure activities is good preparation for the life changes associated with late adulthood.

VII. Preparing for late adulthood

A. Aging changes activities and perspectives in predictable ways. Taking more responsibility for one's own life increases one's sense of mortality.

B. A will is important even if the person does not have property; a will can describe after-death choices.

    1.   An **advance directive** is a legal document specifying what medical care can be given in the event the person becomes unable to make or communicate his or her decisions. There are two types of advance directives.

        a.   A **living will** notifies the person's physician of his or her wishes regarding the withdrawal of life-sustaining equipment even if the result is death.

        b.   A **durable power of attorney for health care** designates a person to make medical decisions on your behalf other than the withdrawal of life-support systems.

    2.   Middle age is the optimal time to make decisions about long-term care.

    3.   Planning for retirement financially and psychologically is another developmental task of middle age.

VIII. Looking back/looking forward

Key Concepts

Directions: Identify each of the following key concepts discussed in this chapter.

1. A(n) _____ is a life transition that occurs within a restricted time period, such as marriage.

2. Being widowed as a young adult and returning to college in middle age are examples of _____.

3. Erikson's theory predicts a normative crisis as the midlife individual faces the task of _____.

4. Radical personality change associated with the midlife reexamination of goals, priorities, and life accomplishments is called a(n) _____.

5. A(n) _____ is a relatively enduring disposition of an individual, a characteristic way of thinking, feeling, and acting.

6. The _____ is a series of predictable stages through which families pass.

7. Marital satisfaction _____ during the parenting of adolescent children. Marital satisfaction appears to follow a(n) _____ path over the family life cycle.

8. With regard to happiness, middle-aged and older marriages are _____ happy than those in the earlier stages.

9. For women, separation and divorce usually _____ the standard of living.

10. The sandwich generation consists of those individuals in middle age who are caught between _____.

11. In the _____, there are more generations but fewer people in each generation.

12. Very early "off-time" grandparenthood can be very _____. Grandmothers report greater _____ than grandfathers from relationships with their grandchildren.

13. When their aging parents require care, _____ are more likely than _____ to provide it.

14. The process of _____ involves getting over another person's death and entails many emotions.

15. Mourning middle-aged sons and daughters go through three stages: _____, _____, and _____.

16. The health of _____ is more negatively affected by the death of a sibling or a spouse than that of other adults.

17. Choosing whatever activities one enjoys and participating in them at one's own pace define _____.

18. Women tend to select leisure activities that are _____ and _____. Men are more likely to be involved in _____ and _____.

19. A(n) _____ is a legal document that can distribute property, appoint a guardian for children, provide for funeral and burial, and appoint an executor.

20. A(n) _____ is a legal document that specifies what medical care can be given if the person cannot make or communicate his or her decisions.

21. A legal document that notifies a person's physician of his or her wishes regarding the withdrawal of life-sustaining equipment even if the result is death is called a(n) _____.

22. A(n) _____ designates a person to make medical decisions on your behalf other than the withdrawal of life-support systems.

Multiple-Choice Self-Test

Factual / Conceptual Questions

1. In a study that looked at how individuals rated various positive and negative traits, it was found that people who were in their _____ had the most positive view.
   a. thirties
   b. forties
   c. fifties
   d. sixties

2. Radical change within the personality associated with reexamination of goals, priorities, and life accomplishments at the midpoint of life has been called the
   a. collective unconscious.
   b. life review.
   c. midlife crisis
   d. midlife transition.

3. All of the following support the view that the midlife period entails a crisis *except*
   a. Costa and McCrea's personality traits.
   b. Gould's UCLA study.
   c. the Harvard Grant study.
   d. Levinson's life structures.

4. As compared to middle-aged couples, elderly couples tend to display more
   a. anger.
   b. humor.
   c. affection.
   d. disgust.

5. Marital satisfaction tends to be lowest
   a. when children are preschoolers.
   b. when children are school-aged.
   c. after children leave home.
   d. before having children.

6. The term *sandwich generation* refers to
   a. young adults who frequent fast-food restaurants.
   b. middle-aged adults who work through lunch hour in order to ensure career advancement.
   c. young adults with children who fail to have family meals together because of conflicting schedules.
   d. middle-aged adults who are called on to help in issues concerning their young adult children and also their elderly parents.

7. Off-time grandparenting is
   a. quite often very distressing.
   b. generally viewed as gratifying.
   c. no different than on-time grandparenthood.
   d. less time-consuming than on-time grandparenthood.

8. Middle-aged siblings tend to
   a. decrease contact in times of divorce.
   b. increase contact when a parent is ill.
   c. increase contact when they first establish their own home.
   d. decrease contact when their own children leave home.

9. When a midlife adult's parent dies, he or she often goes through a period of
   a. extreme depression.
   b. upheaval.
   c. compensation.
   d. physical distress.

10. Longitudinal studies of leisure activities across adulthood suggest that
    a. leisure activities are age-specific.
    b. there is continuity in leisure activities.
    c. leisure time decreases across the entire lifespan.
    d. lower-socioeconomic-status individuals enjoy leisure time more.

Application Questions

1. Forty-six-year-old Anthony feels that his life is at a dead end. He's bored with his job, his family, and his friends. Erikson would say that Anthony is experiencing
   a. despair.
   b. isolation.
   c. stagnation.
   d. resignation.

2. Monica tends to experience fits of fear, anger, and sadness as part of her day-to-day experiences. Costa and McCrea would rate Monica high in
   a. introversion.
   b. neuroticism.
   c. extraversion.
   d. inhibition.

3. Chuck is openly confrontational, tends to have difficulty with interpersonal relationships, and has low regard for authority. Chuck's typology is
   a. punitive-disenchanted.
   b. pseudo-developed.
   c. antihero.
   d. transcendent-generative.

4. On their fiftieth wedding anniversary, Lewis and Carmen were interviewed by a local newspaper reporter, who asked why their marriage was so successful. Lewis's most likely response to this question is
   a. "My wife is my best friend."
   b. "We agree on most major decisions."
   c. "We like to laugh together."
   d. "Marriage is a sacred institution."

5. Julia is trying to balance the needs of her daughter, whose recent marriage is having difficulties, and her aging father, who may need to be admitted to a nursing home due to his confused state. Julia's situation is common to those individuals in
   a. the sandwich generation.
   b. midlife crisis.
   c. the Dream years.
   d. the nightmare years.

6. Louisa's children have all grown up, and the last one has finally left home. Her likely response to this is a(n)
   a. deep sense of loss.
   b. new sense of autonomy.
   c. urge to re-engage with family members.
   d. desire to have more children.

7. Which of these middle-aged adults is likely to have the closest relationship with his or her aging parent?
   a. Tom and his father, Dan
   b. Greg and his mother, Audrey
   c. Sara and her father, Ira
   d. Eleanor and her mother, Virginia

8. Irene and Nell are the daughters of Rose, who has become quite ill and is in need of a primary caretaker. The most likely scenario is that
   a. the younger sibling will take charge of the caregiving.
   b. there will be increased communication between the siblings, but this is likely to create some conflict.
   c. both siblings will join forces to provide for primary care.
   d. each sibling will assume that the other will take care of the problem.

9. Forty-eight-year-old Evelyn's mother has just died. Evelyn reflects on the loss by thinking that her children will not have a grandmother to watch them, that she'll have to make a better attempt to keep in contact with her brother and sisters now that their mother has died, and that she's lost a shopping partner. Evelyn's behavior reflects the tasks associated with
   a. stocktaking.
   b. reminiscence.
   c. internalization.
   d. denial.

10. Darryl has met with a lawyer and drawn up a document that says if he is seriously ill and cannot survive without life-sustaining equipment, no measures should be taken to continue his life. Darryl has made a(n)
    a. will.
    b. durable power of attorney for health care.
    c. advanced directive.
    d. physician-assisted suicide contract.

Answer Key

Key Concepts

1. normative life event
2. nonnormative life events
3. generativity versus stagnation
4. midlife crisis
5. trait
6. family life cycle
7. declines, curvilinear
8. more
9. lowers
10. adjacent generations
11. beanpole family structure
12. distressing, satisfaction
13. daughters, sons
14. bereavement
15. stocktaking, reminiscence of hard and meaningful memories, internalization and passage
16. middle-aged adults
17. leisure
18. social, home-based, exercise, outdoor recreation
19. will
20. advance directive
21. living will
22. durable power of attorney for health care

Multiple-Choice Self-Test: Factual / Conceptual Questions

1. Choice (d) is correct. In reflecting on personality traits, older individuals tend to be much more positive than other age groups. In particular, the study mentioned found the sixty-year-olds to be the most positive.

2. Choice (c) is correct. By definition, this is what a midlife crisis is. Choice (a), collective unconscious, is a Jungian concept that refers to a part of the unconscious shared by a society or a people; choice (b), life review, is something found in the later years as one reflects on one's life; and choice (d), midlife transition, is a lesser form of midlife crisis that does not hypothesize the same level of upheaval.

3. Choice (a) is correct. Costa and McCrea indicated that personality traits remain relatively stable across adulthood, which is contrary to what a mid-life crisis would predict. Gould's UCLA study, choice (b), and the Harvard Grant study, choice (c), as well as Levinson's life structures theory, choice (d), all provide evidence of upheaval during midlife.

4. Choice (c) is correct. Studies show that elderly couples show more affection toward one another when compared to middle-aged couples. No differences are found in anger, humor, or disgust, choices (a), (b), and (d), respectively.

5. Choice (b) is correct. Marital satisfaction shows a U-shaped curve across the family life cycle, with the lowest point being during the school years, right before the children leave home. Choice (d), before having children, is one of the high points of marital satisfaction; choice (c), after children leave home, begins a rise in marital satisfaction; and choice (a), when children are preschoolers, is low, but not the lowest point.

6. Choice (d) is correct. By definition, the sandwich generation refers to the notion that middle-aged individuals are caught between concerns arising from both their children and their parents.

7. Choice (a) is correct. Off-time grandparenthood is often a result of such things as teenage pregnancy, and thus brings on more stress as well as more responsibility. It tends to be distressful when compared to on-time grandparenthood, so choices (b) and (c) are incorrect; it is certainly not less time-consuming, choice (d), and may in fact be more time-consuming, due to the need to help out a bit more.

8. Choice (b) is correct. When a parent is ill, siblings tend to get together more often and communicate more to deal with the family situation. They also tend to increase contact time during other family crises, such as divorce, so choice (a) is incorrect. They tend to decrease contact as they establish their own households, so choice (c) is incorrect; but they increase contact once their children are grown, making choice (d) also incorrect.

9. Choice (b) is correct. Like many crisis situations, the death of a parent often causes an upheaval in which adjustments in the life structures need to be made. Although some middle-aged children get depressed, choice (a), and some even suffer physical distress, choice (d), most do not. Some may also try to compensate for the loss, choice (c), but the prevailing response is upheaval.

10. Choice (b) is correct. Studies have shown that leisure activities in the younger years are rather similar to leisure activities in the later years; thus, there seems to be continuity. Leisure activities are generally not age specific, so choice (a) is incorrect, although some exceptions can be found. Leisure time actually increases in the later years, so choice (c) is incorrect; and higher-socioeconomic-status groups have more leisure time than lower-socioeconomic-status groups, making choice (d) also incorrect.

Multiple-Choice Self-Test: Application Questions

1. Choice (c) is correct. The task Erikson associated with the midlife period is generativity versus stagnation. In Anthony's case, he is not resolving this and is therefore stagnating. Choice (a), despair, is associated with the older age period; choice (b), isolation, is associated with the young adulthood period; and choice (d), resignation, is not one of Erikson's stages.

2. Choice (b) is correct. Costa and McCrea identified what has come to be known as the big five personality traits. The description provided is that of neuroticism in which the individual is not particularly well adjusted. Choices (a), introversion, and (c), extraversion, refer to another of Costa and McCrea's personality traits, which involves how outgoing the person is, while choice (d), inhibition, involves a different personality characteristic, one characterized by reluctance.

3. Choice (c) is correct. Farrell and Rosenberg developed a typology for men's response to the midlife period. The antihero is a highly confrontational, alienated individual who has low regard for authority. He openly confronts stress and is dissatisfied; this description fits Chuck. Choice (a), punitive-disenchanted, is also a dissatisfied person, but one who tends to deny stress; choices (b) and (d), pseudo-developed and transcendent-generative, respectively, are both satisfied—one denies stress and the other is open to it.

4. Choice (a) is correct. The number one reason males give for a long-term successful marriage is that they view their wife as their best friend; women's number one reason is that marriage is a long-term commitment. Although the other choices, (b), (c), and (d), are also reasons given by men, they don't rank as high as choice (a).

5. Choice (a) is correct. Julia's situation involves trying to deal with the concerns of her child, who is in transition, and her father, who is also in transition. Because the issues come from both sides, individuals in middle adulthood have been referred to as the sandwich generation. Although some theories might say these issues are part of a midlife crisis, choice (b), the concept of a midlife crisis does not fully describe the circumstances given. This period of life is not characterized as the Dream years, choice (c); nor is the term *nightmare* used, choice (d).

6. Choice (b) is correct. When children leave, mothers often respond with some degree of happiness, since they gain a new sense of independence (time on the hands). Choices (a), (c), and (d), a deep sense of loss, an urge to re-engage with family members, and a desire to have more children, respectively, are responses consistent with someone suffering from the empty-nest syndrome, which is actually quite rare. (Only about 5 to 15 percent of mothers experience the empty-nest syndrome when their children leave.)

7. Choice (d) is correct. Studies show that the closest relationship between parents and children at the children's midlife is the mother-daughter relationship. The others, although they are more positive than during the young adult and adolescent years, are not as strong as the mother-daughter bond.

8. Choice (b) is correct. In times of family crisis, especially the illness of a parent, middle-aged siblings tend to increase their contact and communication as they try to deal with the situation. With this increased communication, however, there is also increased potential for conflict and misunderstandings. Choice (b) best captures this scenario. The scenarios outlined in choices (a), (c), and (d) can occur but are not as likely.

9. Choice (a) is correct. A common response to the death of a parent is to reflect on how the loss of that person will change other relationships or behavior. In particular, one's own relationship within the broad family structure may change. Reflecting on these changes has been termed *stocktaking*. Choice (b), reminiscence, although similar, typically refers to recalling previous events without looking at how these might affect one's current situation. Choices (c) and (d), internalization and denial, respectively, are not relevant.

10. Choice (c) is correct. Leaving instructions about what should be done in case of serious illness is known as an advanced directive. Choice (a), a will, is a broader document that often deals with possessions; choice (b), a durable power of attorney for health care, is related to an advanced directive in that it names someone who can make those decisions about life and death. Choice (d), a physician-assisted suicide contract, does not exist.

CHAPTER 16

Late Adulthood: Physical and Cognitive Development

Learning Objectives

1. Define what is meant by ageism and discuss the use of aging stereotypes.

2. Discuss the changes that have occurred in life expectancy. Describe how these changes affect population growth and distribution. Identify the leading causes of death in the elderly.

3. Differentiate between cellular and programming theories of aging.

4. Characterize the overall physical changes associated with the late adulthood period, including the loss of efficiency and slowing of some behaviors.

5. Discuss the changes in skin, bone, and muscle as well as the changes in body systems associated with aging.

6. Describe the changes that occur in the various sensory systems with emphasis on visual and auditory changes.

7. Discuss health and fitness during the later years. Identify what kinds of behaviors promote health and what kinds of behaviors detract from health.

8. Identify and describe the major chronic illnesses associated with aging. Discuss the risk factors and means to reduce those risks.

9. Discuss the development of wisdom during the later adulthood years. Differentiate between cognitive mechanisms and cognitive pragmatics.

10. Discuss the issue of cognitive decline in aging and explain what animal and human studies show.

11. Describe the changes in the brain associated with aging. In particular, discuss changes in the nervous system and organic brain syndromes.

12. Describe Alzheimer's disease. Identify the causes, symptoms, and treatment of the disorder. Distinguish Alzheimer's from other disorders, including multiinfarct dementia and senile dementia.

13. Discuss depression in the elderly. Identify the signs and variables associated with depression and suicide.

14. Discuss the process of retirement, including adjustment and variables that determine who is likely to retire.

Chapter Overview

In the United States, elderly people and growing old are viewed negatively. Ageism is the stereotyping of and discrimination against people because they are aging or old. Life expectancy in the United States is seventy-five years, but the maximum lifespan remains one hundred fifteen years and is not expected to change. Gender, race/ethnicity, and socioeconomic status affect mortality. Cellular theories of aging attribute the breakdown of cells, organs, and the organism to "wear and tear" on the cells caused by stressors such as toxins, pollutants, and free radicals. Programming theories consider the maximum lifespan to be built into the genes of each species and beyond human control.

Late adulthood is a time of loss in efficiency of body systems, but it is also a time of compensation. Motor responses, sensory processes, and intellectual functioning slow with age. Some systems experience regeneration and growth due to their plasticity. Skin, bone, and muscle all show age-related changes, as do the cardiovascular and respiratory systems. The rate of aging of these systems is strongly influenced by lifestyle factors, smoking, and exposure to air pollutants. Age-related loss also occurs in all of the senses. Health and fitness continue to be important in the later years. Regular aerobic exercise is needed to prevent hypokinesia and to maintain cardiovascular and respiratory fitness. Chronic illness often begins during middle adulthood or earlier. Cardiovascular disease is responsible for most illness and death of men during the middle years and is associated with risk factors of family history, health-compromising behaviors, personality type, and stress. Cancer refers to more than one hundred diseases characterized by uncontrolled cellular growth. Different cancers have different risk factors. Other chronic illnesses that affect older adults include hypertension and arthritis.

Wisdom is a positive cognitive change associated with later life, and some older adults perform at near-peak levels on wisdom-related tasks. Research with both animals and humans shows that enrichment and training can lead to positive changes in elderly brains and cognitive performance. Normal aging affects the brain, reducing the number of neurons and increasing the density of synapses. Alzheimer's disease is the most common chronic organic brain syndrome. Depression is more common among the elderly than younger adults and can put the elderly at risk for suicide. Several variables, such as health, finances, the nature of work, and work satisfaction affect both the decision to retire and satisfaction after retirement. Many individuals follow nontraditional retirement patterns.

Chapter Outline

I. Aging and ageism

   A. Societies differ in their treatment of the elderly. In some societies, old age is revered.

   B. In the United States, elderly people are viewed negatively, although this was not always the case. Age bias has changed dramatically in the United States over the past three centuries.

   C. **Ageism** is the systematic stereotyping of and discrimination against people because they are old.

1. Stereotypes can be positive or negative.

2. Because stereotypes are based on generalizations of old people rather than on actual appraisals of individuals, they reflect preconceived notions or prejudices.

   a. Stereotypes include physical traits such as slow, feeble, and gray-haired.

   b. Stereotypes include personality traits such as cranky, repetitive, sweet, caring, pleasant, and storytellers.

D. Elderly individuals who defy the stereotypes are perceived as exceptions.

E. Ageism is common among professionals in medicine, psychotherapy, and research.

II. Physical development

Most elderly individuals continue to be productive contributors to their families and their communities.

III. Longevity

The average life expectancy in the United States has gone from forty-seven years in 1900 to seventy-five years today. Eradication of disease and improvements in diet and sanitation increase life expectancy. The population of the United States has been getting more diverse during this century with regard to ethnicity, social class, and income. Poverty levels have declined, and median income for people sixty-five and over has increased, although subgroups of the elderly population live in poverty or near-poverty.

A. Mortality

1. Mortality rates began to fall in the late 1960s because of improvements in medical care and drugs and improved health behaviors.

   a. Men have made larger gains in life expectancy than women except at advanced ages of seventy-five and above.

   b. All age groups have made improvements except the very oldest group (age eighty-five and above).

2. Women and men die from the same causes, although men have higher mortality from all the leading causes of death except diabetes mellitus.

   a. In late adulthood, the gap between men's and women's mortality rates narrows.

   b. The gender gap continues to widen with age for cancer, heart disease, kidney disease, and suicide.

3. There are racial and ethnic differences in mortality rates and mortality crossover.

• A multicultural view: The mortality crossover

B. Life expectancy

1. Although life expectancy has increased, lifespan has not changed because it refers to the maximum possible period of time a species could be expected to live if environmental hazards were eliminated.

2. For humans, the lifespan is one hundred and fifteen years.

3. The oldest verified age to which an individual has lived is just over one hundred and twenty and a half years.

IV. Theories of aging

A. The breakdown of the surveillance, repair, and replacement process of the body is known as **senescence**. This causes an individual to become more vulnerable to disease and mortality. Theories of aging attempt to explain senescence.

B. **Cellular theories**, also known as wear and tear theories, focus on the processes that take place within and between the cells and lead to the breakdown of cells, tissue, and organs.

1. These theories explain the loss of function by repeated errors of transmission of genetic material resulting from toxins, pollutants, free radicals, and other factors that affect cell reproduction.

2. The older the individual, the greater the number of the cells that will have errors and the greater number of the cells that will have multiple errors.

C. **Programming theories** consider the maximum lifespan to be predetermined by the genes in each species through the number of possible cell replications. At birth, our eventual death is already built in; anything less than ideal environmental conditions may shorten our life, but nothing can lengthen it.

V. Physical functioning in late adulthood

Late adulthood is a time of loss in efficiency of body systems, but it is also a time of compensation.

A. Slowing with age

1. Motor responses, sensory processes, and intellectual functioning slow with age.

2. The slowing down may be due to aging in the peripheral nervous system, the sensory receptors, and the nerves that transmit sensations.

3. Health and physical fitness are more closely related to performance than is age.

B. Skin, bone, and muscle changes

1. The most noticeable changes of late adulthood occur to the skin.

a. The skin becomes more wrinkled, dry, sagging, and less regular in pigmentation.

b. The skin is easily bruised, heals more slowly, and grows lesions.

c. Irregularly distributed melanocytes cause "age spots."

2.   Demineralization causes bone degeneration, which is called osteoporosis. Osteoporosis takes place in a two-phase pattern.

   a.   Women experience far greater bone loss than men do.

   b.   Regular weight-bearing exercise, estrogen replacement therapy, and calcium supplements have been effective at slowing and even reversing osteoporosis in postmenopausal women.

3.   A progressive loss of muscle strength and speed occurs.

   a.   Loss of muscle fibers results from atrophy due to disuse or to damage and atrophy of the nerve fibers that carry impulses to the muscles.

   b.   Strength is maintained through physical exercise.

C.   Cardiovascular system changes

1.   The changes in the cardiovascular system that began in early adulthood continue through middle and later adulthood.

2.   The heart has reduced maximum cardiac output and aerobic power.

3.   These changes are kept to a minimum by regular aerobic exercise and good nutrition.

D.   Respiratory system changes

1.   The lungs become smaller and less elastic and are less efficient in gas exchange.

2.   The decrease in function is gradual, but by late adulthood the loss is considerable.

3.   The decreased efficiency of the lungs increases the risk of stroke or loss of brain functions.

4.   Older adults compensate by using accessory muscles to facilitate respiration. Under conditions of stress, an older adult may have difficulty breathing or become fatigued.

5.   These changes make older people more susceptible to chronic bronchitis, emphysema, and pneumonia.

E.   Sensory system changes

1.   Visual loss is part of the primary aging process.

   a.   Loss of accommodation occurs in senescence, leading to the need for reading glasses.

   b.   Cataract is a clouding of the lens and is the most common correctable cause of blindness.

   c.   Glaucoma is increased pressure in the eyeball and can cause blindness.

2.   Hearing loss is also a part of the primary aging process.

  a. Presbycusis is age-related hearing loss caused by changes in the conductive systems in the outer and middle ear and loss of hair cells and nerves in the inner ear, leading to problems with high-pitched sounds and consonants in normal speech.

  b. The percentage of elderly Americans with significant hearing loss increases with age.

  c. Noise is the largest contributor to hearing loss.

  d. Hearing aids can compensate for hearing loss to some extent, but are not helpful in all settings.

 3. Primary aging affects both taste and smell, with age-related declines in smell being greater than those in taste.

  a. Taste buds do show reduction in numbers with age.

  b. The ability to recognize a large number of foods declines with age.

  c. Smell receptors begin to decrease at about thirty years of age with the peak age to detect odors between twenty and fifty.

  d. Research suggests that the ability to smell odors does not decline until the seventies.

- Perspectives: Older adults have healthier lifestyles than young and middle-aged adults

VI. Health behaviors in late adulthood

Increased physical vulnerability may make health and fitness in the later years more important than in early or middle adulthood. Beginning healthy habits in early adulthood can have cumulative benefits in later adult years.

A. Diet

 1. Nutritional concerns increase during late adulthood because at the same time caloric needs decline, the need for many nutrients rises.

 2. Not getting enough vitamins and minerals can increase risk for a variety of health problems.

 3. Activity level, gender, weight, height, genetic make-up, social environment, and socioeconomic status all affect dietary needs and nutritional deficits.

B. Exercise

 1. As people get older, routine physical activity decreases.

 2. **Hypokinesia** is a disease of disuse that causes degeneration and functional loss of muscle and bone tissue.

 3. Regular exercise prevents hypokinesia and has a number of other positive benefits.

4. Although older adults may engage in more health-promoting behaviors than younger adults, they don't necessarily exercise.

    a. Among older adults, more men exercise than women.

    b. Health professionals are often overcautious in prescribing exercises for the elderly.

C. Alcohol consumption

    1. During late adulthood, sensitivity to alcohol increases.

    2. Alcohol can reduce reaction time, impair coordination, and cloud mental abilities.

    3. Levels of alcohol consumption and the number of problem drinkers are lower in older age groups.

    4. For some groups of the elderly population, alcohol consumption remains a problem.

        a. Elderly males are at greater risk for alcoholism than females.

        b. Research shows that health problems are associated with a greater probability of elderly individuals abstaining from alcohol, while financial difficulties are associated with a lower probability of abstaining.

D. Prescription drugs

    1. Elderly individuals are at high risk for adverse drug effects.

    2. Improper medications may cause physical, cognitive, and social dysfunction.

VII. Chronic illnesses

A chronic illness is one that cannot be cured but only managed and is a common feature of late adulthood. Chronic diseases are incremental, universal, and characterized by progressive loss of organ reserve. The key to preventing chronic illness is to delay reaching the clinical threshold. Chronic illnesses tend to affect all aspects of a person's life.

A. Cardiovascular disease

    1. Cardiovascular disease is the major chronic illness in the United States. Athero-sclerosis is the most common heart disorder in the United States and may progress evenly or may result in a sudden catastrophic event.

        a. Narrowed or closed arteries wholly or partially block the flow of oxygen and nutrients to the heart.

        b. Temporary blockage may cause angina pectoris, and severe blockage may result in myocardial infarction.

    2. Coronary heart disease is common among males and elderly people in general. Other risk factors include family history, health-compromising behavior, personality type, and stress.

3. Hypertension, or high blood pressure, can cause deterioration of the arterial walls and of the cell tissue, putting the person at risk for heart attack, kidney damage, and stroke. Risk factors for hypertension include genetic predisposition, obesity, poor diet, and, perhaps, personality characteristics.

B. Cancer

1. Cancer is characterized by uncontrolled cellular growth and reproduction due to a dysfunction of the DNA. Cancerous growths can spread by invading other tissues and organs.

2. Cancer is the second most frequent cause of death in the United States.

   a. Regular breast examination and mammograms are recommended for women forty and older.

   b. Professional digital rectal examination of the prostate is recommended for men starting at age fifty.

3. Some risk factors for cancer include genetic predisposition, gender, socioeconomic status, ethnicity, lifestyle, diet, and marital status.

4. The onset of cancer is related to uncontrollable stress caused by some life event. Stress may suppress the immune system and interfere with DNA repair. Personality also has an influence on the likelihood of developing cancer.

C. Arthritis

1. Arthritis causes the body to incorrectly identify its own tissue as foreign matter and attack it. It is the second leading chronic disease in the United States.

2. Arthritis attacks the joints and connective tissue and causes inflammation, pain, stiffness, and sometimes swelling of the joints.

3. Arthritis can be crippling.

   a. Osteoarthritis is the most common type of arthritis and affects weight-bearing joints.

   b. Rheumatoid arthritis affects the whole body rather than specific, localized joints. It is the most crippling and is most prevalent among people ages forty to sixty.

4. Early diagnosis and treatment can prevent the disabling aspects of rheumatoid arthritis.

D. Common symptoms in later years

1. The kinds of symptoms that bother women and men are very similar, but are more frequent in women.

   a. Women's chronic conditions tend to be nonfatal.

   b. Men's tend to be fatal or precursors to fatal conditions.

2. Incidence of chronic diseases varies among racial/ethnic groups.

3. Chronic diseases generally have their beginning in earlier life stages and often have their onset earlier as well.

    a. The great frequency of chronic illness is a result of people living longer.

    b. Some people adapt and compensate for losses despite suffering from chronic illnesses.

    c. Physical fitness helps to maintain most body systems at high levels of functioning, although the levels are not as high as they were before because primary aging cannot be stopped.

VIII. Cognitive development

Some individuals show significant changes in intellectual performance in midlife, while a few show little decline even into their eighties. Several factors reduce the risk of cognitive loss.

IX. Wisdom

Wisdom, expert knowledge and good judgment about important but uncertain matters of life, is a positive change associated with late life.

A. Cognitive mechanics

    1. Cognitive mechanics refers to basic memory processes, which are likely to decline in late adulthood.

    2. Using techniques to improve memory can help, but the performance of elderly persons is still poor compared to young adults.

B. Cognitive pragmatics

    1. Cognitive pragmatics refers to intellectual problems in which culture-based knowledge and skills are key in managing the peaks and valleys of life.

    2. Older adults can show higher levels of wisdom-related knowledge on tasks specific to their own age group than young adults.

X. Cognitive plasticity and training

Plasticity refers to the ability of other neurons to take over the functions of neurons that have been damaged or lost.

A. Animal research

    1. Research shows that environmental living conditions have an impact on the state of the cerebral cortex.

    2. Young, middle-aged, and old rats raised in an enriched environment show an increase in the growth of dendrites and a thickening of the cerebral cortex.

3. Young, middle-aged, and old rats raised in impoverished environments have diminished cortices.

B. Human research

1. Individual differences exist in age-related changes in cognitive functioning and may be related to environmental factors.

2. Research has focused on retraining abilities and processes that longitudinal studies have shown to exhibit earlier patterns of decline.

3. Intellectual decline is not necessarily irreversible, and intervention strategies may allow for longer maintenance of high levels of intellectual functioning.

XI. The aging brain

Age-related changes occur in the central nervous system. Brain weight and mass start to decrease gradually at age twenty; these changes are very small by age fifty and accelerate after age sixty.

A. Brain changes

1. Most brain changes are not apparent until age sixty, with the greatest loss in the sensory and motor areas and the smallest in the association areas.

2. By age eighty, brain mass has decreased by about 10 percent.

   a. Plasticity enables other neurons to take over the functions of neurons that have been lost.

   b. Some research suggests that the density of synapses increases with age.

3. As the cardiovascular system changes, the blood flow to the brain is reduced.

   a. Some neurons die, and others develop neurofibrillary tangles; the brain develops granulovascular degeneration.

   b. The brains of elderly individuals with senile dementia show these structural changes.

4. Most declines in mental functioning are related to changes in health and are not a function of age.

5. Physical damage to the brain can cause organic brain syndromes.

   a. **Acute brain syndromes** are caused by metabolic malfunctions and medication effects.

   b. **Chronic brain syndromes** are characterized by irreversible changes in the brain and include Alzheimer's disease.

B. Multiinfarct dementia

1. **Multiinfarct dementia** is caused by vascular diseases and is characterized by a series of tiny strokes.

2. The tiny strokes may go unnoticed at the time or may be accompanied by headaches or dizziness.

3. Diagnosing multiinfarct dementia is important because treating the hypertension and underlying vascular disease can slow the progress of the brain disease.

C. Alzheimer's disease

1. Senile dementia of the Alzheimer's type, or **Alzheimer's disease**, affects more than 11 percent of individuals over sixty-five years of age.

2. Alzheimer's disease is caused by degeneration of the brain areas in those portions of the cerebral cortex associated with memory, learning, and judgment.

3. The presence of senile plaques and neurofibrillary tangles in the brain is the basis for the microscopic diagnosis of Alzheimer's disease.

4. Forgetfulness and confusion are typically the first symptoms of Alzheimer's.

    a. As the disease progresses, the confusion becomes more intense and often includes belligerence.

    b. Later symptoms include greater confusion and hyperactivity.

    c. In the final stages sleep increases, then come coma and death.

    d. The course of the disease is usually seven to ten years.

5. Some evidence suggests that genetic defects are involved in causing Alzheimer's disease.

    a. Variations in APOE, a gene on chromosome 19, are associated with Alzheimer's disease.

    b. APOE can be used to identify those who are at greater biological risk for the disease.

6. Older adults may experience anticipatory dementia, which is the concern that normal age-associated memory changes are signs of the onset of Alzheimer's disease. This may discourage people with remediable memory complaints from seeking help.

7. Drugs are sometimes given to lessen the Alzheimer's patient's agitation. Memory aids can help patients in the early stages to maintain their functioning.

*   Working with Mark John Isola, therapeutic recreation director: Helping Alzheimer's patients and their families

D. Senile dementia

1. The loss of brain cells causes **senile dementia**.

2.   Senile dementia impairs orientation, intellect, judgment, and memory.

3.   Slightly fewer than 5 percent of all persons over sixty-five suffer so severely from dementia that they require institutional care or a full-time custodian.

   a.   Mild to moderate dementia requires special attention to care and safety on the part of the family or caregivers.

   b.   It causes much personal anguish to see a family member unable to recognize loved ones.

4.   Most older adults are in good cognitive health. Changes in functioning should not simply be accepted as the inescapable effects of age.

XII.   Mental health and aging

A.   Depression is the most common psychiatric complaint of elderly adults.

B.   Since symptoms associated with depression may be thought to be normal changes associated with aging or illness, they may go undiagnosed.

1.   Elderly patients report physical but not affective symptoms.

2.   Symptoms of depression may mimic dementia, leading to misdiagnosis.

C.   Between 4 and 7 percent of older adults experience depression severe enough to require intervention.

1.   Depression is more common in very old adults.

2.   Chronic diseases and reactions to medications may contribute to depression.

D.   Gender, race/ethnicity, and socioeconomic status are associated with depression among the elderly.

E.   Untreated depression increases the incidence of suicide, especially among elderly, White males.

F.   Effective treatments for elderly depression include antidepressants and psychotherapy.

G.   Men and women who report low physical activity may be at a higher risk for developing depression ten or twenty years later.

XIII.   Work and retirement

Most Americans look forward to retirement in their later years. People who can control whether and when they retire can plan for and anticipate the change. The statistics on when people retire are contradictory.

A.   What is retirement?

1.   Leaving a career job is a significant life event but does not necessarily mean leaving the labor force.

a. Many employees do not stop working when they leave their full-time career jobs.

b. Research shows that those who leave between fifty-eight and sixty-one are the most likely to hold another full-time job.

c. Retirement may mean changed or reduced employment, not simply stopping work.

2. Many adults, especially racial/ethnic minorities, have never held career jobs and thus never consider themselves to be retired.

a. Perceptions of a discontinuous work life make the line between work and nonwork indistinct and create ambiguity of retirement status.

b. In terms of retirement, women face problems similar to those of racial/ethnic minorities.

3. Nontraditional retirement patterns are common among older Americans.

4. Those who retire experience a series of phases as they adjust to their new status.

5. Race/ethnicity, gender, health, pension status, and occupational level all affect retirement possibilities and choices.

a. People with poor health or who perform physically demanding work are more likely to leave the labor force, as are those with pension benefits.

b. Those who are healthy and those without benefits are more likely to continue working.

6. How much individuals enjoy their work also influences retirement decisions.

a. Workers with boring, repetitive jobs are likely to choose retirement as early as they can afford it.

b. Workers with interesting jobs that give them high satisfaction are less likely to retire early and more likely to continue to work.

B. Well-being in retirement

1. Sixty percent of retirees are relatively satisfied and adjust well to their new life circumstances.

2. Health and financial security are the major determinants of life satisfaction after retirement.

3. Occupational status also predicts retirement satisfaction.

Key Concepts

Directions: Identify each of the following key concepts discussed in this chapter.

1. The systematic stereotyping of and discrimination against people because they are old is called _____.

2. The maximum possible period of time a species could be expected to live if environmental hazards were eliminated is known as _____.

3. _____ is the degenerative phase of the aging process.

4. The theories of aging that argue that there is a breakdown of cells, tissue, and organs are the _____.

5. The maximum lifespan is thought to be predetermined by the genes in each species, according to the _____ of aging.

6. Motor responses, sensory processes, and intellectual functioning _____ with age.

7. Bone degeneration is called _____. _____ is increased pressure in the eyeball.

8. A disease or disuse, or _____, causes degeneration and functional loss of muscle and bone tissue.

9. Heart attack is also known as _____. A(n) _____ is a rupture or leak of an arteriole in the brain.

10. The leading cause of cancer deaths for men and women is _____.

11. The most common type of arthritis is _____. The type of arthritis that affects the whole body is _____.

12. Expert knowledge and good judgment about important but uncertain matters of life are known as _____.

13. Content-free wisdom is called _____, while knowledge-rich wisdom is _____.

14. The ability of other neurons to take over the functions of neurons that have been damaged or lost is called _____.

15. Age-related changes in the brain include _____ and _____.

16. Metabolic malfunctions and alcoholism can cause _____, which involve fluctuating periods of awareness.

17. Irreversible changes in the brain cause _____; these include Alzheimer's disease and senile dementia.

18. Blockages in the blood vessels that reduce or prevent blood flow to the brain cause _____.

19. The type of senile dementia that is the result of degeneration of the brain cells in the portions of the cerebral cortex associated with memory, learning, and judgment is known as _____.

20. The fear of Alzheimer's disease is sometimes referred to as _____.

21. The dementia that impairs orientation, intellect, judgment, and memory is called _____.

22. The most common psychiatric complaint of elderly adults is _____.

Multiple-Choice Self-Test

Factual / Conceptual Questions

1. Systematic stereotyping of and discrimination against people because they are old is termed
   a. elder abuse.
   b. grayism.
   c. ageism.
   d. Elderhostel.

2. Currently, the elderly (sixty-five years of age and older) make up approximately _____ percent of the U.S. population.
   a. 4
   b. 9
   c. 13
   d. 22

3. Approximately how old is/was the longest living person in the world?
   a. 113 years
   b. 121 years
   c. 127 years
   d. 134 years

4. Which of the following is *not* a risk factor associated with osteoporosis?
   a. Increasing age
   b. Being male
   c. Smoking
   d. Being chronically overweight

5. All of the following are considered health-promoting tips for older adults *except*
   a. control your feelings.
   b. exercise at least three times a week.
   c. check cholesterol level regularly.
   d. look forward to the future.

6. Which of the following chronic conditions is the most prevalent in women over seventy-five?
   a. High blood pressure
   b. Hearing impairment
   c. Arthritis
   d. Cataracts

7. _____ refers to intellectual problems in which culture-based knowledge and skills are primary.
   a. Wisdom
   b. Cognitive mechanics
   c. Cognitive pragmatics
   d. Expertise

8. By age eighty, brain mass typically declines by about _____ percent.
   a. 5
   b. 10
   c. 15
   d. 20

9. The most common mental health problem of the elderly is
   a. depression.
   b. senility.
   c. phobic reactions.
   d. schizophrenia.

10. The two factors that seem to be the major determinants of life satisfaction after retirement are health and
    a. amount of retirement planning.
    b. personality.
    c. financial security.
    d. marital status.

Application Questions

1. Fred is seventy-two years old. The most likely cause of his death will be
   a. an accident.
   b. cancer.
   c. heart disease.
   d. suicide.

2. Professor Hsieh believes that maximum lifespan is based on a genetic timing mechanism that directs cells to divide only a certain number of times. Her view is most closely associated with
   a. cellular theories of aging.
   b. systems theories of aging.
   c. programming theories of aging.
   d. wear and tear theories of aging.

3. Sixty-year-old Bridget is very light-skinned. As compared to someone with darker skin, the effects of aging will produce
   a. paler skin and fewer age spots.
   b. paler skin and more age spots.
   c. darkening of the skin and fewer age spots.
   d. darkening of the skin and more age spots.

4. Forty-five-year-old Brent has more difficulty focusing his eyes, finds it more difficult to see in low light conditions, and seems to need reading glasses. He is most likely
   a. showing early signs of glaucoma.
   b. showing signs of cataracts.
   c. going blind.
   d. showing signs of normal aging.

5. Paul has high blood pressure; this puts him at higher risk for all of the following *except*
   a. cancer.
   b. heart attack.
   c. kidney damage.
   d. stroke.

6. Jeff has noticed that his eighty-one-year-old grandfather, although healthy, seems to be showing more cognitive decline in recent years. Given that there is nothing medically wrong with Jeff's grandfather, what is the most accurate advice you can provide?
   a. Cognitive decline is inevitable and irreversible; things will only get worse.
   b. Cognitive decline can be halted or slowed, but a reversal is unlikely.
   c. Cognitive decline is not inevitable and can be reversed with appropriate training.
   d. We just don't know whether cognitive decline is inevitable and irreversible.

7. Esther is in the early stages of Alzheimer's disease. She will most likely show
   a. loss of gross motor control.
   b. forgetfulness.
   c. some personality deterioration.
   d. visual impairment.

8. Consider the following family members: sixteen-year-old Jeremy; his forty-two-year-old father, Ronald; and his sixty-seven-year-old grandfather, Alvin. Who is at the greatest risk of suicide?
   a. Jeremy
   b. Ronald
   c. Alvin
   d. Jeremy and Alvin

9. Phil has just retired. According to Atchley, which of the following responses is most likely?
   a. Depression
   b. Euphoria
   c. Exhaustion
   d. Anxiety

10. Who is more likely to retire early?
    a. Arthur, who works on an assembly line for an appliance maker
    b. Winston, who works as a museum curator
    c. Louis, who is a university professor
    d. Abdul, who owns his own shoe store business

Answer Key

Key Concepts

1. ageism
2. lifespan
3. Senescence
4. cellular theories
5. programming theories
6. slow
7. osteoporosis, Glaucoma
8. hypokinesia
9. myocardial infarction, stroke
10. lung cancer
11. osteoarthritis, rheumatoid arthritis
12. wisdom
13. cognitive mechanics, cognitive pragmatics
14. plasticity

15. neuronal loss, increase in density of synapses
16. acute brain syndromes
17. chronic brain syndromes
18. multiinfarct dementia
19. Alzheimer's disease
20. anticipatory dementia
21. senile dementia
22. depression

Multiple-Choice Self-Test: Factual / Conceptual Questions

1. Choice (c) is correct. By definition, ageism is the systematic stereotyping of and discrimination against older individuals. Choice (a), elder abuse, refers to physical, mental, or neglectful cruelty; choice (b), grayism, is not a term generally used; choice (d), Elderhostel, refers to special education programs for the elderly.

2. Choice (c) is correct. Currently the elderly make up about 13 percent of the U.S. population and this figure is growing.

3. Choice (c) is correct. Although there have been claims of older individuals, the oldest verified individual is still alive as of this printing. She is Jeanne Calment, a Frenchwoman, who is over one hundred twenty-one years of age.

4. Choice (b) is correct. Choices (a), (c), and (d)—increasing age, smoking, and being chronically overweight, respectively—all contribute to bone deterioration. Females are more likely to suffer osteoporosis than males.

5. Choice (a) is correct. Choices (b), (c), and (d)—exercise at least three times a week, check cholesterol level frequently, and look forward to the future, respectively—are all linked with healthy lifestyles, but controlling or holding in your feelings has negative consequences. It seems best to express one's feelings.

6. Choice (c) is correct. Arthritis is the number one chronic condition that afflicts women over seventy-five; for men, hearing impairment is number one. Choice (a), high blood pressure, is second choice (b), hearing impairment, is third; and choice (d), cataracts, is fourth.

7. Choice (c) is correct. Cognitive pragmatics stresses the application of knowledge from one's experiences, especially culture, to solving problems. Choice (b), cognitive mechanics, refers to basic memory processes; choices (a) and (d), wisdom and expertise, respectively, refer to expert knowledge.

8. Choice (b) is correct. Studies show an average loss of 10 percent of brain mass by age eighty.

9. Choice (a) is correct. Depression is the number one mental health affliction of the elderly, which may help to account for the higher suicide rate. Although senility, choice (b), phobic reactions, choice (c), and schizophrenia, choice (d), all occur, they are not as prevalent.

10. Choice (c) is correct. Financial security along with health are the two factors that seem to predict the level of adjustment and life satisfaction during retirement. The other choices— amount of retirement planning, personality, and marital status—also influence adjustment and life satisfaction, but not to the same degree.

Multiple-Choice Self-Test: Application Questions

1. Choice (c) is correct. The leading killer of males over age sixty-five is heart disease. Choice (a), an accident, is listed as the seventh leading cause of death; choice (b), cancer, is the second leading killer; and choice (d), suicide, is the ninth leading cause.

2. Choice (c) is correct. Programming theories, like that of Hayflick, propose that cells will divide only a limited number of times, which suggests that we are programmed to wear out. Choices (a) and (d), cellular and wear and tear theories of aging, respectively, refer to theories concerned with the breakdown of cells; choice (b), systems theories of aging, refers to theories that concern coordinating major body functions, such as the immune system.

3. Choice (b) is correct. The effects of aging on the skin involve loss of pigment, thus making the person pale, and the formation of uneven pigmentation known as age spots. These two changes are greater for individuals who have lighter skin.

4. Choice (d) is correct. As the lens becomes more inflexible and less clear, many of the problems described in the question occur. This is part of the normal aging process and not the result of a disease process such as glaucoma, cataracts, or blindness.

5. Choice (a) is correct. High blood pressure increases the risk of heart attack, choice (b), kidney damage, choice (c), and stroke, choice (d), but has not been associated with cancer.

6. Choice (c) is correct. Research suggests that much of the cognitive decline found that is not medically related can be stopped and reversed simply by providing the older individual with problems or challenging experiences. Brain growth, in the form of making new connections, continues throughout the lifespan.

7. Choice (b) is correct. The early symptoms of Alzheimer's typically involve memory loss, confusion, and some minor speech problems. Choices (a) and (c), loss of motor control and personality deterioration, respectively, are symptoms one might find in the later stages of Alzheimer's, while choice (d), visual impairment, is not a symptom of Alzheimer's.

8. Choice (c) is correct. Males over sixty-five have the highest suicide rates—even higher than teenagers.

9. Choice (b) is correct. Atchley indicates that the immediate response to retirement is similar to that found in a newlywed couple: a period of happiness as they play out their fantasies. Later, reality may set in and adjustments may need to be made, which may lead to depression, choice (a). Exhaustion and anxiety, choices (c) and (d), are not observed.

10. Choice (a) is correct. Individuals who have somewhat boring and routine jobs are more likely to retire early. An assembly-line worker fits that description. Self-employed individuals, choice (d), or those with white-collar or more challenging jobs, choices (b) and (c), often choose to retire later.

CHAPTER 17

Late Adulthood: Psychosocial Development

Learning Objectives

1. Identify the factors that contribute to successful physical and mental health in the later years.

2. Discuss Erikson's last stage of development and indicate what is required to achieve it.

3. Compare and contrast the activity and disengagement theories of successful aging.

4. Describe the role of marriage in late adulthood. Discuss how husbands and wives view each other.

5. Discuss the elderly spouse as a caregiver in cases of illness.

6. Discuss the effects of the death of a spouse on the surviving spouse.

7. Discuss dating and remarriage in the elderly. Identify the qualities that an elderly person looks for in a mate.

8. Discuss how older lesbians and gay men and older never-married adults deal with relationships during the later years.

9. Describe the older adult's relationships with family and friends.

10. Describe the housing circumstances for the elderly. Identify where they live and how they function.

11. Differentiate between assisted living and long-term-care facilities for the elderly. Discuss the role of control in living conditions.

12. Describe the elderly's level of community involvement.

13. Discuss the role of religion and religious institutions in the lives of the elderly.

14. Discuss the role of reminiscence and life review in the adjustment process of older adults.

Chapter Overview

Successful aging refers to the maintenance of psychological adjustment and well-being across the full lifespan. Longitudinal studies show considerable evidence for continuity of psychological adjustment into late adulthood. Neither activity theory nor disengagement theory can account for successful aging. Although remaining active has been associated with high life satisfaction, successfully aging individuals exhibit a range of activity levels based on their life experiences and personalities.

Older married people appear to be happier, be healthier, and live longer than widowed and divorced people of the same age. As couples face retirement, relocation, and declining health, the marital relationship plays important support functions, especially for men. Wives tend to be spousal caregivers more often than husbands. The death of a spouse causes disruption to self-identity and relationships with others, but does not appear to have negative impacts on subsequent health, ability to function, or well-being. Successful late-life remarriage is more likely when there has been a long prior friendship. Older lesbian and gay couples have satisfaction in their relationships and concerns similar to those of most aging couples. Never-married adults learn to cope with aloneness and to be autonomous and self-reliant. Social convoys and continuous relationships develop and change over time.

Siblings provide the strongest bond outside of spouses, parents, and children. Adult grandchildren continue their bonds with their grandparents and tend to be closer to grandmothers than to grandfathers. Interaction with friends in later life is more important to the well-being of older adults and more subject to variation than relationships with family members. Fictive kin are constructed relationships that sometimes blur the distinction between friends and family. Childless older adults develop ties with friends and other relatives.

Elderly people generally prefer to grow older in place. They are likely to relinquish their own households only when they have limited economic resources and become frail or widowed. There are different options available for housing, such as independent living, naturally occurring retirement communities, assisted living, and long-term care. The level of self-determination in these settings is related to levels of satisfaction and health. Though formal volunteering among the elderly is rather low, most older adults volunteer their time in formal and informal ways and can provide positive effects. Memberships in religious institutions are higher at older ages and decline more slowly than other community memberships. Reminiscence and life review are two contemplative activities that are related to adjustment in older adults.

Chapter Outline

I. Personality development in late adulthood

The vast majority of older men and women who are not cognitively impaired show considerable psychological resilience in the face of stress. They are more satisfied than younger adults with their lives, except with regard to their health. Old age brings many adaptational challenges.

A. Continuity and change in late life

1. Vaillant and Vaillant, using the Harvard Grant study, found five variables that contribute to late-life adjustment.

a. Long-lived ancestors predict physical health only.

b. Sustained family relationships predict physical and mental health.

     c.   Maturity of ego defenses assessed before age fifty contributes to psychosocial adjustment at age sixty-five.

     d.   Absence of alcoholism promotes health.

     e.   Absence of depression disorders promotes health.

  2.   There are several important limitations of the Harvard Grant study that prevent conclusions about women, less privileged men, or people in old-old and very-old late adulthood.

  3.   The Berkeley Older Generation study reveals five personality components that appear to be stationary across two time periods: intellect, agreeableness, satisfaction, energy, and extraversion.

     a.   The most stable trait was satisfaction.

     b.   The data show stability in satisfaction and intellect well into very old age, an increase in agreeableness, and a decline in extraversion.

B. Integrity versus despair

  1.   **Integrity versus despair** is the developmental task of late adulthood according to Erikson.

  2.   Wisdom comes from the conflict between integrity and despair.

C. Theories of successful aging

  1.   **Activity theory** argues that the maintenance of social, physical, and intellectual activity contributes to successful aging.

     a.   Older people who are aging optimally stay active and maintain activities or find substitutes for the ones they must give up.

     b.   One can be active without maintaining levels of activity typical of middle age.

     c.   Research found that activity level did not predict mortality or life satisfaction.

  2.   **Disengagement theory** views the reduction in the social involvement of the elderly to be the consequence of a mutual process between the elderly and society.

     a.   It assumes that aging individuals experience inevitable decline in abilities and want to be released from societal expectations.

     b.   There is little evidence that disengagement is normative.

  3.   Both theories place the burden of adjustment on aging individuals, independently of the circumstances in the world around them. Neither theory can account for the range of activity and life of successfully aging individuals; people have different levels of activity and satisfaction based on their personalities and life experiences.

II. Marriage and singlehood

Older married people appear to be happier, be healthier, and live longer than widowed and divorced people of the same age. As couples face retirement, relocation, and declining health, the marital relationship plays important support functions, especially for men.

A. Spouses as caregivers

1. Spouses serve as the first line of defense in coping with disease and disability.

2. Caregiving by spouses is unlikely to stop until deterioration of health of the caregiving spouse prevents it.

3. Chronic illness affects plans for daily living and requires that individuals integrate their illness into their lives.

4. Chronic illnesses can lead to interpersonal strains for patients and their families.

5. Chronic illnesses can also lead to positive outcomes.

6. Spousal caregivers are subject to emotional, social, economic, and physical strain.

   a. The illness of the spouse removes emotional and social support and limits the personal freedom of the caregiver.

   b. Stresses may be greater on recently married older couples who do not have a lifetime of shared experiences to draw on.

7. More women than men provide spousal care.

   a. Research has found differences in husbands' and wives' responses to their spouse's need for help among the frail elderly.

   b. Men and women experience spousal caregiving differently.

   c. The relationship before the disease or disability influences how couples cope with it.

   d. Since wives already do most of the household tasks, the change is greater for caregiving husbands than for caregiving wives.

B. Widowhood

1. The death of a spouse causes disruption to self-identity and relationships with others.

2. The impact of widowhood depends on the age and social class of the widow.

3. Family relationships are affected by widowhood.

4. Men typically have other roles besides husband that are important to them, which may make widowerhood a less severe identity crisis for them. However, men rely more exclusively on wives as confidants.

5. Being widowed does not increase the risk of earlier mortality, but does have a significant impact on lifestyle. It also reduces family income for both genders.

6. Strong signs of psychological resilience from bereavement and the burdens of widowhood have been found.

- Perspectives: The double standard of sexuality in late adulthood

C. Dating and remarriage

1. Socially active older adults are more likely to meet people who are potential dating partners.

2. Health, driving ability, organizational memberships, and contact with siblings are all positively associated with dating.

3. Older adults tend to place more emphasis on companionship and are not experimenting with marital roles.

4. Dating has positive effects on feeling desirable and finding an avenue for self-disclosure.

5. Marriage in later life is not uncommon, but it is likely to be remarriage, with the major reasons being companionship and economic resources.

6. Older adults choose mates who have similar backgrounds and interests.

7. Successful late-life remarriage is more likely when there has been a long prior friendship.

D. Older lesbians and gay men

1. An estimated 10 percent of older adults are lesbian women and gay men.

2. Long-term relationships are much more frequent among gay men and lesbians than is commonly assumed.

3. Lesbian, gay, and heterosexual couples do not differ on standard measures of relationship quality or satisfaction.

4. In a study, areas of concern for gay and lesbian correspondents were primarily the same as those for most aging adults: loneliness, health, and income.

5. Discrimination and stigma have profoundly affected their aging experience, life satisfaction, and quality of life.

E. Never-married older adults

1. Only about 5 percent of older adults in the United States have never been married.

2. Never-married adults have learned to cope with aloneness and to be autonomous and self-reliant.

3. Married and never-married people report less loneliness than those formerly married.

III. Relationships with family and friends

Social convoy is used to describe the dynamic concept of lifelong social networks. Attachment and social support are important throughout the life course. Older adults tend to provide support for fewer network members than younger adults. The most important relationships are with spouses, parents, and children.

A. Siblings

1. Older adult siblings often form one of the strongest social support systems for the older adult, during good times and bad.

2. Siblings can act as confidants, caregivers, and cherished friends.

3. The death of a sibling changes the family constellation, and those who remain feel less buffered from their own mortality.

4. Research shows that African Americans tend to report more positive attitudes toward their siblings and to show greater interest in providing support for them than do Whites.

5. Gender is important to sibling relationships.

    a. A living sister is associated with large increases in sibling contact.

    b. Sister-sister ties are the strongest, and brother-brother ties are the weakest.

6. Siblings can be a source of social support.

B. Adult grandchildren

1. There is a continuation of the bond between grandparents and grandchildren that begins early in the grandchildren's lives.

2. On average, adult grandchildren did more activities with their grandmothers than with their grandfathers.

3. Grandchildren report being more influenced by their grandmothers than by their grandfathers in religious beliefs, sexual beliefs, family ideals, educational beliefs, moral beliefs, and personal identity issues.

4. Grandchildren rate their relationships with their grandmothers to be stronger than their relationships with their grandfathers.

5. Age, location, level of relationship, and contact level with parents influenced the contact between grandchildren and grandparents.

6. Culture provides different attitudes toward behaviors in different ethnic groups.

    a. Having many grandchildren may have an effect on grandchildren-grandparent relations.

C. Friends

1. Interaction with friends is more important to everyday well-being in later life.

2. Of all types of support, friends most often provide emotional intimacy and companionship.

3. Contact with friends is less consistent than with family. Health, economic problems, distance, retirement, or neighborhood changes may make interaction difficult.

4. The research on the effects of gender on relationships in later life is inconclusive.

   a. Some research shows that men tend to have larger friendship networks and engage in more frequent interactions with their friends.

   b. Some research shows that women place greater importance on friendship and engage in more intimate relationships.

D. Fictive kin

1. Sometimes, the relationships between kin and friends become blurred.

2. The merging of voluntary and obligatory relations sometimes produces **fictive kin**, or constructed relationships.

3. Fictive kin provide flexibility in family caregiving for elderly adults but are not expected to fulfill the responsibilities of kin.

E. Childlessness

1. Studies indicate that being without children does not have a negative impact on well-being in later life.

2. Childless women tend to develop ties with friends as both companions and confidants to a greater extent than older adults who are parents.

3. Childless men place greater emphasis on friends as companions as well, but turn to relatives for confidants.

4. Siblings become a more important part of adults' social support networks in the absence of living parents or children.

IV. Problems of living: The housing continuum

Aging in place is the ideal for both gerontologists and elderly people. Elderly people prefer to grow older where they have been younger. They are likely to relinquish their own households only when they have limited economic resources and become frail or widowed. Frailty brings the need for housing modifications and special services.

A. Independent living

1. Homeownership is common among the elderly.

2. Taxes and home maintenance costs can be a financial burden for older adults, especially when health problems and functional impairments accumulate.

3.   Elderly homeowners are more likely to become isolated or to receive less adequate care than apartment dwellers.

4.   Elderly renters tend to be older than elderly homeowners and are more likely to be women and disproportionately African Americans.

5.   Renting provides close-by neighbors, some security, and some social support, and renters are not responsible for yard and building maintenance. On the other hand, renters may not be allowed to modify their homes to help their functioning.

6.   **Naturally occurring retirement communities (NORCs)** are housing developments that are not planned or designed for older people but attract a majority of residents age sixty or more.

   a.   NORCs provide supportive social environments and access to services and facilities that can prolong independent living.

   b.   Safety of the neighborhood is of primary importance to both young and old.

   c.   Some NORCs located in the inner city lack necessary services and security.

B.   Assisted living

1.   **Assisted living** refers to some degree of help with daily living that enables older adults to age in place.

2.   Assisted living provides formal and informal support.

3.   Retirement communities provide a range of options from independent living to twenty-four-hour skilled nursing.

4.   An elderly person needs assistance when unable to perform at least one daily activity.

   a.   The largest source of help is relatives.

   b.   With advancing age, more people rely on formal support.

5.   Elderly or senior housing is federally subsidized and specially designed to meet the needs of old and disabled adults who are poor and have few other options.

6.   Retirement communities are private, age-specific housing alternatives.

7.   **Congregate housing** provides some communal services, such as a central kitchen and dining room.

•   Working with Debbie Holt, homemaking/companion: Helping community-living elderly adults

C.   Long-term care

1.   Long-term care is a broad concept that refers to ongoing assistance to people with chronic illnesses and disabilities in a wide variety of settings.

2.   Most long-term care is personal care and consists of help with everyday activities.

3.   Between 30 and 50 percent of older people will spend a short time in a nursing home after an early discharge from the hospital.

4.   Paid help is important and often combines informal caregiving with some formal services.

5.   Adult day care can supplement family caregiving.

   a.   It is a community-based group program designed to meet the needs of adults with functional impairments.

   b.   A comprehensive program of social, physical, cognitive, and functional activities is offered to maximize remaining strengths and minimize deficits.

D.   Control over living conditions

1.   If the elderly person has to move for whatever reason, it is preferable to move to some space that he or she personally controls.

2.   Satisfaction is related to degree of personal control over living conditions.

3.   Negative effects on the health of older people have been found when their personal control is restricted.

4.   A number of variables are improved when elderly are given responsibility.

5.   Choice becomes one of the most important aspects of the housing continuum.

V.   Interests and activities

The socioeconomic standing of the individual to a large extent influences how he or she spends his or her time. Health acts as a threshold for leisure, and financial security plays a critical role in supporting various activities. Education and occupation influence preference for activities. Developing **activity competence** is generally established in earlier adult years. Leisure pursuits of older people vary greatly. Past patterns of activity shape the way older adults use their time.

A.   Community involvement

1.   Community organizations include many different types of organizations designed to achieve a purpose or pursue some shared interest.

2.   There is much stability in the people's general levels of participation in community organizations from middle age until their sixties, when involvement gradually decreases.

3.   Volunteerism provides a link with the community.

   a.   Only about 16 percent of people over sixty-five are volunteers.

   b.   If the definition of volunteerism is broadened to include informal services, almost all retired adults do volunteer work.

4.   Older volunteers face some problems.

       a. They may be assigned tasks that are beneath their knowledge, experience, and dignity.

       b. Sometimes volunteers are placed in positions without sufficient training.

       c. Some volunteers prefer paid part-time work.

       d. People who are retired may be unwilling to commit to a rigid volunteer schedule that might limit their freedom to travel.

       e. Transportation is often a problem for older volunteers.

   5. Elderhostel programs are another kind of community involvement.

       a. These programs offer continuing higher education.

  B. Religion and spirituality

   1. Churches or synagogues are the organizations to which older people most frequently belong.

   2. There is greater involvement of people over age sixty-five.

   3. Lack of church or synagogue attendance does not necessarily mean lack of religious involvement.

   4. Religious institutions form an important source of social support among racial/ethnic minorities.

   5. The few longitudinal studies of religiosity show that cohort differences may be more important than age differences.

       a. Religion generally refers to organized religion.

       b. **Spirituality** refers to the human need to construct a sense of meaning in life and can occur within or outside of a specifically religious context.

   6. Spiritual development appears to be age related but not age determined.

   7. Spirituality has been found to influence one's perception of quality of life and will to live, even in the face of loss and infirmity.

   8. Solitary activities can promote spiritual integration.

       a. **Reminiscence** is the recall of past experiences and events and occurs among people of all ages.

       b. **Life review** is an evaluative universal inner experience of older people that enables them to take stock of their lives as well as to prepare for death.

  • A multicultural view: Can individuals postpone dying for a special event?

VI. Looking back/looking forward

Key Concepts

Directions: Identify each of the following key concepts discussed in this chapter.

1. Erikson's stage of _____ describes the developmental task of older adults.

2. The theory that argues that maintenance of social, physical, and intellectual activity contributes to successful aging is the _____.

3. The _____ theory views the reduction in elderly adults' social involvement as the effect of a mutual process between the elderly and society.

4. Marital satisfaction generally _____ among long-term married couples.

5. _____ serve as the first line of defense in coping with disease and disability.

6. More _____ than _____ provide spousal care.

7. The notion that getting older enhances a man's value but diminishes a woman's is known as the _____.

8. The major reasons for marriage in late adulthood are _____ and _____.

9. _____ refers to the dynamic concept of lifelong social networks.

10. Adult grandchildren report their relationships with their _____ to be stronger than their relationships with their _____.

11. The merging of voluntary and obligatory relations produces _____.

12. Most older adults would prefer to live _____.

13. Housing developments that are not planned or designed for older people but attract a majority of residents age sixty or more are called _____.

14. _____, or semi-independent living, refers to some degree of help with daily living.

15. An option for housing for older adults where there are some communal services is called _____.

16. _____ is ongoing assistance to people with chronic illnesses.

17. _____ over living conditions is important in the health and satisfaction of older adults.

18. The skills and knowledge needed to take advantage of opportunities for activities are called _____.

19. When formal and informal volunteer activities are included, _____ older adults volunteer.

20. _____ is a nationwide program of continuing higher education programs for older adults.

21. When a person recalls past experiences and events, it is called _____.

22. _____ is a universal inner experience of older people to remember past experiences or unresolved conflicts that can now be reintegrated.

Multiple-Choice Self-Test

Factual / Conceptual Questions

1. In the Harvard Grant study, the variable that strongly predicted physical and mental health in older adults was
   a. maturity of ego defenses.
   b. socioeconomic status.
   c. sustained family relationships.
   d. intelligence.

2. For Erikson, the last developmental task involves the establishment of
   a. expertise.
   b. generativity.
   c. morality.
   d. integrity.

3. According to activity theory, decreased social interactions in old age come from
   a. society withdrawing from the aging person.
   b. the aging person withdrawing from society.
   c. the aging person and society mutually withdrawing from each other.
   d. the aging person and society remaining connected but to a lesser degree.

4. As compared to older women, older men tend to view wives as
   a. caregivers.
   b. companions.
   c. confidants.
   d. friends.

5. Which of the following is *not* one of the differences between male and female caregivers in the case of a sick spouse?
   a. Husbands tend to get less outside help than wives.
   b. Wives are more tolerant of caregiving burdens.
   c. Husbands tend to emphasize structural activities.
   d. Wives tend to focus on the changes in the marital relationship.

6. Older lesbian and gay couples tend to be
   a. more content in their relationships than older heterosexual couples.
   b. less content in their relationships than middle-aged lesbian and gay couples.
   c. just as content in their relationships as older heterosexual couples.
   d. less content in their relationships than middle-aged heterosexual couples.

7. Sibling relationships during the older years are best categorized as
   a. apathetic.
   b. congenial.
   c. intimate.
   d. loyal.

8. Individuals who do not have close friends are more likely to be all of the following *except*
   a. city dwellers.
   b. male.
   c. older.
   d. working class.

9. As compared to older adults with children, childless older adults tend to
   a. be more lonely.
   b. have more extensive social networks.
   c. value sibling ties more.
   d. show significant drops in social networks.

10. As compared to younger adults, people over sixty-five years of age tend to be involved in volunteer activities
    a. about three times as much.
    b. about twice as much.
    c. at about the same rate.
    d. less.

Application Questions

1. Sam, who was very active in the community as well as his job, has gradually reduced his involvement since his retirement. Sam says that he's paid his dues and now it's time for some younger blood to take over while he sits back and enjoys the rest of his life. Sam's attitude and behavior reflect the
   a. activity theory.
   b. disengagement theory.
   c. reintegrative theory.
   d. role abandonment theory.

2. Sixty-seven-year-old Florence has cancer and has been bedridden at home for about two months. In this situation, who is likely to be the primary caregiver?
   a. A home health nurse
   b. Her husband
   c. Her older daughter
   d. A relative other than husband or older daughter

3. Sixty-eight-year-old Constance, whose husband died four years ago, is now dating. Which of the following roles is she *least* likely to be concerned about in a potential mate?
   a. Caregiver
   b. Confidant
   c. Friend
   d. Lover

4. According to the social convoy model of relations, which of the following relationships should be the *least* important for Clarence, a married man in his early sixties?
   a. His aging father
   b. His wife
   c. His friend of over five years
   d. His thirty-eight-year-old son

5. Sixty-four-year-old Harold is likely to find his strongest support group in his older years to be his
   a. coworkers.
   b. church members.
   c. neighbors.
   d. siblings.

6. Jared has a typical relationship with his grandparents. Which of the following statements describes that relationship most accurately?
   a. He interacts with his grandparents at least once a week.
   b. He is more likely to participate in activities with his grandmother than with his grandfather.
   c. In the area of religion and moral beliefs, he's influenced more by his grandfather than by his grandmother.
   d. In the area of sexual beliefs and family ideals, he's influenced more by his grandfather than by his grandmother.

7. Anna and Sheldon have been long-term neighbors of Allan and Shirley and encourage their children to refer to them as Aunt Anna and Uncle Sheldon. The term that best describes the relationship between Anna and Sheldon and the children is
   a. fictive kin.
   b. godparents.
   c. pseudo relatives.
   d. surrogate aunt and uncle.

8. Seventy-year-old Morris and his wife are a typical older couple. They most likely
   a. live in an apartment.
   b. own their own home.
   c. are in a special retirement community.
   d. moved to a different house shortly after retirement.

9. Bea has daily help available to provide some light cleaning, and she participates in the meals-on-wheels program. Bea's housing situation is best characterized as
   a. personal care home.
   b. fully independent living.
   c. assisted living.
   d. congregate housing.

10. After not seeing his son for over thirty years because of a major conflict, seventy-year-old Salvatore has taken steps to reconnect with his son and finally resolve the issue. Salvatore's actions can best be understood in the context of
    a. a life review.
    b. reminiscence.
    c. a religious revelation.
    d. a premonition of death.

Answer Key

Key Concepts

1. integrity versus despair
2. activity theory
3. disengagement
4. increases
5. Spouses
6. women, men
7. double standard of aging
8. companionship, economic resources
9. Social convoy
10. grandmothers, grandfathers
11. fictive kin
12. in their own homes
13. naturally occurring retirement communities
14. Assisted living
15. congregate housing
16. Long-term care
17. Control
18. activity competence
19. most
20. Elderhostel
21. reminiscence
22. Life review

Multiple-Choice Self-Test: Factual / Conceptual Questions

1. Choice (c) is correct. By far the most powerful variable that determined adjustment in the elderly was the degree to which their family relationships were intact. Individuals with good family relationships were more adjusted than those with poor relationships. Choices (a), (b), and (d)—maturity of ego defenses, socioeconomic status, and intelligence, respectively—did not show any overall effects.

2. Choice (d) is correct. Erikson's last stage is integrity versus despair, which involves looking back over one's life and deciding whether it has truly meant something. Choice (b), generativity, is a middle-adulthood issue, while choices (a) and (c), expertise and morality, respectively, are not issues in Erikson's theory.

3. Choice (a) is correct. Activity theory posits that society withdraws from the person while the person tries to maintain contact and resist the withdrawal. Those who can maintain the contact are better adjusted.

4. Choice (c) is correct. Males tend to view their wives as confidants and the primary figure within their social network. Females, on the other hand, often see their husbands as companions, choice (b), and, although important, not the core of their social network. Choice (d), friends, and especially choice (a), caregivers, are other roles they may play.

5. Choice (a) is correct. Choices (b), (c), and (d) are all trends found in caregiving, but husbands actually tend to get more outside help than wives when caring for their spouses.

6. Choice (c) is correct. Studies suggest that lesbian and gay couples that have had long-term relationships and are now in their later years are very similar to heterosexual couples in the satisfaction level of their relationship. Thus, choices (a), (b), and (d) are inaccurate.

7. Choice (d) is correct. In a study that examined sibling relationships in the later years, about 45 percent rated their relationship as loyal, while only 25 percent rated it congenial, choice (b); 17 percent rated it as intimate, choice (c); and only 5 percent rated it as apathetic, choice (a).

8. Choice (a) is correct. Older adults who lacked friends were more likely to be males, choice (b); older, choice (c); and working class, choice (d). City dwellers tended to have more friends than rural individuals.

9. Choice (c) is correct. Contrary to some popular beliefs, childless older adults are not lonelier, choice (a). They have similar-sized social networks, so choices (b) and (d) are incorrect, but do tend to value siblings even more.

10. Choice (d) is correct. Unfortunately, the elderly population tends to volunteer less than the adult population; about 16 percent of the elderly volunteer in some way, while 23 percent of the general adult population volunteers.

Multiple-Choice Self-Test: Application Questions

1. Choice (b) is correct. Sam seems to be withdrawing from society and views that as an appropriate transition to successful aging. This is most consistent with the disengagement theory. Choice (a), activity theory, would have the society (community) withdrawing from him, much to his disdain. Choices (c) and (d), reintegrative theory and role abandonment theory, respectively, are not regarded as aging theories.

2. Choice (b) is correct. The spouse, in this case, the husband, is most likely to be the primary caregiver in instances like this as long as he is physically and mentally able. A home health nurse, her older daughter, or another relative—choices (a), (c), and (d), respectively—may help, but tend not to be primary caretakers.

3. Choice (a) is correct. For both elderly males and females, the caregiver role is not a major consideration when looking for a mate, while choices (b), (c), and (d)—confidant, friend, and lover—are all important roles.

4. Choice (c) is correct. The notion that blood is thicker than water holds here. Based on the convoy model, family relationships, choices (a), (b), and (d), are more important than friendships.

5. Choice (d) is correct. Family relationships and, in particular, siblings seem to make up a large portion of an individual's support group. Nonrelatives, choices (a), (b), and (c), tend to play lesser roles.

6. Choice (b) is correct. Studies suggest that grandchildren tend to interact more with their grandmothers than with their grandfathers. Also, grandmothers have more influence on religion, moral beliefs, sexual belief, and family ideals than grandfathers, making choices (c) and (d) incorrect. Grandchildren tend to interact with grandparents about once a month, so choice (a) is also incorrect.

7. Choice (a) is correct. *Fictive kin* is the term given to individuals who are so close they take on the status of relatives even though they are not related. The other terms—godparents, pseudo relatives, and surrogate aunt and uncle—are not used.

8. Choice (b) is correct. Seventy-five percent of the elderly own and live in their own homes. Only a small percentage move after retirement, so choices (c) and (d) are incorrect, and most have homes, not apartments, so choice (a) is also incorrect.

9. Choice (c) is correct. Bea gets some help but still lives independently, thus she's involved in an assisted living arrangement. Choice (b), fully independent living, has no help, while choices (a) and (d), personal care home and congregate housing, respectively, have a greater degree of assistance.

10. Choice (a) is correct. A life review involves looking over the past and seeing what unresolved conflicts need to be resolved as one approaches the end of life. Although reminiscence, choice (b), may be part of the process, the life review involves action as well as simply looking back. The other choices, a religious revelation, choice (c), and a premonition of death, choice (d), may help motivate a life review, but they don't quite capture the scenario described here.

CHAPTER 18

Death, Dying, and Bereavement

Learning Objectives

1. Identify how death and the causes of death have changed over the century.

2. Discuss how attitudes about death have changed and identify the factors that contributed to those changes.

3. Describe how people think about their own death. Indicate how individuals of different ages view the experience.

4. Discuss the factors that contribute to suicide in the elderly.

5. Identify and describe Kübler-Ross's stages of dying. Discuss the data that support her view.

6. Define what is meant by a "good death" and discuss some of the cultural differences in dying.

7. Discuss the ways in which we care for the dying and cite the factors that have promoted the reemergence of dying at home.

8. Describe the role and philosophy of the hospice.

9. Differentiate among the various forms of assisted suicide for terminally ill patients.

10. Define what is meant by bereavement and differentiate between grief and mourning.

11. Describe how a parent experiences the death of a child at different life stages.

12. Describe the process of anticipatory grief.

13. Describe the function of funerals and other ritual practices that deal with death. Identify cultural differences in these practices.

14. Describe the process of mourning. Indicate how different ethnic and cultural backgrounds respond to death and its aftermath.

15. Discuss the recovery process and the role of support groups in the adjustment to the death of a loved one.

Chapter Overview

Social and technological changes in the twentieth century have led to a separation of death from everyday life and to an attitude that denies death. Recently the death awareness movement has promoted the idea of the good death and raised awareness about issues of dying and bereavement. Aging is associated with increasing acceptance of death and increased concern about the process of dying. Suicide rates are higher in later life, especially among white males. Kübler-Ross has outlined five stages of reactions to dying that have been widely accepted by clinicians but have been questioned by theory and research. A good death is one that enables the dying individual to experience growth in this final stage of life. Nursing homes, hospices, and home care provide terminal care alternatives to hospital death. Home death provides familiarity and greater opportunities for sustaining relationships, but also may pose many difficult aspects. Much controversy surrounds the issues of assisted suicide and euthanasia.

Differences are seen in grief depending on the nature of the relationship, the on-time or off-time nature of the loss, and whether there is time to anticipate loss. Funerals and other ritual practices serve several functions for mourners. Different ethnic cultural traditions have different expectations about grief and bereavement. Support groups have been established to bring people together to provide empathy and to encourage survivors to feel normal about grief reactions. Recovery consists of growth and change as a survivor returns to previous levels of functioning while making adjustments to the transition.

Chapter Outline

- Perspectives: How children understand death

I. Attitudes toward death

   Most Americans will live past age sixty-five and die from **degenerative diseases**, compared to in the past when most deaths, young and old, were from **communicable diseases**.

   A. Death has become less familiar in the twentieth century than ever before because of social and technological changes.

   B. The attitude toward death has been described as death denied.

      1. Death has become private.

      2. Mourning is denied.

      3. Funerary rites are included that erase signs of death.

   C. The result of the "death denied" attitude is that people feel uncomfortable about death, and adults send confusing messages about death to children.

   D. Because of contemporary attitudes toward death, the dying often experience a social death before their biological death.

   E. The **death awareness movement** has attempted to give people the opportunities to learn about death and dying.

II. Facing one's own death

In 1990, 72 percent of deaths in the United States were among people age sixty-five and older. As people age, recognition of their mortality increases. In middle adulthood, people start to estimate the amount of time they have left before they are likely to die.

A. Death acceptance

1. People both accept and deny the reality of their dying.

2. Late adulthood is associated with an increasing acceptance of death and increasing concern about the process of dying.

3. Fewer than one in five American adults have actually prepared any written advance directive.

4. Older people talk about death more than younger people do and seem to be less fearful of it, but there are differences among male and female perceptions of death; fear of death is also related to religiosity.

5. There are a number of explanations of why older people are less fearful of death.

6. Unfinished business can interfere with the normative process of accepting death as one gets old.

B. Elder suicide

1. It is important not to confuse age-related death acceptance with desire for death.

2. Leave-taking can help individuals control anxiety and reduce impulses to end their life through suicide, assisted suicide, or euthanasia.

3. Suicide rates are higher in later life, but cross-sectional and longitudinal data present different pictures.

4. Not all elderly are equally likely to attempt or commit suicide. There are several factors that put an individual at high risk for suicide, such as living alone, poor health, and being a white male.

5. Older suicides may be harder to predict and prevent compared to younger suicides, and older adults seem to communicate warnings of suicide less frequently.

6. Suicide at any age appears sudden and unexpected to the people left behind.

C. The dying process

1. Kübler-Ross interviewed more than two hundred dying patients and proposed five distinct stages through which individuals pass.

a. Denial is the initial response; it is the refusal to believe the terminal diagnosis.

b. Anger then may be displaced onto the family or medical staff.

c. Bargaining with a higher being and asking for more time to do something good may occur next.

      d. Depression is the stage in which the individual begins to acknowledge and mourn the impending loss.

      e. The final stage, acceptance, is reached only if the person is allowed to express and work out earlier feelings.

  2. Research has challenged Kübler-Ross's stage formulation.

D. The good death

  1. **The good death** is one that is appropriate to the person who is dying.

  2. Improving the quality of end-of-life care in hospitals will require changes in the organization and culture of the hospital and active support from hospital leaders.

  3. The death awareness movement has promoted conditions that can make the good death possible.

III. Caring for the dying

The way the dying are cared for influences the quality of their deaths.

A. Terminal care alternatives

  1. Grief work is an initial phase of the bereavement process that entails anger, self-recrimination, depression, and taking care of unfinished business.

  2. Home used to be where most elderly people died in the United States. Most deaths now occur outside of the home.

  3. **Hospice** takes a holistic approach to death by attending to the physical, emotional, spiritual, and aesthetic needs of patients and their families, predominantly in their own homes. It is formally recognized by Medicare and private insurance companies.

  4. The decision to die at home brings with it several difficult aspects for which many families are unprepared.

      a. Today's dying typically are much sicker and more fragile than they used to be.

      b. The most likely caregiver is a woman, and today a higher portion of women are employed outside the home. This situation increases the risk for potential emotional, physical, and financial stress.

      c. Home care is most appropriate when the patient is alert enough to relate to the caregiver and benefit from the familiar surroundings.

  5. Nursing homes are the institutions other than hospitals in which Americans most frequently die.

  6. **Palliative care** is designed to manage the pain and other symptoms so that the dying person can enjoy what remains of life; it is a part of hospice care.

      a. Hospice includes trained medical staff and trained volunteers; family members serve as caregivers.

      b.   Hospice facilities are designed more like homes than hospitals.

      c.   Most hospice care is provided at home.

B. Assisted suicide

    1.   Some terminally ill people choose to end their lives while they are still rational rather than suffer and be a burden to their loved ones.

    2.   Euthanasia is the voluntary ending of life when illness makes it intolerable.

      a.   **Passive euthanasia** refers to not doing something to prolong life.

      b.   **Active euthanasia** refers to taking steps to end life.

    3.   There is much debate over euthanasia and especially assisted suicide. Some believe that patients should have self-determination regarding the termination of their lives. Others argue that loosening the restraints on active euthanasia could lead to abuses by unethical and incompetent doctors.

- Working with Susan Gardner, social worker: Helping the dying and bereaved

IV. Bereavement

Bereavement is the experience of loss of a loved one through death. During late adulthood, deaths of loved ones become more frequent. Bereavement is made up of **grief**, which is the emotional response to one's loss, and **mourning**, the actions and manner of expressing grief.

A. Grief

    1.   Grief occurs when we lose certain primary relationships.

      a.   Relationships of attachment include spouses or partners, parents, and children. We count on these relationships for security. Grief follows the death of any single relationship of attachment.

      b.   Relationships of community include friends, work colleagues, and other family relationships. Death is followed by distress and sadness, but not persisting grief.

    2.   Grief is a natural process that occurs after the loss of a loved one, although it is very personalized and is influenced by the age of the deceased person and the relationship.

    3.   The grief process has three overlapping phases.

    4.   The grief one feels before the death of a loved one occurs is called **anticipatory grief**.

      a.   A study showed that anticipatory grief is more likely if the elderly parent is ill for a long time and is not cognitively intact.

      b.   Providing care during a prolonged illness can result in grief before the death and relief after the death.

    5.   Grief is a powerful emotion that is stimulated by the actual death of a loved one.

- A multicultural view: Men and grief

B. Funeral and ritual practices

1. Funerals are ritual practices associated with death; modern rituals focus on the expression of both grief and hope.

2. Funeral rituals have three functions.

   a. They organize the appropriate disposal of the body.

   b. They contribute to the realization of the implications of the death.

   c. They assist in social reintegration and meaningful ongoing life.

3. The functions of funerals take different forms in different cultures.

4. Funeral rituals take different forms in different circumstances in the same culture.

5. Funerals in America have been criticized for being too elaborate because of commercial pressure.

6. There has been a countermovement toward simpler funerals and cremation rather than burial.

C. Mourning

1. Mourning is the social experience of grief.

2. In all cultures, there are some restrictions and some obligations for mourning.

   a. American society does not approve of mourning except within the rigid confines of the funeral.

   b. Jewish law and custom give mourners a structure that encourages feeling their loss and thus healing.

   c. Hispanic Americans also believe it is important to take time to express one's feelings of grief.

   d. Many Asian Americans believe death allows for a continued relationship between the deceased and the survivors.

D. Support groups

1. Bereavement programs have been developed to encourage survivors to feel normal about their grief reactions and to offer empathy.

2. Bereavement groups take several forms such as self-help groups, groups organized by hospices, and groups led by trained professionals.

E. Recovery

1. Grief involves a process of transition. Survivors take on new roles and see themselves from a new perspective.

2. Grief leads not simply to recovery but to change and transformation.

3. Recovery is a return to previous levels of functioning, and there are several indicators of this return.

4. Not everyone goes through the same grieving process to reach recovery.

Key Concepts

Directions: Identify each of the following key concepts discussed in this chapter.

1. Cardiovascular disease and cancer are examples of _____ diseases, while influenza, cholera, and measles are examples of _____ diseases.

2. The attitude that is prevalent regarding death and dying in the United States is referred to as _____.

3. The purpose of the _____ movement is to teach people about death and dying.

4. Late adulthood is associated with a(n) _____ acceptance of death.

5. _____ are at most risk for elder suicide.

6. The five stages of the dying process, according to Kübler-Ross, are _____, _____, _____, _____, and _____.

7. The _____ is one that is appropriate to the person who is dying.

8. _____ is an initial phase of the bereavement process; it entails anger, self-recrimination, depression, and taking care of unfinished business.

9. The movement called _____ takes a holistic approach to death by attending to the physical, emotional, spiritual, and aesthetic needs of patients and their families.

10. _____ is managing pain and other symptoms so that the dying person can enjoy the rest of his or her life.

11. _____ is the type of euthanasia that refers to not doing something to prolong life. _____, on the other hand, refers to taking steps to end life.

12. The experience of loss of a loved one through death is called _____.

13. _____ is the emotional response to one's loss; _____ refers to the actions and manner of expressing grief.

14. The grief one feels before the death of a loved one occurs is known as _____.

15. _____ are ritual practices associated with death.

16. Recovery is best understood as a return to _____.

Multiple-Choice Self-Test

Factual / Conceptual Questions

1. What percentage of deaths takes place in hospitals?
   a. 60 percent
   b. 70 percent
   c. 80 percent
   d. 90 percent

2. Most people feel uncomfortable around death because
   a. they fear their own death.
   b. horror movies often portray the dead as being monsters.
   c. they feel that a dead body may carry disease.
   d. they have often had very little experience with death.

3. At what period of life do people typically begin to estimate the amount of time they have left before they are likely to die?
   a. Adolescence
   b. Early adulthood
   c. Midlife
   d. Just before retirement

4. As age increases, fear of death tends to
   a. decrease.
   b. increase.
   c. remain relatively stable.
   d. initially decrease until midlife, at which time it begins a sharp increase.

5. Which of the following is *not* true concerning Kübler-Ross's stages of dying?
   a. They are distinctive.
   b. They overlap.
   c. They are sequential.
   d. They are primarily based on cancer patients.

6. When asked how they viewed their deathbed scene, most college students described
   a. a quick death most often caused by an accident.
   b. a death in the hospital while connected to various pieces of high-tech equipment and in a semiconscious state.
   c. being at home with family and friends while being very alert, lucid, and aware that death was approaching.
   d. a painful experience, in a hospital, shifting in and out of consciousness.

7. All of the following have contributed to the reemergence of home death *except*
   a. the hospice movement.
   b. better emergency medical services.
   c. insurance companies limiting hospital stays.
   d. the death awareness movement.

8. The emotional response to the loss of a loved one is termed
   a. grief.
   b. mourning.
   c. bereavement.
   d. death anxiety.

9. Funerals do all of the following *except*
   a. provide an endpoint to the grief process for nonrelatives.
   b. organize proper disposal of the body.
   c. contribute to the realization of death and its implications.
   d. assist in social reintegration.

10. Grief, especially for a family member who has died, should be viewed as a process of
    a. recapturing the past.
    b. getting back to normal.
    c. transition and change.
    d. preparing for one's own death.

Application Questions

1. Sixty-five-year-old Myron is most likely to die
   a. in an accident.
   b. of a communicative disease.
   c. of a degenerative disease.
   d. of natural causes.

2. Sixteen-year-old Alysha's concept of her own death is likely to
   a. portray it as only a temporary experience.
   b. involve seeing herself as invincible.
   c. produce a sense of anger and unfairness.
   d. include the concept of severe pain.

3. Who is likely to show the greatest amount of death anxiety?
   a. Walter, an atheist
   b. Mack, a strongly religious person
   c. Gavin, a person with a strong personal philosophy
   d. Stanley, a sporadically religious person

4. Of the following, who is most likely to commit suicide?
   a. Stanley, an eighty-six-year-old White male
   b. Lucia, an eighty-seven-year-old White female
   c. Desmond, an eighty-eight-year-old African American male
   d. Patrice, an eighty-six-year-old African American female

5. A person asking the question "Why me?" is likely to be at Kübler-Ross's _____ stage of dying.
   a. anger
   b. bargaining
   c. denial
   d. depression

6. John has just been admitted to the hospice. He can expect that
   a. he will be left alone to die.
   b. every effort will be made to maintain his life.
   c. he is likely to die at home or in a homelike facility.
   d. he will not receive any drugs or medications for his symptoms.

7. Rita, who is terminally ill with cancer, has developed an infection in her lungs that if not treated with antibiotics will cause her death. Her doctor does not prescribe any medication for the infection, but gives her drugs to reduce the pain. This would be considered
   a. malpractice.
   b. passive euthanasia.
   c. active euthanasia.
   d. physician-assisted suicide.

8. The McNaughtons' two-month-old infant has just died of sudden infant death syndrome. Their emotional response to the loss is most likely to be
   a. anger.
   b. guilt.
   c. denial.
   d. total numbness.

9. The day after her husband's funeral, Grace returned to work wearing a very attractive cream-colored outfit. How are her colleagues likely to respond to her return and to her outfit?
   a. They are likely to be accepting.
   b. They are likely to take her aside and tell her she should take some time off and wear black.
   c. They are likely to give her the silent treatment.
   d. Most will be appalled at her return and the lack of black and may express some direct anger or dismay.

10. A friend of your seems to be having difficulty adjusting to the death of a loved one who died four months ago. What is the best advice you can offer your friend?
    a. Say, "Don't worry, you'll get over it."
    b. Mention that there are support groups for people who have lost loved ones.
    c. Tell your friend that he or she needs professional help.
    d. Ignore it, hoping it will pass soon.

Answer Key

Key Concepts

1. degenerative, communicable
2. death denied
3. death awareness
4. increasing
5. White males
6. denial, anger, bargaining, depression, acceptance
7. good death
8. Grief work
9. hospice
10. Palliative care
11. Passive euthanasia, Active euthanasia
12. bereavement
13. Grief, mourning
14. anticipatory grief
15. Funerals
16. previous levels of functioning

Multiple-Choice Self-Test: Factual / Conceptual Questions

1. Choice (c) is correct. Current data indicate that about 80 percent of all deaths occur in hospitals.

2. Choice (d) is correct. Death tends to be more hidden today than in the past and it is this lack of experience with death that seems to make people uncomfortable. Although some may also fear their own death, choice (a), this fear tends to decrease with age. Choices (b) and (c), the effects of horror movies and fear of disease, respectively, are not widely accepted.

3. Choice (c) is correct. Keith (1982) found that many people, but not all, first looked at how much time they may have to live during the midlife period, which was part of the planning process for the rest of their lives.

4. Choice (a) is correct. Older individuals tend to talk about death more and fear it less.

5. Choice (c) is correct. Kübler-Ross's stages are distinctive stages, choice (a), that may overlap, choice (b), but they are not necessarily sequential, choice (c). They were also formulated mainly using young and middle-aged adult cancer patients, choice (d).

6. Choice (c) is correct. College students painted a somewhat pleasant experience, dying surrounded by friends and family. This ignored many of the current realities, which involve institutions, long-term illness, and pain, choices (a), (b), and (d).

7. Choice (b) is correct. The hospice, choice (a), and death awareness movements, choice (d), have both contributed to examining death with dignity at home, which has been further encouraged by insurance companies that will no longer pay for a long-term hospital stay, choice (c). Although emergency medical services have improved greatly, they are designed more to sustain life using all possible methods and then to transfer people to the hospital setting.

8. Choice (a) is correct. By definition, grief is the emotional response to loss, while mourning, choice (b), refers to actions and manner of expressing grief; choice (c), bereavement, is the experience of loss, which encompasses both grief and mourning; and choice (d), death anxiety, is the fear of death.

9. Choice (a) is correct. Even for nonrelatives the emotional response to the death of a friend does not end with the funeral but may continue for some time. The other choices are all functions of a funeral, ranging from very practical purposes—the proper disposal of the body, choice (b)—to more emotional and social support functions, like contribute to the realization of death and its implications, choice (c), and assist in social reintegration, choice (d).

10. Choice (c) is correct. After the death of a loved one, there is always some adjustment to the loss. The closer the person was to the deceased, the more the adjustment. This adjustment brings on new growth and thus should be viewed as a period of transition and change. One does not simply recapture the past, choice (a), or return to how things were, choice (b). Although there may be some reflection about one's own mortality, choice (d), choice (c) captures best the typical response to the death.

Multiple-Choice Self-Test: Application Questions

1. Choice (c) is correct. Degenerative diseases are currently the most likely cause of death. Choice (b), communicative disease, was once true, but many of those diseases are now preventable or treatable. Choice (a), an accident, occurs more often in younger years but is not as common for older individuals, and choice (d), natural causes, tends to be higher in the very, very old.

2. Choice (b) is correct. Teenagers tend to understand death from a cognitive standpoint but still feel that it will not happen to them because they are special. They therefore sometimes feel invincible, which makes it all the more difficult when someone their age dies.

3. Choice (d) is correct. The highest levels of death anxiety are found in individuals who are uncertain about their beliefs. Choices (a), (b), and (c)—atheist, strongly religious, and strong personal philosophy, respectively—would have strong beliefs.

4. Choice (a) is correct. White males over age eighty-five have the highest suicide rates. The other three choices, (b), (c), and (d), are considerably lower.

5. Choice (a) is correct. Kübler-Ross indicated that during the anger stage of death and dying, the person asks the question "Why me?" People in the bargaining stage, choice (b), often ask, "Yes me, but . . . " People in the denial stage, choice (c), say, "Not me." People in the depression stage, choice (d), say, "Yes me" and then mourn the loss.

6. Choice (c) is correct. Most hospices are home-care based and try to allow the person to die in the family setting. If that is not possible, a homelike setting is desired. Hospice does not abandon the dying to die, choice (a), but rather provides support for the dying and their families. Entry into a hospice means that the person is terminally ill and no heroic measures will be taken to sustain life, so choice (b) is incorrect; but drugs and medication are used, contrary to choice (d), particularly to deal with pain, so the person may die with dignity.

7. Choice (b) is correct. This case involves the withholding of medication that would otherwise prolong the life of the person. It is not malpractice, since all parties must agree to the process, choice (a); nor is it an active process where something is given to speed up the process, choices (c) and (d).

8. Choice (b) is correct. Although anger, denial, and total numbness—choices (a), (c), and (d), respectively—can all occur, the most likely response is guilt in that parents wonder if there was something they could have done to prevent the death. The death of an infant is clearly an off-time event that parents have great difficulty adjusting to.

9. Choice (a) is correct. Recent studies suggest that wearing black and staying away from work are actually unimportant, although this response may vary in some ethnic groups. Thus her colleagues will most likely be understanding and accepting of her behavior and not follow any of the options described in choices (b), (c), or (d).

10. Choice (b) is correct. Perhaps the best advice is to simply make the person aware that if he or she is having some difficulty, there are places to turn to for help. Even more important, but not listed as an option here, is for you to be there in case the person wishes to talk a little. Choice (a), saying, "Don't worry, you'll get over it," is not appropriate since it tends to belittle the person's emotions; choice (c), telling your friend that he or she needs help, is also an extreme response that implies your friend is very troubled; and choice (d), ignoring it, although a common response, is not as helpful or supportive as choice (b).

r